Thinking Orientals

THINKING ORIENTALS

Migration,
Contact, and
Exoticism in
Modern America

HENRY YU

UNIVERSITY PRESS

2001

OXFORD
UNIVERSITY PRESS

Oxford   New York
Athens   Auckland   Bangkok   Bogotá   Buenos Aires   Calcutta
Cape Town   Chennai   Dar es Salaam   Delhi   Florence   Hong Kong   Istanbul
Karachi   Kuala Lumpur   Madrid   Melbourne   Mexico City   Mumbai
Nairobi   Paris   São Paulo   Singapore   Shanghai   Taipei   Tokyo   Toronto   Warsaw

and associated companies in
Berlin   Ibadan

Published by Oxford University Press, Inc.
198 Madison Avenue, New York, New York 10016

Oxford is a registered trademark of Oxford University Press.

Library of Congress Cataloging-in-Publication Data
Yu, Henry, 1967–
Thinking Orientals : migration, contact, and exoticism in modern America /
Henry Yu.
p.   cm.
Includes bibliographical reference and index.
ISBN 0-19-511660-7
1. Asian Americans—Social conditions—20th century.   2. Asian Americans—
Ethnic identity—Philosophy.   3. Chicago schools of sociology.   4. Sociology—
United States—History—20th century.   5. United States—Race relations—
Philosophy.   I. Title.
E184.O6 Y8 2001
305.895073—dc21   00-022570

Acknowledgment is made to New York University Press for permission to use
"Mixing Bodies and Culture: The Meaning of America's Fascination with Sex between
Orietals and Whites," in *Sex, Love, Race*, ed. Martha Hodes (1998).

9 8 7 6 5 4 3 2 1

Printed in the United States of America
on acid-free paper

PREFACE

Migration and
Knowledge Created
about and by
Asian Americans

Although this book was written in Princeton, New Jersey, and Los Angeles, California, many of its ideas crystallized during the four solo driving trips I took across the United States during graduate school. While stopping for gas on the interstates or during meals in diners and restaurants, I hurriedly scribbled thoughts that had occurred during my driving. Through those long hours on America's roads, I realized that coming to know something is often a physical as well as an intellectual movement, that coming to knowledge is not something that occurs only in a study room or a research lab somewhere in a university; sometimes it is an act strewn across a landscape of ignorance. It is a leaving of some familiar place in order to trace a series of journeys into the unknown.

The physical location of the unknown, a sense that it is elsewhere, is an aspect of the mystery of knowledge that is often forgotten when we have overcome our ignorance. We come to feel more at home with something, we are comfortable in knowing more about it, we no longer fear to tread its unknown streets. The excitement of being lost, of being confused, or even afraid, is replaced. Knowing is a secure place to be.

In driving the freeways, I have come to understand how a traveler might begin to feel and think as a stranger to the world. As a Canadian studying and migrating within America, I have often thought about the intellectual benefits and drawbacks of being a self-conscious outsider. As a Canadian whose parents, and grandfather and great-grandfather long before them, each came to North America from China, I have also felt deeply the bittersweet condition of being the stranger.

This study has been an attempt to answer why it is that an Asian American in the United States, no matter how long and for how many generations he or she might have been here, will still be regularly asked "Where are you from?" The inquisitors are never satisfied with the answers of Los Angeles, or Vancouver, or Canada. You are seen as an "Oriental" of some sort, and they need to sort you according to some foreign distinction. And so you must answer, "I am 'originally' from Japan," even though you have never been to Japan, or "My parents (or grandparents) are Chinese." To feel like an outsider is an existential phenomenon on the individual level, but it is also the result of journeying through a certain kind of landscape. It is this terrain of race relations in the United States that I have come to know through my travels.

So much writing about race relations in America continues to ignore everything except the dichotomy between black and white. Asians, Hispanics, and basically everybody else in the complex mix of American society are evaluated as unimportant or uninteresting. This study shows how crucial thinking about Orientals has been to the formulations of the most prominent theorists of race and culture in modern American intellectual life.

The Department of Sociology at the University of Chicago serves as the central locus for almost everything in this book. This does not mean that everything took place in Chicago, but that everything can somehow be traced there. The connections to the university wind through a series of sociological texts, a mass of research questions and projects. Beyond the texts themselves, I am interested in the personal contacts that we can see through the refraction of these texts—adviser-student relationships, collegial scholars, and chance encounters (the contact may have been as impersonal as someone reading someone else's book). My interest is not arbitrary, but contingent, because it is the very contingent fact that people came to be a part of this network of intellectual dialogues that makes them interesting to me: how they came to it, how they spoke and wrote within it, how their thinking came to be affected by the methodologies and ideas they learned, how their own interests and lives intersected with the "problems" as defined by the body of texts.

This book is divided into two main parts, each of which is dominated by a particular kind of physical and intellectual movement. In the first movement, a series of social scientists and reformers come to the West Coast of the United States to try to understand what they perceive as the "Oriental Problem" in America. In the second movement, a series of students with Chinese and Japanese backgrounds come to Chicago to study and research various aspects of this problem. The two movements are generally distinct in time, with one following the other, but they are also existentially different, involving very different positions in the institutional structure of American academia. In the conclusion, I retrace how Orientals came to be valued for being exotic and representative of a faraway place that was defined as being un-American, and how this helped to define what was American. As a shorthand, the first movement describes how some people wanted to know about Orientals and how it helped define themselves as white; the second movement describes how Orientals dealt with this, thought about it, survived, and at times even thrived within a structure built upon white curiosity; the conclusion retraces the legacy of Chicago theories in so much thinking about race and culture in modern America, and what we should do about it.

I have deliberately chosen to focus in the first movement on how the stage was initially set by the white Americans who came to learn about Orientals on the West Coast. There is a point to telling my story with Chinese Americans and Japanese Americans coming in the second movement to a stage already set. I want to emphasize the constraints that limited the possibilities for Asian American intellectuals in the twentieth century. Asian Americans, like African Americans and other intellectuals of color in the United States, did not (and in many ways still do not) have the range of possibilities that white scholars enjoyed. I could have opened with two simultaneous movements, with Asians coming to America, meeting with midwesterners coming to the Pacific Ocean. Such a setting for my story, however, would have implied that the meeting was between two groups with an equal say in how the meeting would be defined and understood.

To have narrated my story as if Chinese American and Japanese American intellectuals had as loud a voice in academia as their white colleagues would be misleading. This is not to suggest that they did not have as much to say, just that their possibilities for being heard and validated were much more restricted. The white, Protestant men who came to understand Orientals in the early twentieth century had first say in defining the meaning of Orientals in America. The Chinese Americans and Japanese Americans who came to sociology in the twentieth century said and did a great number of things, but they performed on a stage that was mostly not of their own making.[1]

In the second movement of this book, I describe how Chinese Americans and Japanese Americans came to know themselves through theories and institutions of "Orientalism." Edward Said used the term "Orientalism" to trace the long history of how people in Europe and the United States created an idea of an "Orient" that was the opposite of everything "Occidental." Said has also described a process of second-order Orientalism, the result of the power of Orientalist knowledge to so shape the possibilities of meaning that people "Orientalize" themselves.[2] One of the main ways this happened was through a language of self-identity that turned race into a performance. A theatrical metaphor for identity—calling skin color a costume or a mask—emphasized race as a set of acts performed in front of non-Asian audiences. The social possibilities that such a dramatic language allowed for Asian Americans were limited by the demand for Oriental performances, so that non–Asian Americans established the market for what was valuable. There was room for Asian American intellectuals to maneuver, to negotiate, and to choose different paths for understanding. It was, however, a highly constrained set of roles.

It is the nature of these constraints, and what they say about the ways that American intellectuals have treated race and culture in the twentieth century, that is the legacy of American Orientalism. By analyzing the institutions that white intellectuals created to understand Orientals in America, I am also describing the historical transition from gentlemanly to institutional Orientalism. In the nineteenth and early twentieth centuries, individual amateurs fascinated by the exotic, often missionaries, created knowledge about what they labeled the "Orient." This book describes the eventual creation of a professional discipline of sociology interested in Orientals in the United States and Asia.

This book is not a comprehensive study of American Orientalism. There have been a number of fine studies of Orientalist scholarship in regard to American knowledge about China and Japan, and therefore I have focused on how knowledge about Asian migrants to the United States was produced. This has allowed me to combine an examination of an Orientalist institution with the effects it had on Asian Americans who were both its subjects and its researchers. It has also allowed me to tie American Orientalism with race relations in the United States, countering a tendency to associate it only with knowledge produced about Asia. Delineating how American Orientalism focused so exclusively on China and Japan also explains how other groups, in particular those from the Philippines, were left out of definitions of who was Oriental. Those exclusions have continued to plague Asian American history.

The very term "Asian American" was coined by activists and intellectuals in the 1960s and 1970s as a reaction to the exotic connotations of the term "Oriental."[3] Valuing a past that had its roots in Asia, yet emphatically sounding a right to be treated as Americans, Asian American activists turned Orientalism on its head. The pursuit of Asian American studies arose as part of a larger social and political challenge to the oppression and marginalization of Asians in the United States and around the world, particularly in light of the racism displayed during American wars in Southeast Asia. There are, however, legacies from the past of American Orientalism that still need to be examined, and the connections between earlier definitions of the Oriental Problem and the current state of knowledge about Asian America form part of the epilogue of this book.

During a recent discussion of the difference between the label "Oriental" and the term "Asian American," a student in one of my classes at UCLA observed that an Oriental is an object—like a carpet or a meal or a vase—whereas an Asian American is a person. In the end, she captured perhaps the essential difference on which this whole book is structured. Throughout the history of the United States, Asian Americans have been objectified, in all the senses which that word connotes. Who has treated them as objects, and what about them as objects has made them interesting or valuable, and how they have responded to their treatment as objects—these are the interesting questions that follow from that simple formulation.

It is a common and trite observation that all scholarly research is in some way autobiographical. I had hoped rather than feared that mine would bear out this truth, and I have always tried to see this work as a personal journey as much as an intellectual exploration. And so I wish to thank all those who have been my fellow travelers during this long voyage. This study would not have been possible without John Kuo Wei Tchen, whose footnote in his edition of Paul Siu's work on the Chinese laundryman started off all of this. Without Jack's help and encouragement, this venture would never have begun. The same goes for my adviser, Dan Rodgers, whose intelligence and insight have provided an inspiring and necessary vigilance to my work. A research paper for his intellectual history seminar marked my first floundering into the depths of this topic, and without him as a mentor, my academic life would certainly have drowned long ago. Nell Painter provided valuable support and an admirable academic model for my decision to turn from studying European to American history, and Jim McPherson's kind encouragement and ecumenical approach allowed me the freedom to search and research.

Since the first moments of this project, I have held the conviction that the research of a number of students at the University of Chicago, written over half a century ago, is intrinsically interesting and deserves a close examination. For most of its history Regenstein Library at the University of Chicago used sign-out cards to keep track of loans. One of the pure joys of my research was to see the individual signatures and addresses of the sociologists who studied the Chinese and Japanese in America, neatly handwritten inside the covers of each other's dissertations and theses, complete with the dates borrowed and returned. Thus we can see the material traces of something as ephemeral as textual contact.

The most interesting times I had during my research travels, however, came not from examining archives and reading texts but from conversations with those sociologists from the University of Chicago whom I was able to interview. Like the texts they wrote so many years ago, these individuals were an illuminating conduit to those times in which I am interested and through which they lived. But they were also much more. It was an honor and a pleasure to talk with them not only about those years in the past but also about other years, other events, and other matters that had nothing to do with my study—the things out of which wonderful conversations are made. To Robert Faris, Clarence and Doris Glick, Carrell Horton, Ralph Hum, Beulah Ong Kwoh, Yuan Liang, Katherine Lind, Elizabeth Marwick, Jitsuichi and Edna Masuoka, Frank Miyamoto, Setsuko Nishi, Tom Shibutani, Eugene Uyeki, and all the people who helped me immeasurably by sharing their memories of past years, my deep thanks. Thanks especially to Elaine Lee, daughter of Rose Hum Lee, whose time and generosity with her mother's correspondence made possible some of my most interesting research.

Many thanks to the staffs of the Hoover Institution at Stanford University, the Bancroft Library at Berkeley, the Roosevelt University Library Special Collections in Chicago, the Regenstein Special Collections at the University of Chicago, the Social Welfare History Archive at the University of Minnesota, the Fisk University Library Special Collections, and the National Archives in Philadelphia and in Chicago, as well as to Marleen Tuttle of the University of Chicago Alumni Association, John W. Hughes Jr. of the Butte–Silver Bow Public Library, and Lon Johnson of the Mai Wah Society of Butte, Montana.

My research was supported by Princeton University and by a dissertation grant from the Social Sciences and Humanities Research Council of Canada. I benefited from the congenial support and food of the Woodrow Wilson Society of Fellows of Princeton and of my wonderful colleagues at the Department of History and the Asian American Studies Center at UCLA, in particular chairs Ron Mellor, Brenda Stevenson, and Don Nakanishi, who were kind enough to give me a job and several leaves in which to finish my work. The Institute of American Cultures, the Dean of Social Sciences Scott Waugh, and the Academic Senate of UCLA provided funding for converting my dissertation into a book. Portions of my manuscript were revised while I was at the University of California Humanities Research Institute at Irvine, the Center for the Humanities at Wesleyan University, the departments of American Studies and of History at Yale University, and the Balch Institute of Ethnic Studies in Philadelphia. I express my gratitude to those people who have encouraged me during this project, by correspondence and in person: Kay Anderson, Alan

Brinkley, John Burnham, Philip Choy, Sarah Deutsch, Cindy Fan, John Faragher, Shank Gilkeson, Art Hansen, Evelyn Hu-deHart, Shirley Hune, Yuji Ichioka, Walter Jackson, Victor Jew, Robert Johnston, Peter Kwong, Him Mark Lai, Barbara Ballis Lal, Stanford Lyman, Valerie Matsumoto, Fred Matthews, Muriel McClendon, Monica McCormick, David Montgomery, Stephen O. Murray, Don Nakanishi, Gary Nash, Franklin Ng, Mae Ngai, Frank Odo, Gary Okihiro, Peggy Pascoe, Rosane Rocher, Michael Salman, Ron Takaki, Brigitta van Rheinberg, Fred Wacker, Kay Warren, Sian Hunter White, Min Zhou, and especially Sucheng Chan and Scott Wong, who arranged my first publication, and Judy Yung, who generously shared material on Flora Belle Jan and Rose Hum Lee. Russell Leong advised changing the title to better capture the focus of my book, and among a number of valuable suggestions made during a term in Berkeley, Ling-chi Wang pushed me to pursue the story of Rose Hum Lee. His advice and Michael Omi's classes were crucial not only to this book but also to my understanding of Asian American history.

Many thanks to the manuscript reviewers who recommended this book for publication and who gave such valuable suggestions for revision. My particular gratitude to Andrew Abbot of the University of Chicago's Department of Sociology, an early supporter of the project who took the time to show me the icons of the department's history. His extensive and vehement criticism of my manuscript led to a number of serious reconsiderations that I hope have resulted in a better book. Randolf Arguelles, Chris Gantner, Lisa Itagaki, and Greg Vanderbilt contributed to this book as research assistants, and conversations with them and with students in my classes sharpened my arguments. Thanks to Sheldon Meyer, Thomas LeBien, Susan Ferber, and Will Moore of Oxford University Press for getting this book published and for their editorial suggestions.

I owe a debt of gratitude to my elementary and high school teachers, whose early belief in me imparted scholastic faith. My professors at the University of British Columbia—Janos Bak, Ed Hundert, Daniel Overmyer, Allan Sinel, Chris Stocker, and Steve Straker—introduced me to history, and Ed Wickberg taught me Chinese Canadian history. At Princeton I want to give thanks to Faye Angelozzi, Jean Babey, Kathy Baima, Patti Byrne, Bill and Christine Jordan, Steve Kotkin, Pamela Long, Arno Mayer, John and Mary Murrin (if not for a timely chat over coffee with John, I would have left Princeton for law school), Phil Nord, and Peggy Reilly. Thanks to my graduate school companions, in particular Alastair Bellany, Vince DiGirolomo, John and Marisa Giggie, Sally and Dan Gordon, Gary Hewitt, my roomate and intellectual confidant Walter Johnson, Steve Kantrowitz, Grazia Lolla, April Masten, Madére Olivar Hewitt, Jerry Podair, Ben Weiss, and John and Glenda Wertheimer for helping me survive. At both Princeton and UCLA, Steve Aron, Amy Green, Teo Ruiz, and Scarlett Freund have been dear friends, supporters, and dinner companions.

Kariann Yokota understands the ideas in this study better than I do. I have known from the moment I met her that she is much smarter than I am. During countless discussions about the place of Asians in America, she sharpened arguments and gave me the gift of her own ideas. Without her expertise and knowledge of Asian American and U.S. history, I could never have completed this project. She read the manuscript with extraordinary care and improved virtually every sentence and phrase. She has been an intellectual collaborator in writing this story, and, more than anybody else, she has contributed to its every idea. There is more in here that is taken from her than there is that I can call my own.

Finally, the largest debt of all, to my family. To the Yokota and Ichiho families—in particular Keiko, Tak, Audrey, and Roger—who have given me their home and made me one of their own. To my wife, for whom I have been searching all my life—for you, my love, the simplest wish—may you always be here. To my sister, and to my brother and his family, who have traveled with me and made the journey that much richer. To my grandparents and great-grandparents, who struggled and hoped, and that has meant everything. To my parents, who supported me in every sense, and whose dreams brought me to this point. They have made me who I am.

Los Angeles, California   H. Y.
May 2000

CONTENTS

NOTES ON TERMS AND TRANSLATIONS

This book describes how certain conceptual categories such as "race," "culture," and "identity" developed as markers of social belonging. A number of terms are enclosed in quotation marks when they first appear in the text to emphasize a critical perspective upon how institutional practices produced them as categories of social existence. In particular, the term "Oriental" appears in this book not because I condone its contemporary use as a label but because it reflects a specific historical category and the social relations associated with it. Relatedly, I use the term "white" for that constellation of people who benefited from inclusion into the category of "whiteness" by being defined and treated in practice as different from Americans of "color." Finally, most Chinese terms appear in a transliterated form of Cantonese rather than the modern phonetic pinyin form.

Thinking Orientals

AN INVOCATION

Life differs from death in the matter of movement.

—Roderick Duncan McKenzie, "Movement and the
Ability to Live," 1926

Let us start with a map. Unfold like a painted fan a mercator projection, a view from high above the earth encompassing the Pacific Ocean, with Asia on the left and the Americas on the right. The arc of the Pacific Rim sweeps from the blotch of Australia to Indonesia and Southeast Asia, up the coast of China past the Korean peninsula and Japan, around Alaska and down the West Coast of Canada and the United States, tailing off to the tip of South America. Imagine the map as a parchment through which to relive the past, a chart to trace the stories of people as they move about, leaving a trail of dotted lines that follow them from place to place. The story of these people is one of movement, and like a travel-worn atlas that shows the scrawled markings of roads taken and places seen, this map will show journeys and tell stories of how people came to see things previously unseen, how they tried to understand what they saw, and how they often kept going somewhere farther in order to understand what they had just seen. Place-names coalesce on this imaginary map, given meaning within and connected to the lives of our travelers. Guangdong Province in southern China, Japan, Hawaii, Seattle, San Francisco, Stockton, Los Angeles, Butte, Tule Lake, Iowa City, Nashville, and, on the extreme edge of our map, Chicago.

This story is about a group of people from disparate backgrounds and differing places. It describes how their paths came to cross, and how by crossing paths they came to an understanding of each other and of themselves. Ultimately, this story traces how, in this world of movement and migration, of people in new places, some travelers came to an agreement about who they were, where they were, and what they meant to each other. . . .

INTRODUCTION

The Locations of History

It might be tempting to think of Asian immigration to the United States in mythic terms, of migrants from the Far East coming to the West Coast of the United States and crossing the continent eastward, passing fleeing Indians and westering white settlers. Figuring Asian immigrants as a sort of anti–frontier myth would be appealing, a powerful way (along with the story of Hispanic Americans who were in California, Texas, and New Mexico long before it was the American West) of subverting Frederick Jackson Turner's conception of the western frontier. Turner's 1892 thesis placed white European Americans at the center of history, situated at a frontier moving steadily westward, occupying the boundary between civilization and savagery. Telling a story about Asians from a different shore— people who crossed the Pacific instead of the Atlantic and created their own eastern frontier—might seem a welcome corrective to Eurocentric American history. But the notion of an Asian diaspora spreading outward from China and Japan into Southeast Asia, Australia, Hawaii, South America, and finally Canada and the United States would only place Asians instead of Europeans at the center of history.[1]

It would be more interesting to talk about locations, about points between which people move. Getting away from the metaphors of homeland and destination that make America the end of long journeys, this story is about various sites. These places were the central nodes for the production and distribution of knowledge, the founts for creating the forms of consciousness that result from contact. In migrating, and in imagining the differences between the places we have come to and the places we have left behind, new forms of knowledge are created. Often, this knowledge is predicated on a definition of the exotic, of what is absolutely foreign and different about one place or the other. Racial and ethnic identity was defined during this period, a subset of a larger phenomenon labeled "cultural consciousness."

The concept of "culture" was a way of getting away from biological theories of race that had served a similar function of categorizing similarities and differences between humans. Cultural theory was a knowledge system arising from the categorization of differences—between American and Chinese, between American and Japanese, between Japanese and Chinese, between "Negro" and "Oriental," between white and "colored." At the same time, it created a sense of similarity among people who purportedly shared the same culture.

These systematic comparisons were made at certain locations. And thus Honolulu, Seattle, San Francisco, Los Angeles, and Chicago were sites for the production of knowledge about the exotic. The knowledge that was produced was linked to other theories about the geographic origin of cultural differences: Where did difference arise? Who brought it, and from where? Questions were asked and knowledge was made. The locations were meeting points, sites from which and to which people moved. Knowledge production within the institutions that researched the Oriental Problem involved both physical migration and intellectual change. Migrating intellectuals carried ideas between places—they also created new ideas, moving from one way of seeing the world to another.

There was a point in American history when social theories about race, migration, and culture provided a resonant description of everyday life. Ideas about Asian Americans formed a central part of such theories. Global labor migration and population displacement caused by industrialization and colonization led to massive immigration in the nineteenth and early twentieth centuries. By the 1920s, social scientists had created a body of theories for understanding race and culture that had grown out of this world of mass movement.

Immigration legislation in 1924 ended large-scale migration to the United States. In the period between 1924 and 1965, the social landscape of the United States changed, and theories about culture, assimilation, and racial consciousness lost their emphasis on migration and movement. In a world where new immigrants were few, ethnicity became a matter of eradication and loss, a process of forgetting. By 1965, when the doors to the United States were reopened to migrants, analyses of race and culture reflected the demographic history of the exclusion period; when ethnicity as a matter of migration was recalled, it was within the memories of grandparents. The history of "Orientals" within the United States reflects this larger periodization within American history.

The era of 1924 to 1965 is an aberration in American history rather than the model. At every other point in U.S. history, significant new migration to the nation has been the rule. Before and during the 1920s, social thinkers tried to make sense of race and culture as processes of movement and contact. With an estimated 35 million new immigrants coming to the United States in the century before the 1924 immigration act, conceptions of America as the final destination of long journeys dominated. In the four decades of immigration exclusion between 1924 and 1965, social theories increasingly reflected the deluded belief that race and culture were static entities, categories of social life within a United States that had clear boundaries. During that era, conceptions of race and culture became shorthand labels for long-term histories of migration. In the past three decades, Americans have reawakened to a world of movement. The place of Asian migrants in such a world still needs to be adequately imagined, but until we understand the legacy of earlier theories about "Orientals," reflecting earlier histories, such a project is born of amnesia.

Asians have been understood within American social thought in two major ways—as a racial "problem" and as a racial "solution." From the time Chinese arrived in the mid–nineteenth century, migrants from Asia were considered a threat to white labor and American society. Categorized as Orientals, these immigrants were demonized as exotic and non-American. From violent lynchings through the internment of Japanese Americans during World War II, Asian Americans were treated as a problem. Since the 1960s, they have seemingly become the opposite, sanctified as the "model minority" solution to racial and economic ills. This new notion about Asians, however, still depends on an exoticization of them as somehow not American, and it traces a theoretical lineage to early sociological studies about the importance of race and culture in the United States.

In the early twentieth century, a number of American Protestant missionaries, along with scholars at the University of Chicago's Department of Sociology, became interested in Orientals in America. Their interest led to Americans born of Chinese and Japanese ancestry being concerned with the same questions, and the result was a series of scholarly texts produced by whites and Asian Americans about the so-called Oriental Problem in America.

The Chicago sociologists came up with a number of approaches and theories in order to understand the Oriental in America, and they often used these same theories in their studies of race relations in general. Their ideas about the Oriental Problem thus had connections to definitions of race and culture in modern America that went far beyond the Chinese and Japanese who were their initial subjects. The sociologists deliberately connected their study of the Oriental Problem both to their theories about European immigrants and to their interest in what they called the "Negro Problem" in America. The Oriental represented a way for them to bridge these two separate issues, a subject that could amalgamate their studies of immigration and of race.

In connecting racial theory to the phenomenon of immigration, Chicago sociologists provided a rich antecedent to contemporary examinations of race and culture in a transnational context. They were theorists of migration as the main constituent of modern life, and though we have lost many of the ways in which these sociologists analyzed social life, there remain many important legacies, as well as forgotten lessons that are still salvageable.

Chicago sociologists wrote often about what they called modernity, which, for them, was about movement, contact, and change. In migrating, and in imagining the differences between the places come to and the places left behind, new kinds of knowledge are created. Often, this knowledge is predicated on a definition of the exotic, of what is absolutely foreign and different about one place or the other. The Chicago sociologists emphasized the forms of consciousness that contact created, the stories of marginalization and narratives of exclusion that almost always resulted from new contacts between groups of people. By the 1950s, the main legacy of Chicago formulations of social interaction in America could be found in symbolic interaction theory, a focus on the formation of group identity and consciousness as the main constituent of race, culture, and ethnicity.

The central importance of Robert Park's theories in popular and politically dominant understandings of race and ethnicity in America is unquestionable. The "assimilation cycle" and theories about "race prejudice" and "marginality" had a formative effect on American social thought. Even more important, sociological theories had a profound effect on the expansion in the twentieth century of ethnicity and racial identity as means of self-description and understanding. For example, Richard Wright, author of the novel *Native Son*, explained in 1945 that his intellectual understanding of his experiences growing up a "Negro" in America owed much to the theories of Chicago sociology. Wright's experiences of racism were not created by Chicago sociology, but the manner in which he analyzed and narrated his racial identity in his writings was informed by these sociological explanations.[2] Identity itself as a theory and mode of self-understanding came into importance along with the rising rhetorical power of social science.

In focusing so much of social scientific theory on identity and the ethnic awareness of racialized groups, the Chicago school highlighted racial consciousness as the most interesting phenomenon in race relations. These sociologists were aware of the unequal constraints and limitations in possibilities for consciousness that a racist social structure in the United States had produced. However, in targeting consciousness as a main subject of study, Chicago theorists helped popularize an appreciation of racial identity that made it into an aesthetic object. They produced an institutional structure that valued the exotic nature of the knowledge possessed by Orientals and other "ethnics." They also defined the dominant forms through which such knowledge should be expressed.

This is a story about the origins and consequences of a widespread fascination with the Oriental in the United States.[3] Social scientists became interested in Orientals, and in doing so they created an intellectual and institutional construction. This construction was a framework of theories that defined who Orientals were, as well as their place in America. It was also the social practices of a network of academics and researchers who produced these ideas and who were connected to each other through the University of Chicago and their research on the Oriental Problem.

The intellectual construction of the Oriental Problem came to shape almost all academic thinking about Asian immigrants in America during the first half of the twentieth century. This happened because the institutional construction created a demand for Chinese American and Japanese American informants and researchers. These Asian American scholars, along with their non-Asian colleagues, produced a coherent body of knowledge about Orientals in the United States. Distributed by the institutional networks of Chicago sociology into universities and teaching colleges across the nation, this knowledge of Orientals came to dominate how Asian Americans were defined by others and how they understood themselves.

The Asian American intellectuals who came to be a part of the institutional construction associated with the Oriental Problem were given a chance to conduct sociological research, and they took advantage of the rare opportunity to enter careers in academia. The theories and definitions of the Oriental Problem also had a formative effect on the self-identities of the intellectuals involved, giving them a new sense of who they were and of their place in American society. Their understandings of themselves were often profoundly affected by their contact with the intellectual construction of the Oriental Problem. As an institution, social science reproduced its members socially at the same time that it replicated its knowledge intellectually.

At the heart of this professional process lay the entwined practices of how to evaluate exotic knowledge and how to be an elite white. Unlike the value of whiteness described by historian David Roediger, as a metaphorical wage from which certain workers benefited by their inclusion into the category of white, the extolment of whiteness in the institutional practices of American Orientalism lay hidden at the center.[4] Professional academics, in defining an interest in the exotic, and at the same time producing knowledge about the unknown, also produced themselves as the expert knowers. Seeing themselves as enlightened and cosmopolitan at the same time they defined working-class racists as ignorant and provincial, progressive and liberal elites crafted themselves as the knowing subject through which others became important.

For much of the twentieth century, analyses of racism have centered on the working classes. It was economic competition, combined with unenlightened ignorance, that was at the root of all racial conflict and prejudice. Elite ideas of race and culture were understood to be in opposition to working-class racism. As such, they were assumed to be antiracist. That story has always benefited educated elites in the United States, since their own economic status allowed them the privilege of dabbling in knowledge of the exotic. It is time to see elite definitions of racial and cultural difference from another perspective.

The desire to know the unknown, to acquire the exotic, is not restricted to knowledge about Orientals. But if the pursuit of knowledge about the unknown has marked the modern sciences, it has had a peculiar character and power in the institutional form of Orientalism. This is not to say that the white sociologists in this book are bad men. Indeed, they were some of the few allies that Asian immigrants to the United States ever had. Without these men (there were few women in positions of power), none of the Asian American intellectuals discussed in this book would have had the chance to enter academia. During their time, the Chicago sociologists were some of the few academics who recruited Asian Americans and African Americans as colleagues. By examining what they thought they were doing in studying Asians, my goal is to explain how their intellectual project was a progressive program, but also how it built an institutional structure that was Orientalist. In other words, individual sociologists and their intentions cannot be divorced from the structural effects of their practices.

It is crucial to understand the importance of institutional practices in the creation of knowledge. Even today, inequities still gird the evaluation of exotic identities within the United States. Ethnic and racial groups in America are seen to possess seemingly unique forms of knowledge, a situation that both helps and hinders them. Able to offer knowledge to those who are curious, racial groups and the identities they possess become objects of exchange.

From Oriental Problem to "model minority," Asian Americans have both suffered and benefited from definitions of their exoticism. Unlike European immigrants who blended into whiteness, Asian Americans, like

African Americans, have been both valued and denigrated for what was assumed to be different about them. Always tied to some other place far away, and marked with the desire for and abhorrence of the foreign that suffuses any use of the term "Oriental," Asian Americans still struggle to define themselves as part of the American social body.

Set apart from the rest of America, Asian American intellectuals have fought hard to define for themselves a place in the United States. For the last seventy years, Asian American academics have been caught between the need to create knowledge that is valuable to an academia dominated by the curiosity of white Americans and a desire to help, through their knowledge, others who have been similarly treated as "Orientals." They have been valued for being exotic and different at the same time that they have been marginalized for the same reasons. They began as representatives of a "problem" to be solved, and in the last thirty years have perversely come to be valued as the potential solution to the race problems of this country.

Race, according to sociologist Robert Park, was in the mind, a matter of consciousness. Park left a legacy of believing that race was only a matter of thinking: if we just stopped thinking about race, it would go away. But in a strange twist on Descartes, in thinking about race continually, Park brought it continually into existence. We think race, therefore race exists. Just how difficult a feat it is to forget race is proven by how impossible an accomplishment it was for the Chicago sociologists, all of them professional thinkers. More important, even if every single American did stop thinking about race, this would not erase the legacy of a history of thinking about it and practicing it for so long that every element and relationship in society has been structured upon its definitions. Indeed, forgetting about race would only freeze the historical inequities that existed because of racial thinking.

We put much moral judgment on the weighing of intent—if someone did not mean to hurt you, then, morally, that is better than if he did intend to hurt you. If someone did not intend to be a racist, then she is a better person than someone whose ideas and thoughts are prejudiced. We often judge people on whether they meant what they said or whether they meant to do what they did. In contrast, however, we might put much stock in deeds rather than words—actions, it is said, speak louder than words.

It is the link between intention and consequences, thinking and doing, theory and practice—this is how we might understand the Oriental Problem as both an intellectual and an institutional construction. Describing the Oriental Problem as a set of institutional practices connects the theories of Chicago sociology to a set of relationships between people. Ideas, in other words, are produced and reproduced by networks of people, and the ways in which these people understand and use these ideas are embedded in a particular set of social practices.

Social theory is a rhetorical language. Its explanations become true in the way in which any group of words and ideas can achieve truth, which is true to a group of people. Truth is sought in social contexts. Only when people speak with each other, argue and decide upon what something is to mean, what something is worth, only then is truth—and falsehood—created. For too long, we have thought that white men in academia sought Truth (with a capital *T*) and that women and minority scholars pursuing gender, racial, and ethnic studies studied only themselves. In the beginning all knowledge is tied to personal concerns. What is interesting and in need of knowing is always tied to the knower who asks.

Understanding social practices unites both acts and ideas, without one being prior to the other. Social practices embody the power relations that shape the ways in which knowledge is created and validated. It is not the ideas of the Oriental Problem that have had the greatest effect on Asian Americans—it is the social practices that these ideas have accompanied. The production of ideas reflects a pattern of institutional practices. By examining these practices, we can come to understand the very different paths that people treated as Oriental, in contrast to those treated as white, have had to tread in the United States. The unintended and often ironic consequences of the Oriental Problem as a set of practices have had a significant effect on the history of Asians in America.

FIRST MOVEMENT

Coming to the West

Constructing the Oriental Problem

A SETTING

Backdrop a mural, with the terrified faces of Chinese men running away from an explosion, their long hair ponytailed into distinctive queues, flapping in the wind of their flight. Behind them, torching the buildings and homes of the Chinese laborers, stands a lynch mob of bearded white men, carrying shotguns and makeshift clubs. The scene might have a date marked in bold letters, perhaps 1877, perhaps 1885. The specific location? It could be Tacoma, Washington, or Rock Springs, Wyoming, or Snake River, Idaho, or a dozen small towns in California, from Redding to Bakersfield. It does not matter, as long as the image is retained: a memory of Chinese workers and merchants being driven out of frontier towns, herded in a long march to the ghettos of San Francisco and Vancouver, British Columbia.[1]

Imagine a man in a suit, circa 1920, a lawyer perhaps, a man comfortable addressing a crowd, comfortable in his persuasion. He gives a speech, punctuated by cheers and chants of "No Japs":

> It takes dynamite to stir up Americans when their country is in danger. But when we get aroused watch out. This is not a question of racial equality. It is simply the incompatibility of the white and yellow races. We cannot mingle, socially, industrially, economically, or politically. Once a Jap always a Jap. . . .
>
> The churches have been our biggest obstacle in the fight against the Japanese. We have had to fight propaganda of the golden rule, the brotherhood of man, live and let live philosophy and all the other countless unthinking, sentimental arguments that our religious dictators

would have us follow. The churches have been easy prey for the propa-
gandists of the Mikado, as also have many of our universities, like Stanford
and Columbia.

Loud, prolonged cheering echoes as the man works the crowd: "Let's
stick together and the Japs will have to leave. They have had to do it everywhere else, when public opinion demanded it. We can save them all their
nickels and dimes by making them stay down town in their 'Little Tokio,'
where they belong."[2]

1923.

If you live on the West Coast of the United States and you happen to
have come from somewhere in Asia, you live a restricted existence. As an
"Asiatic," a "Mongolian," an "Oriental," you are "ineligible for citizenship,"
unable to become a naturalized American, and if you are in California, you
are forbidden by law from owning land.[3] If you happen to have been born
in the United States, you are legally a citizen, but you face widespread
discrimination in work, housing, and the law. If you are Chinese, chances
are that you are male, since exclusionary laws have kept Chinese women
out of the country since 1882, and thus fewer than one out of eight people
with Chinese ancestry are female.[4] You would find it difficult to live outside of a Chinatown—almost no one except other Chinese would rent or
sell to you. If you are from the Philippines, chances are even higher that
you are male—one in twenty immigrants are women—and you probably
work as a migrant agricultural laborer. If you are from Japan, chances are
closer to even that you are female. You might be a "picture bride" brought
over in an arranged marriage to a Japanese man already in the country,
and any children you produce would immediately be American citizens by
birth. Although the practice of bringing over arranged brides has just been
stopped, there are enough Japanese women in the United States to lead
to a sizable American-born generation of children, particularly in comparison to the Chinese and the Filipino communities.[5] As for the Chinese,
however, anti-Asian practices often restrict you to ghettos such as "Little
Tokyo."

Being considered an Oriental, you find your prospects for prosperity
and your choice of employment and housing curtailed by a long history of
anti-Asian agitation by labor groups and nativist organizations such as the
Sons and Daughters of the Golden West and the American Legion. The
U.S. Congress is just about to pass a series of new immigration laws that
will virtually cut off all immigration from Asia. However, this final solution to Oriental immigration to the West Coast is still not enough for
many—some people want to deprive American-born Orientals of their
citizenship and drive all "Asiatics" out of the country. Many of the exclu-

sionist groups proudly point to a violent past of so-called sandlot agitation, mythologizing the vigilante actions of lynch mobs that drove the Chinese out of most of the American West during the 1870s and 1880s. By 1923, these groups perceive the Japanese in the country to be the latest manifestation of the "Yellow Peril" to "white civilization." If you are of Asian ancestry in the United States in 1923, you are seen as "alien"—very few people see you as "American." Even among those who tolerate you and your existence, there is an overwhelming sense that you are an unknown, a mystery, perhaps even inscrutable. . . .

Professions of Faith:
Missionaries, Sociologists, and the
Survey of Race Relations,
1924–1926

In the first week of June 1924 a middle-aged missionary named
J. Merle Davis paid a visit to the Chinatown of Fresno, California. The
Chinatown was small, only a block or so along Tulare Street, and Davis would
have had no trouble locating the building for which he was looking. If it
had been nighttime, he could have been guided by the brilliant neon sign
that announced the Yet Far Low Restaurant, but even in daylight the elec-
tric sign on the corner of Tulare and China Alley was easily visible.

Merle Davis was not a Californian. His father had been an American
missionary to Japan, and Davis had grown up there. After graduating from
college in the United States, Davis had returned to Japan to serve as the
secretary of the Tokyo Young Men's Christian Association (YMCA), and
only recently had he moved to the United States. At this moment, he was
on his way to meet Flora Belle Jan, the seventeen-year-old daughter of the
man who owned the Yet Far Low chop suey restaurant. Although Jan's
family was well-off by Chinatown standards, none of this wealth was apparent in the living quarters attached to the restaurant. They were crowded,
dark, and, according to Davis, dirty and reeking of Chinatown smells.
Within this humble home, Flora Belle Jan slept in a half loft, one side of
which was divided into a place for clucking hens.

Davis was fascinated by the young woman. This was his second visit,
and despite the crude surroundings, he saw enormous potential in her. Jan
was witty, poised, and talkative, with a penchant for being modern and
unconventional in the manner of a young flapper. Armed with a vivacious
intelligence and imagination, she had ambitions to be a writer, and several

of her stories had been published in William Randolph Hearst's prestigious *San Francisco Examiner*. During his visit, Davis chatted with Jan about her parents' disapproval of her conduct, and how she was afraid they would not support her wish to attend Berkeley and further her career. Afterward, he left convinced that with the "right handling and leadership she might make a great deal of herself and become a real help to her own people."[1]

Why was this missionary from Boston through Japan so interested in this young Chinese American flapper? What did he see in her? More important, how did she see herself? From this initial location in the Yet Far Low chop suey restaurant in Fresno, we can fan out in a number of directions. In one, we can follow the question of what had brought this Protestant missionary, and behind him his network of evangelical brothers, to this small Chinatown in California. In another, we can trace a story of how these missionaries brought in a related network of social scientists who had their own interests in this woman and her community. We can also see how this young "Oriental American," and many others like her, fit into the description that the missionaries and sociologists presented of the Oriental Problem.

American missionaries connected the conversion of Orientals in Asia with the sociological study of Orientals in America. Beginning with the Survey of Race Relations on the Pacific Coast of the United States between 1924 and 1926 and continuing through the formation of the Institute of Pacific Relations in Hawaii in 1926, a network of American missionaries and social scientists crisscrossed Asia, North America, and Hawaii, producing knowledge about the relations between people living in each of these locations. In the course of their explorations of what they labeled the Pacific frontier, they created a body of theories about the differences between Orientals and "Occidentals."

Furthermore, the American missionaries and sociologists would entrench their scholarly knowledge within a set of academic and funding institutions that would disseminate and reproduce their definitions of the "Orient."[2] The first third of this book, therefore, examines how an American institution of Orientalism arose in the 1920s, putting in place definitions of the great physical and cultural distance between "Orientals" and "Americans" that would have long-term effects on how Asian Americans were understood within the United States for the rest of the twentieth century.

The Japan Gang

What was the missionary J. Merle Davis doing in California? He had been sent on a reconnaissance trip to the West Coast by the Institute of Social and Religious Research, a New York–based organization that channeled Rockefeller Foundation money into what it deemed worthy social research projects. The stated purpose of the institute, which was run by a number of Protestant ministers with a deep concern over social welfare and the state of religiosity in the United States (they were often connected with the label of "Social Gospel"), was to finance scientific research that would serve the aim of social reform.[3] One of the institute's key members was John R. Mott, a leader in the YMCA movement in the United States and the founder of the YMCA International.

The YMCA movement had been planned in the last two decades of the nineteenth century as an attempt to make Christianity a practical element of everyday modern life, targeting the urban centers of America and the world. The mission of the YMCA was to promote goodwill and harmony through institutions that organized social activities that encouraged "fair play" and "cooperation." As an act of Social Gospel, the YMCA was an attempt to expand religiosity from a private, individual orientation into the social acts of everyday life.

Since the first anti-Chinese riots of the 1870s, Protestant missionaries were among the few allies of Asian immigrants in the United States. Concurrent with their Far Eastern missions, Baptists, Methodists, and Presbyterians set up missions to "heathens" in America. Beyond the goals of conversion and saving souls, these missionaries were also concerned with the social welfare of immigrants. They believed that the numerous laws passed by state and federal legislatures that discriminated against "Asiatics" in America made mission work in Asian countries more difficult. But despite the fact that it was in the missionaries' own interests to lessen the harsh treatment of Orientals in America, their condemnations of American injustice were nonetheless heartfelt.[4]

The missionaries had a long history of involvement in the effort to counter anti-Asian agitation. For example, the most prominent friend of the Japanese in the country, the Reverend Sidney Gulick, had been born in Japan and had spent most of his life there. As "Oriental secretary" for the Federal Council of Churches of Christ in America, he published a series of pamphlets and books attacking restrictive American immigration and landowning legislation in regard to Asians and calling for equal and just treatment of immigrants and aliens regardless of race, color, or religion.[5] In addition to immigration reform, the Federal Council had tried to promote "friendly relations" between the United States and Asian countries by calling for such acts as the elimination of the opium trade, universal disarmament, and Philippine independence. Sidney Gulick, J. Merle Davis, George Gleason, and Galen Fisher were members of the network that composed the Federal Council, the American Board of Foreign Missions, the YMCA and Young Women's Christian Association (YWCA), and the Institute of Social and Religious Research.

In 1922, George Gleason of Los Angeles and Galen Fisher of New York, both returned from mission work at the YMCA in Tokyo, called for an investigation of widespread anti-Japanese agitation on the West Coast.[6] J. Merle Davis was sent to the West Coast in 1922 to find out what could be done about anti-Japanese agitation. By the end of 1923, he had decided that the Institute of Social and Religious Research should pledge $55,000 toward the Survey on Race Relations on the Pacific Coast. This ambitious effort was aimed not only at discovering the facts about the "racial situation" in the West but also at bringing pro- and anti-Asian groups together.[7] Because of the political polarization over Oriental immigration, Davis believed that just getting the opposing sides to talk would be difficult. In accordance with the missionaries' larger aims of goodwill and peaceful reconciliation, he felt that bringing everyone together into a mutual dialogue about "objective" facts would be one of the greatest accomplishments of the survey.[8]

Davis recognized that the missionaries and the nativists had opposing sympathies in regard to Orientals. He attributed this divergence to their vastly different backgrounds. In private letters, the missionaries pinned the causes of anti-Oriental sentiments among West Coast whites on several factors: their lack of education, their origins in the American South or Catholic Ireland, and their ignorance of Oriental culture. It was no coincidence that the backgrounds of the Protestant ministers were quite different; they all were college educated, originated from the northeastern United States, and had spent significant time in the Orient.[9] The missionaries believed that their experience in dealing with the supposed subtleties of Oriental culture made them uniquely qualified to overcome the conflicts between groups on the West Coast. In recommending his friend Merle Davis to lead the survey, George Gleason referred to the time that all of them had spent in Japan. Political divisions in the survey made it necessary to "have an executive head who possesses the kind of tact which years of experience in Japan seem to develop in us." Gleason questioned "whether any man on the Coast, or any ordinary man who has not lived in the Far East, could do the job that needs to be done."[10]

The missionaries knew the Japanese from firsthand experience, and they had been frustrated in dealing with Orientals who seemed to take offense at the slightest mistake. They blamed the offenses, of course, on the strict demands of social etiquette and politeness that Japanese society demanded, and not on their own ignorance or tendency to misread social cues. In the end, however, they felt that after dealing with such an exotic and intricate culture as the Japanese, handling the nativists would be relatively easy.

"Is there an Oriental Problem in America?" an article describing the survey asked. "If so, where is it? What are its manifestations? What do we know of our Chinese, East Indians, Filipinos, and Japanese?"[11] In setting out to research race relations on the West Coast, both missionaries and white supremacists agreed that the Oriental Problem was the central concern. But who was an Oriental? And what was the "problem"? The answers to these questions, not surprisingly, depended on who was being asked.

For the Asiatic Exclusion League, the Sons of the Golden West, the American Legion, and other nativist organizations, "Oriental" was a racial classification that not only was bounded by presumed origins in Asia and the Far East (the mythical Orient) but also reflected a history of struggles over the threat of cheap labor to supposedly "native whites." After the Civil War and the end of the enslavement of African Americans, labor organizations and unions on the West Coast had portrayed Chinese "coolie" workers as the newest threat to "free" (as opposed to "enslaved") labor. Excluding Chinese from their organizational efforts, unions used them as the whip to bring white labor into line. At the same time, the claim that Chinese immigrants were "nonnative" somehow transformed immigrants from Ireland, Great Britain, and European countries into "native" Americans. This was accomplished by equating white and native, leaving out all those classified as nonwhite, even if they had arrived in the United States earlier and had lived and worked in the country much longer.[12]

By 1923, the Chinese had been so effectively excluded from most occupations that they were no longer considered a threat. But the nativist rhetoric of a Yellow Peril and the threat of Orientals to America rested upon the continuing memory of how the Chinese "problem" was overcome. When large numbers of Japanese immigrants came to the West Coast at the turn of the century, they were designated as the latest "Oriental invasion." Just like the Chinese before them, the Japanese were portrayed as creating unfair competition because of their work habits and their ability to endure hardship and sacrifice, threatening to crowd out helpless white workers and farmers who could not compete. Anti-Japanese organizations pointed to what they saw as unnaturally productive farming practices (when compared with the relatively inefficient methods of most European American farmers) as an indication that the growing numbers of Japanese were about to take over the West.

The nativists were further enraged by the strength of the Japanese government in protecting Japanese nationals in the United States. Unlike the Chinese government, which had been relatively powerless to stop the Chinese Exclusion Act of 1882, the Japanese government had been able to forestall any federal legislation in the United States that discriminated against Japanese immigrants. Until the 1920s, successful anti-Japanese legislation had almost all been on the state level, and nativist groups in the West called for a strong federal exclusion act.[13] Not until the new federal immigration laws of 1924, which barred Asians along with almost all other immigrants from entry into America, did the U.S. government finally seem to act against the "Oriental invasion."[14]

The tendency of nativist and labor groups to link racial definitions of Orientals with perceived economic conflicts led to an extension of Oriental classification to East Indian and Filipino migrant agricultural workers, even though during the early 1920s there were many fewer members of these groups than there were Chinese and Japanese in the United States.[15] To the undiscerning eye that could not tell a "Chinaman" from a "Jap," the perceived visual difference between traditional Orientals and East Indians and Filipinos was bridged by their similar economic threat.

Stretching the category of Orientals even wider, Korean immigrants were entering Hawaii and the United States in relatively small numbers. Korean migrants, however, were restricted from leaving home by the Japanese colonial government that controlled Korea at that time. The few Koreans who did manage to come to Hawaii and the mainland United States were legally counted as Japanese nationals, and within the context of the survey they generally were taken for being Japanese.

During the early days of the Survey of Race Relations, Davis even responded to the suggestions of labor leaders to consider including Mexicans in the survey's purview, since they were seen as one of the larger racial labor forces. However, he eventually decided that the definition of Oriental would not stretch that far. The practical focus of the survey was to be Asian migrants, in particular Chinese and Japanese.[16] East Indians and Filipinos would receive little attention.

The survey's eventual focus on Chinese and Japanese as the main Oriental subgroups had everything to do with its missionary organizers. Davis, Gleason, and Fisher had begun their project because of their background in Japan and their concern over anti–Japanese agitation; they expanded the focus of the survey to include the Chinese at a much later date. Surprisingly, this expansion was less in response to labor leaders, who no longer had much "problem" with the Chinese, than to the many missionaries who worked among the Chinese in both China and the United States.

In the end, the definition of who was an Oriental was connected with the missionaries' interest in the Orient as the geographic location of their mission. They empathized with Orientals in America because they viewed them in the same way that they viewed Orientals in the Orient: as potential converts. Organizations such as the YMCA International professed a global vision of not only Christianization but also Americanization, spreading the "good word" about the American way of life, which they saw as a concurrent goal. The Survey of Race Relations was only one of many steps toward the remaking of the Oriental at home and abroad.[17]

For missionaries, the Oriental Problem lay not with the threat of Chinese and Japanese labor but with West Coast whites and their terrible treatment of Orientals in America.[18] Davis, Gleason, Fisher, and Gulick had all known Christianized Orientals in Japan, and many converted Orientals had migrated to the United States. The missionaries truly believed that if the American public could come to see Orientals as they did, as potential and successful converts to Christianity, then all would be well. The economic threat of Oriental labor was a nonissue once Orientals were recognized as fellow Christians and Americans. The definition of Christian also stood for Protestant. Many Filipinos were devout Catholics from centuries of Spanish rule, but their assimilation into America also entailed denominational conversion.

In an attempt to dispel the illusion that there was a Yellow Peril in the United States, the Reverend Sidney Gulick tried to prove that Asians were "assimilable." His book *The American Japanese Problem* included chapters answering yes to questions such as "Are Japanese assimilable?" and "Can Americans assimilate Japanese?" Pictures of "Americanized" children from Japan in Christian homes and schools, wearing Western dress and hairstyles, exemplified the "assimilability" of the Japanese. One of the captions announced that the "American-Japanese" man in the photograph could "speak no Japanese" and was a graduate of Yale, proof that he had reached the pinnacle of white Protestant achievement in America.[19]

External signs such as clothing and hairstyle became the proof of outright assimilation, since they signified the "loss" of traditional dress and speech. Gulick and other pro-Japanese writers often used these signs as a rhetorical weapon to combat the fears of anything less than "100% Americanism" that the nativist organizations were propagating. Americanization was a focal term in the debate that surrounded the image of America as a "melting pot," and the question of assimilation became the center of the Oriental Problem. A key claim of the missionaries' argument against nativist groups such as the American Legion and the Sons of the Golden West was that Orientals were in fact assimilable to American life, as proven by their adoption of superficial signs of Americanization such as clothing, speech, and hairstyle. American manners and Christian beliefs would surely follow.

The fascination of Merle Davis with Flora Belle Jan, the young daughter of the chop suey restaurateur, was part of the missionaries' desire for symbols of effective assimilation. Jan was American-born, had the mannerisms of a young American flapper, and proved to all who met her that she was not like the typical Oriental. As Davis gushed, Jan was "the only Oriental in town apparently who has the charm, wit and nerve to enter good White society. She has been accepted."[20] In the eyes of Davis, Flora Belle Jan was the perfect embodiment of successful Americanization, and as such was the very type of person for which the survey was searching. For these reasons, she would be used over and over again as an exemplar of successful assimilation of the Oriental in America.

The difference, in the end, between the nativists' and the missionaries' definitions of the Oriental Problem was that the nativists believed that the Orientals were the problem, and the missionaries believed that both the nativists and the unconverted Orientals were the problem. In trying to bring together everyone concerned during the Survey of Race Relations, the missionaries recruited a group of sociologists to study the problems in a scientific manner. For them, the Oriental Problem was limited to neither the Orientals nor the nativists; according to Robert E. Park, the most prominent of the sociologists, the missionaries were part of the problem, too.

A Profession of Faith of a Different Order

During the early planning stages of the Survey of Race Relations, Merle Davis saw a way to overcome the gulf between the pro- and anti-Oriental forces: the survey needed to bring in scientific experts who seemingly had no political stake in the debate over Asian immigration. The experts would have to come from the outside, since some of the West Coast academic institutions, such as Stanford University, had become associated with pro–Oriental stands.[21] Davis believed that as long as the surveyors could claim to be conducting scientific research and merely "gathering facts," the survey would appear politically neutral.[22]

The aura of knowledge and expertise that surrounded the notion of the university campus was one of the rhetorical myths into which the surveyors wanted to tap. Like the shrine of a local Shinto deity or a Catholic pilgrimage site, the university campus was a location suffused with powerful meanings: research, facts, learning, and, above all, knowledge. For those who believed in enlightenment through greater knowledge, the scientific experts from the hallowed ground of elite universities could make a rhetorical claim for the greatness of fact in a way that the missionaries could not. A correspondent for the *Chicago Daily News* noted that the survey would mark the beginning of a "permanent surveillance of interracial movements" on the Pacific Coast. "Scholarship will inspire and control the work," he stated, and all would be controlled from the central head-quarters of the universities.[23] The grand claims of true enlightenment and surveillance were partly a product of the missionaries' desire for impartial fact-finding, but they also reflected the current claims of social science.

Although scientific sociology as an academic discipline was barely thirty years old, it had already carved out an impressive niche in almost all elite universities in the United States. Perhaps the most famous social scientist of those years was the University of Wisconsin's E. A. Ross, a former Stanford University professor and prominent Progressive Party intellectual who had advocated an instrumental role for social science in the control and progress of society.[24] Ross and many of his contemporaries pioneered a vision of social science that shared a tenet with the missions of the Protestant ministers—social reform planned and implemented by highly educated elites.[25] Indeed, many of the early sociologists had been ministers or missionaries themselves before converting to social science.

The ties between social science and the Social Gospel remained strong.[26] Enlightenment was a means to a better world, and the pursuit of knowledge about race relations on the West Coast was an end in itself. This goal reflected a belief in the value of learning, as well as a reflection of a deep faith in the socially regenerative power of applied knowledge, held by both Protestant missionaries and social scientists. The project of the social scientists cannot be understood apart from the religious reform-ers who shared such similar backgrounds and goals.

As examples, consider Emory Bogardus and William Carlson Smith, both professors of sociology at the University of Southern California who became involved with the Survey of Race Relations through their con-nection with George Gleason and the YMCA of Los Angeles. Bogardus had grown up on a farm outside of the small town of Belvidere, Illinois. When he moved to Chicago to attend college, he had been shocked and forever changed by the cosmopolitan world he encountered, explaining that until that time he had accepted without question the literal interpre-tation of the Bible. The YMCA movement affected him powerfully, and for the rest of his life Bogardus struggled to fulfill the tenets of "practical" religion: "I learned that real tests of religion are what one does with his religious beliefs, what they do for one, and that daily behavior is a yard-stick of what a person's religion means to him." He served as the director of the School of Social Work at the University of Southern California (USC) and the head of the Department of Sociology; he also was instru-mental in the Goodwill Industries of Los Angeles, which collected donated goods and sold them to raise funds for charity work.[27]

The Social Gospel, which advocated daily efforts to make the world a better place, underwrote every moment of Bogardus and Smith's work in social science. Their devotion to sociology cannot be understood without taking into account their involvement in programs of personal and social improvement. Smith had been a teacher in Assam, India, with the American Baptist Foreign Mission Society before attending graduate school in sociology, and his dissertation at the University of Chicago was based upon his mission experiences among the Ao Naga tribe in India.[28] The overlapping backgrounds and shared sense of social mission of the Protestant ministers and the social scientists ran deep.

This overlap, however, led the head researcher of the Survey of Race Relations, Robert E. Park, to consistently criticize the missionaries who were his allies. Park, a member of Chicago's Department of Sociology and Anthropology, felt that sociology had been closely allied with missionaries for too long, and he tried to distance social science from religious organizations. One of the most prominent social scientists in the country at the time, Park had been chosen by Merle Davis and the Institute of Social and Religious Research to become the research director of the Survey of Race Relations. He brought to the survey not only a badge of scientific expertise but also a very different outlook on social science than that held by many of his colleagues.

Unlike some famous sociologists, such as Progressive reformer E. A. Ross, Robert Park did not consider it his job to advocate for social reform. To him, the role of sociology was not the improvement of society but the description of society and how it worked. For Park, sociology would not create reform programs but help those who built such programs do so more "intelligently."[29] To the eventual consternation of many of the missionaries, Park became the most influential of the survey researchers.

According to Robert Park, the science of sociology could not be concerned with morality. Park often professed a deep-felt distaste for the motives of do-gooders. Sociologists could not be in the business of "improving" people. "The trouble with our sociology in America," he claimed, "is that it has had so much to do with churches and preachers." The sociologist could not "condemn some people and praise others." The sociologist should be able to understand a social situation from the point of view of all its participants—moral approval or disapproval merely blinded the sociologist to the "inner world" of other people. Park had been a journalist before coming to sociology, and his style of empirical sociology relied on empathy and description rather than the social prescriptions that the ministers expected from him.[30]

Robert Park tried very hard to distinguish the sociologists from the missionary reformers, but during the Survey of Race Relations, the distinction was often difficult to maintain. Without the ministers' network of connections up and down the West Coast, the sociologists would never have been able to contact someone like Flora Belle Jan. Protestant church workers were often some of the few whites who had close personal contact with large numbers of the Chinese and Japanese on the West Coast.[31] Although Jan professed herself to be "quite out of sympathy with the Baptist Mission people" and "emancipated from all religious influence," Merle Davis was alerted to Jan's presence through his contacts with the Fresno Baptist Mission.[32]

The reliance of the Survey of Race Relations on the network of Protestant churches and missions on the West Coast had several important ramifications. For one, the sociologists, because they felt their project was entwined and conflated with the missionaries, tried to distance themselves rhetorically from the missionary reformers. The strident tone of Park's attempts to distinguish the work of social science from the work of religion reflected just how closely they were connected.[33] Social science was a profession of faith of a different order from that of the missionaries, one that emphasized a belief in objectivity and science rather than salvation and mission.

Park, however, was forced to exaggerate the chasm that lay between the two disciplines. Within the context of a missionary project in which the sociologists were inextricably bound, Park's insistence on the sociologists' difference from the social reformers took on much more meaning. The social scientists' belief in what they were doing was predicated on their not having to justify the ultimate good of their research. The justification was self-apparent within the larger aim of social reform that sociologists shared with the reformers. Both the Protestant ministers and the Chicago sociologists believed in the ultimate good of enlightenment and knowledge; they just disagreed on how direct the application of that knowledge would be. Park's unease with his allies, however, persisted throughout the survey, and many of the missionaries became increasingly disillusioned with Park's management of the survey research.[34]

The second major result of the Survey of Race Relations' reliance on the Protestant missions was the lasting definition of who and what Orientals were. Because the missionaries often could speak Chinese and Japanese and the sociologists could not, early on the researchers had to rely on the church network for translation and interpretation. Since the missionaries had a preponderance of contacts with the Chinese and Japanese on the West Coast, and in particular Christianized members of these communities, most of the interviews and life histories collected by the survey and subsequent research results reflected these connections.

There was virtually no contact with the smaller numbers of Filipino and East Indian migrant workers on the Coast; therefore, these groups dropped out of the definition of the Oriental Problem. After the 1924 immigration laws cut off Japanese immigration (Chinese immigration had already been effectively halted since 1882), immigrants from the Philippines arrived in greater numbers. They were allowed into the Country because the Philippines had been colonized by the United States after the Spanish-American War of 1898, and legally they were not migrants from a foreign nation. But despite their significant numbers, they remained mostly outside the purview of the Oriental Problem as a research program.

This definition of who was Oriental had long-term consequences for the history of Asian Americans. Because immigrants from India, the Philippines, and Korea were largely ignored within the Oriental Problem, their experiences were excluded from academic knowledge about being Asian in America.[35] Even after migrants from Korea, South Asia, Southeast Asia, and Pacific islands such as the Philippines, Samoa, and Guam began arriving in numbers that rivaled or surpassed the number of Chinese Americans and Japanese Americans, the historical legacy of this initial theoretical focus on Chinese and Japanese has been profound.

The Survey of Race Relations was the first major intersection between American missionary efforts among Orientals and American sociology's research interests with Oriental immigrants. The fascination of the Protestant ministers with Orientals such as Flora Belle Jan—American-born, enlightened, and modern—both overlapped with and provided the context for the interest of Chicago sociologists in the Americanization and cultural assimilation of Orientals. The intimate connection of ministers with sociologists underwrote the sociological perspective as a social good. Without the missionaries' connections to Chinese and Japanese in Asia and the United States, the institutional formation of expert Orientalism would not have been possible.

2

Thinking about Orientals:
Chicago Sociologists and the
Oriental Problem

In 1924, Robert Park set up a team of social scientists as his first
move in organizing the research for the Survey of Race Relations. All the
prominent universities on the West Coast were represented, from the
University of British Columbia in Vancouver to the University of Southern California in Los Angeles. Almost half of the researchers were graduates of the University of Chicago: Emory Bogardus of USC received his
Ph.D. from Chicago in 1911; William Carlson Smith, also at USC, received
his doctorate from Chicago in 1920; and Roderick McKenzie of the University of Washington in Seattle was a student of Park's who received his
Ph.D. from Chicago in 1921. The list of researchers and their ties to Chicago is remarkable yet, at closer glance, perhaps not altogether surprising.

The University of Chicago had been founded in 1892. Funded by a
sizable grant from John D. Rockefeller, the university turned into a neo-
Gothic incarnation of Oxford and Cambridge in the American Midwest,
a school to rival the Ivy League. The university was built on and near the
land recently occupied by the exhibits of the great Columbian Exposition,
which celebrated the four hundredth anniversary of Columbus's landing
in America. The campus in South Chicago was a model of Oxbridge pre-
tensions, mimicking the medieval monastic architecture of the English
college quadrangles. Facing the open, grassy midway where the Columbian
Exposition's temporary buildings had once been centered, the sociology
department was housed in heavy stone walls complete with fortress tow-
ers. The University of Chicago was a location where serious minds could
do intellectual battle.

Armed with the generous endowment from Standard Oil's Rockefeller, the school immediately set out to hire the best and brightest thinkers in America. John Dewey was persuaded to teach in the philosophy department. His former student George Herbert Mead taught with him, and Mead's course on social psychology became one of the strongest influences on graduate students in sociology. Thorstein Veblen, whose conception of conspicuous consumption shaped American ideas about consumer society, made a name for himself while at Chicago.

The University of Chicago was the first school in the United States to make an institutional commitment to the emerging science of sociology, appointing Albion Small as its first Head Professor of Sociology in 1892. In 1924, it was one of the few renowned institutions, along with Columbia, for graduate studies in sociology. Therefore, it was no surprise that Robert Park would gather a research staff for the survey made up of Chicago alumni, many of whom were now heads of fledgling sociology departments around the country.[1]

Strangers from the Midwest:
Robert Ezra Park and Other Men with Three Names

Who were these Chicago sociologists? Where had they come from? And why were they so interested in Orientals? There is a way in which Chicago sociologists, in coming to think about Orientals in America, were always thinking at the same time about themselves. In order to understand the ideas and perspectives of this group of sociologists, we need to go through their texts and examine how they understood their own backgrounds, in particular their small-town origins.

Almost every Chicago sociologist was from a small rural town, often in what was seen as the West (now the Midwest) of America, and the recurring three-word mantras of their names bespoke white Protestant family heritages. Robert Ezra Park grew up in Red Wing, Minnesota, on the banks of the Mississippi River; William Carlson Smith hailed from the Great Plains town of Grand Island, Nebraska; and Emory Stephen Bogardus was raised on a farm outside of Belvidere, Illinois. William Isaac Thomas, the son of a Methodist minister, was born and raised on a farm in Russell County, Virginia. Roderick Duncan McKenzie came from a rural background on the Canadian prairies, the son of Scottish immigrant farmers outside Carmen, Manitoba. Ernest Watson Burgess, the son of an Anglican minister, lived in the small town of Tilbury, Ontario, before moving as an infant to Whitehall, Michigan.

The rural imagination became a common theme in the rhetoric of the sociologists as they interpreted social phenomena. Bogardus, working as director of boys' clubs at the Northwestern University Settlement Project, made a statement that echoed many of the Chicago sociologists' feelings of coming from small towns to the slums of Chicago: "My rural simple-mindedness was no match for their urban toughmindedness. It was a situation of a lack of sophistication versus unlimited sophistication."[2] Bogardus, Park, and many of the other social scientists often referred to a curiosity for the greater world that had taken them out of the small towns where they grew up; for them, sociology encapsulated the knowledge gained along the physical and imaginative journey from rural to modern America.[3]

The small-town, rural backgrounds of the sociologists became a descriptive metaphor for their strong sense of being outsiders to the phenomena they studied, and this sense of coming from a different world was reified in the pairs of opposing categories that structured their understanding of American society. The opposition between rural and urban lined up with a number of other pairs of theoretical distinctions. For instance, the well-ordered rural villages, where "social organization" and "social control" over individual behavior were strict, were contrasted with cities, where social "disorganization" was high and social control was loose. From the particular outlook of the Chicago sociologists, having come from small towns where everybody seemed to know each other and each other's business, the city appeared a highly individuated, cosmopolitan arena where everyone was a stranger.

The Chicago sociologists saw themselves as strangers to the urban community and thus could describe and explain it in a way only outsiders could. The sense of coming to a situation as an outsider was first embodied in the powerful epiphany of traveling the road from a small town to the confusion and sophistication of the big city. The memory of this journey was never lost on many of the sociologists, who repeatedly used narratives of that experience as an example of the power of social transformations in America. Where the sociologists actually came from, how they felt when they left, and where they ended up are not the interesting details—it is what they thought about the journey long afterward that matters. Across the board, sociological explanations for the transition from rural to urban followed similar patterns.[4]

The Chicago sociologists borrowed German sociologist Ferdinand Tonnies's gemeinschaft/gesellschaft distinction to describe the difference between the social organization of small villages and big cities. Gemeinschaft communities were marked by social relations in which people knew each other well enough that there was an enormous amount of social cohesion and control. Honor and social reputation were important enough that people acted in concordance with accepted social mores out of a fear of being socially ostracized. A gesellschaft society, in contrast, was one where people did not know each other very well, and thus social disapproval played a less significant role in ruling or restraining behavior.

In using the theoretical distinction between gemeinschaft and gesellschaft to understand social life in America, Chicago sociologists applied the theory to a myriad of changes—rural to urban, traditional to modern, Old World to New World. Descriptions of such social change could be narrated in a number of ways. For instance, the rise of a "faceless" city life could be bemoaned as a tragic loss of "traditional" community. Nostalgia for the security and comfort of small-town life and morality could translate into a fear or condemnation of the immorality and licentiousness of "modern," urban life. No one cared about anybody else in the big city, and callous disregard replaced neighborly concern for the person living next door.

In contrast to this nostalgic tale of the transition from rural to urban society, another story might describe the oppressive social control and the lack of personal freedom and privacy that small-minded, bigoted village life represented. The city, in this description, would thus be the emancipated, enlightened place where cosmopolitan acceptance of diversity and difference could be celebrated. People left you alone to pursue your own business, and nobody meddled or gossiped about your personal life.

For Chicago sociologists who had grown up in small midwestern towns and rural settings, their own personal journeys to the big city of Chicago were to resonate within their sociological theories and descriptions. A plethora of people were moving from small towns to big cities in turn-of-the-century America, and understandings of and reactions to that change were as varied as any human experience.[5] The social scientists created a powerful theoretical apparatus for explaining the difference between rural and urban, and they continually described other social transformations using those theories as an analogy.

The sociologists' point of view as outsiders was reflected in their sense of being strangers to the world. What did it mean to have the outlook of an outsider? To be an outsider was more than merely having come from somewhere else. If you were a social scientist who came to the Survey of Race Relations, to be an outsider would mean having a certain outlook on life, as well as a certain position in relation to the world around you, in particular to the people you studied. Like a traveler in a foreign country, an outsider would see everything with fresh eyes and without preconceptions. To be an outsider would mean being impartial—since you had no stake in local affairs, you withheld judgment until the situation had been fully understood. To be an outsider would be to see the world every day as a stranger in a strange land, to find the customs unfamiliar, to be curious about their meanings, functions, and outcomes.[6]

At the same time that the sociologists from Chicago were studying race relations on the West Coast, anthropologists were producing ethnographic field reports on "natives" in colonial locations ranging from the South Sea Islands to southern Sudan. At the University of Chicago, the disciplines of anthropology and sociology were institutionally connected. Chicago anthropologists remained in the sociology department until 1928, and Robert Redfield, a student who would become the most famous of Chicago anthropologists, worked with Robert Park and later married his daughter Margaret. Park's sociology and Redfield's anthropology shared a similar outlook with the contemporary work in ethnography of E. E. Evans-Pritchard and Bronislaw Malinowski.

From the travelogue of Marco Polo in Cathay six centuries earlier to the anthropological fieldwork of Evans-Pritchard among the Azande and Malinowski among the Trobianders, the point of view of the stranger in a strange land had been used as a narrative device for a long time.[7] The primary aspect of the stranger's travelogue and the ethnographic genre was to establish a place as unfamiliar, as strange and exotic. But to stop at that would have been to leave it as a fantastic tale; it would remain mere exotica until an attempt had been made to explain the unfamiliar and to render it familiar. The ethnographic imagination lay in making a place seem strange and then gradually replacing the confusion with knowledge that made the place and the people seem familiar enough to be understandable and perhaps even admirable.

During the early twentieth century, the occasions for anthropologists and sociologists to encounter the seemingly strange had multiplied with the increased migrations and movements of people resulting from labor migration, imperial invasion, and colonial domination. Both academic disciplines had been formed in response to the need to study the people encountered. This need, however, was also the result of a deliberate interest in the strange, and both sociologists and anthropologists traveled great distances to find sites for contact with the unknown. Park had come to the West Coast because he viewed it as the meeting ground between East and West, the Orient and the Occident, the Oriental and the white.

Coming to know the strange, coming to know the Oriental, and coming to the West Coast were all synonymous movements, and the intellectual consciousness of movement was often experienced as a process of transformation and overcoming. Winifred Raushenbush, Park's personal assistant during the Survey of Race Relations, and daughter of famed Social Gospel minister Walter Rauschenbush, summarized what the sociologists felt when studying the "Oriental." She noted that after associating for a while with a "strange people," what was once strange became familiar. "I have had experience myself," Raushenbush stated, "in getting acquainted with Chinamen in Vancouver, and after a little while they did not seem strange to me." They also became more likable. The cosmopolitan thinker, however, needed to remember the intellectual distance he or she had traveled, while unenlightened people remained behind. When Raushenbush spoke to Canadians or Americans about "these people," she had to remember "my own first feelings about them, that to Americans they were still strange."[8]

Such an ability to make the exotic seem familiar was a challenge. Raushenbush was particularly proud when she showed a picture of the young flapper Flora Belle Jan, whom she explained was an example of how some Orientals were so completely "Americanized" that they acted just like other young Americans. The Oriental, Raushenbush argued, was not always so strange.

A second aspect of the outlook of the stranger was even more applicable to the sociologists. To be a stranger in your own land was to enable you to render the familiar unfamiliar, to see your own culture or society as if you were a stranger traveling through it. Readers were given the sensation of seeing themselves from the outside. This twist on the "stranger in a strange land" also had a long history in narrative form, mostly in imaginary travelogues that portrayed a familiar place from the point of view of a foreigner who was unfamiliar with the local mores and customs.[9] American sociology in the early decades of the twentieth century might be understood as a mixture of these possible points of view of the stranger: the first, an attempt to make sense of the strange, as in the sociologists' interest in the unknown Oriental, and, the second, an attempt to make strange that which was unquestioned, to defamiliarize the familiar and see American society as a whole in a new manner.[10]

This aspect of the sociologist as outsider to his own society was what made sociology different from most anthropology of the day. Rather than restricting itself to imaginatively transforming the outlook of white, outside observers into that of various native insiders, sociology transformed the point of view of the outsider into the permanent point of view of the "objective" social scientific observer. All knowledge, not just that of the unknown and the strange but also the already known, was to be from the point of view of the outsider.

The outlook of the outsider and the stranger is central to understanding Robert Park's vision of what he and the other sociologists were trying to accomplish on the West Coast. Park considered it the height of achievement for a sociologist to be able to see a situation from the points of view of those involved, to be able to understand the attitudes of all the different participants, and this ability was derived not from a native or insider perspective but from an outsider perspective. Only by adopting the standpoint of an outsider could one freely step in and out of the local attitudes.

This was the first attribute of what one of the Chicago sociologists termed the "sociological eye"—the ability to see a social situation from a broader perspective and to empathize with different people without judging them. Unlike many cultural anthropologists at the time, the sociologists were not merely interested in the exotic other. Although they came to the West Coast to understand Orientals, they also came to understand the nativists and, at times, even themselves. Because the sociologists stood outside the local situation, everyone was up for examination.

Perhaps more than any other American sociologist or anthropologist at the time, Park emphasized that in a modern world with increasing human migration and movement, the subject matter of sociology should be the encounters between people. Anthropologists viewed exotic "cultures" and "societies" as objects to be examined, to be recorded and saved for posterity before they were destroyed by outside contacts, including themselves. In contrast, Park focused on the actual encounters between different cultures as the interesting subject for sociology. He elevated the point of view of the stranger to the ultimate objective outlook, estranged in the end from any native culture, society, or social group. The sociologists were not of any community except perhaps that of sociologists; they were outsiders and strangers who could examine their own societies with the same detachment with which they studied strange and alien groups.

Park had been greatly impressed by the work of sociologist Georg Simmel, with whom he did graduate work in Germany. Park often cited a convoluted passage in Simmel's text on sociology that described the point of view of the stranger. "The stranger is not taken here," Park quoted, "in the sense frequently employed, of the wanderer who comes today and goes tomorrow, but rather of the . . . potential wanderer, so to speak, who, although he has gone no further, has not quite got over the freedom of coming and going."[11] Although related to actual movement in space, the stranger embodied an outlook on the world, a sense of not belonging anywhere in particular. It was this sense of a perpetual stranger, with its connection to both physical and imagined movement through space, that Robert Park made into the ideal outlook of the cosmopolitan Chicago sociologist.

An America That Would Not Melt:
Polish Peasants, the Negro Problem, and the Oriental

If W.E.B. Du Bois defined the problem of the twentieth century as the problem of the color line, for most social thinkers up to the present, the color line in the United States has been that between black and white. On the West Coast of the 1920s, however, the problem of race was not one of black and white but of white and Oriental. It was this very different world of race relations that brought Park to the West Coast, full of unanswered questions. To understand Robert Park's construction of the Oriental Problem in America, we must place his interest in Orientals within the context of his earlier research work.[12] Park brought to his study of Orientals two important intellectual interests and textual antecedents: a particular understanding of race relations between black and white in America, and extensive research on European immigrants in America.

Park's interest in what was popularly labeled the "Negro Problem" in America was long-standing, and the parallels between his visions of the Negro Problem and the Oriental Problem were extensive. Before joining the University of Chicago, Park had worked as a journalist and a public relations man; for seven years he had served as Booker T. Washington's press secretary at the Tuskegee Institute in Alabama. In addition to touring with the African American educator and issuing press releases on Tuskegee's activities, Park had helped write some of Washington's speeches and books. During his stay in the South, Park took voluminous research notes on "race psychology" and the conditions of southern black farmers.[13]

The other important context for Park's intellectual construction of the Oriental Problem was his interest in immigration. Park and William Isaac Thomas, a close friend and colleague at Chicago, completed *Old World Traits Transplanted*, a long study examining European immigrants, in 1921.[14] Thomas, who brought Park from Tuskegee to the sociology department at Chicago in 1913, was the coauthor of what at the time was probably the most important study ever published concerning American immigration, *The Polish Peasant in Europe and America*.

According to Park and Thomas, Americanization was a complex process that paralleled the sociologists' description of changes between rural and urban, between tight social control and individual freedom, between strict family structures and increased individual mobility. The first two decades of the twentieth century had been marked by social scientists' growing interest in immigration. Recent migrants from eastern and southern Europe seemed unassimilable to "old stock," "Anglo-Saxon" American society because of formidable differences in the way they understood the world. A new conception of America was needed.

Combined with the violent oppression of African Americans exemplified by the Jim Crow society of the American South, immigration and race relations were prime subjects of interest among intellectuals. Progressive reformers believed the world could be made into a better place—progress could be defined in a myriad of ways, but the hope for societal improvement linked political Progressives. In particular, East Coast intellectuals such as Horace Kallen (who coined the term "cultural pluralism") had begun to focus their attention on the myriad of racial and ethnic communities in American society.[15]

Although Park had a deep interest in all aspects of the assimilation of immigrant groups in America, he had little experience with Asian immigrants. A chapter on Japanese immigrants had been included in *Old World Traits Transplanted*, but it was based almost entirely on data that others had collected. For the bulk of the study, Park and Thomas had conducted personal research on New York's Lower East Side, giving the work a marked leaning toward eastern European immigration.[16] The Survey of Race Relations on the Pacific Coast offered Park a firsthand opportunity to see both race relations and immigration on the West Coast and to apply his knowledge of southern race relations and European immigration to the problems between Orientals and whites in the American West.[17]

As both immigrants and a "nonwhite" race, Orientals provided the ideal link between the Polish peasant and the Negro Problem. All three of these research interests—race relations between Negroes and whites, the adjustment experiences of European immigrants, and race relations between Orientals and whites—were linked by one foundational theory. The Chicago sociologists' conception of the interaction cycle, otherwise known as the race relations cycle, or the assimilation cycle, structured social research during the Survey of Race Relations. It would prove to be the most important concept within the Oriental Problem for the next forty years.

The Green Bible:
Chicago Sociologists and Their Definitions

It was a shade of forest green, distinctively bound like an oversized Gideon Bible. At just over a thousand pages, *Introduction to the Science of Sociology* was about the same length as the Good Book. But for the thousands of sociology students who used it, there was no mistaking Robert Park and Ernest Burgess's canonical text, which was first published in 1921, with a second edition in 1924. Over thirty thousand copies were printed of what quickly became known as the "Green Bible," the standard textbook in American sociology. Proselytizing through its pages, the Chicago disciples spread their vision of social science. Like the Good Book, *Introduction to the Science of Sociology* was a collection of excerpts and writings of various authors, from Rousseau and Adam Smith to Durkheim and Darwin, to Chicago men such as Albion Small, W. I. Thomas, and Park himself. Organized into thematic chapters under headings such as "Human Nature," "Social Interaction," "Social Forces," "Social Control," and "Collective Behavior," the Green Bible revealed Burgess and Park's understanding of the science of sociology.

Although eclectic and suggestive of many possible approaches, the Green Bible focused on what Park and Burgess termed "social interaction." The subject of sociology involved questions about how human beings developed consciousness about themselves as individuals and as members of groups, and how they acquired certain attitudes toward objects or other people through their interactions with each other. The tools and methodologies for understanding these social interactions were myriad, ranging from theoretical concepts such as social disorganization to analytical tools such as maps.

One of the most important theories in the Green Bible was the interaction cycle. When dealing with contact between races, Park called the process the race relations cycle; when dealing with the adjustments of immigrants to America, he called it the assimilation or Americanization cycle. Park had characterized the contact between any two well-formed social groups as following a series of progressive stages of interaction. This cycle of stages was a universal, natural process, and whether it took place between "American Negroes" and "American Whites" or between Polish immigrants and previous settlers, the character of the interaction remained the same. Two groups coming in contact always underwent a similar series of social interactions: competition, conflict, accommodation, and assimilation. This natural process began with competition, the bedrock of Chicago theories of social interaction. As groups in contact vied economically for limited resources (such as jobs, space), the competition between them, which heretofore might not have been conscious, transformed into a declared conflict between the self-conscious groups.

Park emphasized the role of conflict in the process of actually producing a group by defining awareness of boundaries. The accommodation stage occurred when the conflict was either won by one of the groups or, more commonly, whenever some lessening of the conflict was achieved. For instance, accommodation occurred if one of the groups withdrew into a ghetto or was forced into a subordinate economic status. Assimilation, the natural end to the cycle, was inevitable as groups in social contact communicated and began to share memories, experiences, and histories; social intercourse was virtually unavoidable, and the mixing of disparate peoples was the rule rather than the exception.

Park and his colleagues brought to the West Coast a ready theoretical construct through which to interpret the process of race relations and assimilation. The Oriental Problem on the West Coast was a regional manifestation of the migration that was affecting the whole world, a result of increased contacts between heretofore separate groups of people. The natural end of the assimilation cycle in the American West, as between any two social groups, was theoretically inevitable.

For the Chicago sociologists, there was a large payoff in connecting the study of European immigration with the study of racial conflict. According to the evidence of their own studies, the Americanization of European immigrants seemed inevitable. In contrast, conflicts between black and white or Oriental and white seemed interminable: that was why they were problems for the sociologists. With the universal application of the interaction cycle, however, the desired end of all three situations was in theory the same. Increased social contacts and the eventual sharing of memories would bring all Americans together in a common consciousness.

But unlike European immigration, there was an additional problem with Negroes and Orientals. In 1914, ten years before the Survey of Race Relations, Park had already linked the situation of Japanese immigrants with that of the Chinese and the Negro in America. Noting that "Japanese, Chinese, and Negroes" were segregated from other Americans, he feared that they had become exceptions to the rule of the interaction cycle. Consciousness of race led to prejudice, and since prejudice could be overcome only by sharing experiences and memories (producing the empathy and understanding that characterized assimilation, as defined by Park), the isolation caused by prejudice cut off communication. Even more prejudice was then produced. Isolation, defined as "exclusion from communication," was thus a dead-end result defying the interaction cycle: the natural end of the cycle, assimilation, was not being achieved.[18]

The main aspect of what Park saw as the Oriental Problem was the inability of Orientals to achieve the last step of the assimilation cycle because of "race consciousness" among whites. It is important to note that Park was not repudiating the theoretical validity of the assimilation cycle. According to him, just because Negroes and Orientals had not yet been assimilated into American society did not mean that they could not or would not be assimilated. The vicious cycle of isolation and prejudice was a problem to be described by the sociologists, but the interaction cycle remained valid.

Not all the survey researchers agreed with Park's connection between the Negro Problem and the Oriental Problem. Economist Eliot G. Mears of Stanford University, who did not share the Chicago sociologists' outlook on race and immigration, stated: "Analogies made between Orientals on the Pacific Coast and Negroes in the Southern States fail."[19] Mears saw too many important differences between the West Coast and the South, and he doubted that linking Orientals and Negroes was useful for understanding their very different situations. A dissenting voice among the survey researchers, Mears conducted his work in isolation from the Chicago social scientists.

Whatever the difficulties with their approach, the sociologists tried hard to link race consciousness—the Oriental Problem and the Negro Problem—with their theories on immigration. They realized that it was a move fraught with hope in the inclusive nature of not only America but also the world. Soon after the Survey of Race Relations was conducted, Park translated his understanding of the United States into that of the globe: "Every nation, upon examination, turns out to have been a more or less successful melting-pot." The mingling of peoples all over the world followed the progressive stages of the interaction cycle. Although the melting pot seemed a uniquely American image for the mixing of disparate peoples, Park asserted that it was a universal process: "Fundamentally, prejudice against the Japanese in the United States is *merely* the prejudice which attaches to every alien and immigrant people" (emphasis mine).[20]

But why did Park use the word "merely"? Why not just state without qualification that it was the same? Robert Park was not coming all the way out to the West Coast just to argue that anti-Asian prejudice was the same as other forms of prejudice. After all, if Asian migrants were, as Park claimed, "merely" another alien immigrant group, why go through all the trouble to launch a massive research survey? The danger that the Chicago sociologists needed to deny was the possibility that racial prejudice was not like other forms, that prejudice against Negroes and Orientals was somehow different. The more general problem for the sociologists was that if they were wrong about anti-Asian prejudice, then there was no hope for America and the world. For them, Asian immigrants could not prove to be an exception.

Race and Culture:
The Repudiation of Biological Hierarchy

The challenge presented by Park's theories can be understood only within the context of other views on race that were current at the time. By placing his statements within the debates over race, we can see how much they were arguments against the biological basis of social differences. Park focused on the *awareness* of physical difference as the important cause of distinctions between races.[21]

According to him, the physical traits themselves—skin color, hair color, facial features—carried no inherent characteristics and would reveal nothing about racial traits. What made Orientals distinct was not their physical differences but people's awareness of these differences. The subject of study for sociology was the mental—the "subjective attitudes" and "race consciousness" that people displayed. It was not physical difference or incompatibility that led to racial conflict and antagonism. It was the awareness of physical difference that was the problem, particularly among one of the social groups that such an awareness created and reinforced: whites.

In the United States, a heterogeneous group of people could become white by emphasizing their physical difference from supposedly nonwhite people. Using the term "race" to refer to any group of particular ancestry and geographic origin, such as Irish or Polish, Park noted how some races of immigrants could become white. Orientals, however, were different. The Japanese were "not the right color," Park determined, asserting that the "Japanese, like the Negro, is condemned to remain among us an abstraction, a symbol." The "us" that was created by not being Oriental or Negro allowed European immigrants to become "mere individuals" among a sea of whites, "indistinguishable in the cosmopolitan mass of the population."

It was the attitude of white Americans that determined at the same time the "attitude of the yellow man toward the white."[22] Conflict and antagonism led to further consciousness of race on both sides. The "gulf of self-consciousness" affected even the most culturally assimilated Orientals. As Flora Belle Jan, the young Chinese American flapper, wrote in a letter to Park during the Survey of Race Relations: "The more I learn about American men and boys, and some girls, the more I think that friendly relations, at least in California, are for the most part impossible."

Jan's pessimism came from racial remarks that inevitably reminded her that she was different. No matter whether they were common or rare, just a single instance was enough to remind her that she did not belong. "I know that I have penetrated more American homes than any other Chinese girl, and I have found many people cordial. . . . But some one some time must make comments, and these do not fall gently on my ears."[23] Even when people were kind, she carried the awareness that at any moment a casual or not so casual remark would reinforce the difference between white and nonwhite.

Robert Park's attempts to understand race psychology, and how Negroes and Orientals became isolated in American society, were an intellectual quest. Long before coming to the Survey of Race Relations, Park had been on a journey to understand himself as a white man in relation to other races. Contained in almost all of Park's writings in the 1920s on race and culture, for instance, were indications of what the Tuskegee experience two decades before had meant to him. His understandings of Orientals and other immigrants continually engaged with his understandings of the "Negro race."

Park's sympathy for those who suffered from white prejudice was genuine and perhaps unsurprising. After all, he belonged to a profession that was closely allied to missionaries who were "friends" to Negroes and Orientals. Upon leaving Tuskegee in 1912, Park had written in a letter to Booker T. Washington: "Some of the best friends I have in the world are at Tuskegee. I feel and shall always feel that I belong, in a sort of way, to the Negro race and shall continue to share, through good and evil, all its joys and sorrows." Park had great empathy for the suffering of Negroes and Orientals, a rare trait. But in the end, he was neither Negro nor Oriental, and he realized that his knowledge of nonwhites had made him the best that a white man could hope to be: "I am very grateful to you for the privilege of knowing you as intimately as I have. I feel that I am a better man for having been here."[24]

The sentiments expressed by Park in his letter to Washington—that he was a "better man" for knowing Negroes, that he felt as if he was a member of the race—were heartfelt. However trite such remarks might seem (he was, after all, not a black man or woman in a society that enforced racial segregation through lynching), they bespoke a cosmopolitan empathy that was still rare even among elite Progressive whites of that period. Like his profusion of sympathy for the "Negro race," his ability to see the world from the very different perspectives of a Negro American may seem unremarkable to readers today, perhaps even obvious to the point of triviality.

However, it is an indication of how pervasive a hold the Chicago sociologists' analysis had on twentieth-century race relations theory that contemporary sensibilities take many of Park's points as given. To live in American society as a white person was not the same as to live in it as a racial minority. Park and his colleagues argued that the proper perspective of cosmopolitan whites was to recognize the very different lives of other people. In alliance with missionaries, they defined those who disagreed with them as ignorant or uneducated. Enlightenment, in the form of spreading knowledge along with this point of view, would bring about a cosmopolitan world. From the hindsight of the third millennium, the sociologists and missionary reformers seemed to have succeeded in their goal. But this should not blind us to the fact that, at the time, Park's analysis and his pride in association with African Americans were not widely shared among white Americans.

The survey researchers found that their reading of the situation on the West Coast was definitely that of a small minority. Because of the pervasive use of racial categories at the time, associations between physical race and differences in social behavior were almost universal. Discussions about "race fitness" were common in academia.[25] Eugenic theories, first popularized by Charles Darwin's cousin Francis Galton, promoted sterilization and controlled breeding to improve the biological fitness of humanity. In addition, men such as Henry Pratt Fairchild pushed for an end to large-scale American immigration because of the supposed biological incompatibility with "non-white races."[26]

The Chicago sociologists were trying to spread a new gospel about culture as an explanation for race. They saw themselves on the forefront of academic thinking about race in America, allied with such intellectuals as Franz Boas, a professor of anthropology at Columbia University. Boas was perhaps the most famous proponent in the United States at that time of a cultural versus biological definition of race. His commitment to a cultural basis for racial difference, as well as the difference between "primitive" and "civilized" cultures, had come to dominate anthropology by the 1920s.[27]

Not all of the Chicago sociologists, however, had been converted by Park. Charles Henderson, a humanitarian reformer and an early Chicago professor of sociology, had been a leading eugenicist. At the time of the survey, William Carlson Smith at USC was still a little unclear about race as a purely cultural phenomenon and had even taught courses in eugenics. The presence of such thinking showed how uncommon and new the ideas about culture still were, and how far the Chicago sociologists had to go in convincing even their own colleagues and acolytes.[28]

Chicago sociologists helped create a new outlook on race and culture in American social thought. They advocated theories of racial difference that focused on the divergent consciousness of groups. If a group of people shared a similar way of understanding the world, then they shared a culture; therefore, if a group shared a similar consciousness of their place in the world because they were conscious of their physical difference from others, then they shared a racial culture. Racial consciousness was equivalent to cultural difference.

The physicality of race became secondary to cultural consciousness. It was this tenet of Chicago sociology that profoundly marked American social thought, creating an interest in what eventually became termed "identity," the forms of consciousness that surrounded definitions of the "self" and of how individuals became groups. The great legacy of Chicago theories of race and culture was their focus on the consciousness of identity as the singular interesting phenomenon behind all racial and ethnic difference.

However, if Chicago sociologists aimed to remove the physical body from cultural consciousness by eliminating biology as a consideration, they merely shifted the importance of the physical into another realm. Because of their interests in immigration and the historical movement of people from one place to another, Chicago theorists such as Robert Park strongly linked cultural consciousness with the body's origins in physical space. If the physical body itself was not the creator of mental differences, the body's movement through space would bear that burden.

3

Orientalism and the Mapping of Race

Chicago sociologists tied race to cultural consciousness, not to biological differences between human bodies. In the end, however, these cultural differences were often associated with the foreign origins of certain human bodies. For Orientals in particular, the cultural differences between them and white Americans were tied to the origins of biological ancestors from Asia. Despite the exclusively social origins of cultural difference, sociologists visualized such differences in the form of maps and other spatial diagrams. Such spatial representations depended on an imagined link that connected the physical spaces of Chinatowns or Japantowns in the United States with the mythical space of the Orient somewhere in Asia.

Mapping was a process of identity formation in and of itself, defining the boundaries between groups. Chicago sociologists at the time were creating the techniques of urban studies, and one of the most important of their tools was mapmaking. Sociologists created charts and diagrams that defined where racial groups existed in space, fixing their places in the world vis-à-vis white America. The sociologists' technique of mapping cultural difference reinforced and further popularized spatial understandings of culture and race, making such categories part of everyone's consciousness of the physical landscape. Where you lived and where you came from became important elements of your cultural identity.

Robert Park and his colleagues Emory Bogardus and Roderick McKenzie would try again and again to connect their cultural descriptions of race with an attempt to map the urban spaces of America. By 1924, Park and his colleagues at the University of Chicago had been busily studying Chicago for a decade, transforming it (in their words) into an urban "laboratory"; Bogardus, as the chair of the sociology department at USC, and McKenzie, in the same capacity at the University of Washington, were in the midst of creating research programs to investigate the urban landscapes of Los Angeles and Seattle.[1]

In Los Angeles, racial segregation had been a part of urban development. Neighborhood housing covenants banning home sales to nonwhite and Jewish Americans were prevalent and became a systematic part of Los Angeles housing. Residential patterns thus reflected the exclusivity of the practices of white supremacy. In Los Angeles, a "Chinatown," a "Little Tokyo," and a "black ghetto" were clustered together, defined overall by the area where nonwhites were allowed to live.[2]

The Chicago sociologists wanted to map where people of different races lived and how they interacted in physical space. Because of the ways in which white supremacy had segregated nonwhites into ghettos, the connection of cultural theory with physical space rang true. But it was the racist practices of housing segregation that such mapping actually described, not a connection between culture and space. The sociologists' strong linkage of Oriental culture with Oriental locations was an illusion. It came, in the beginning, from their assumption that the Orient was the absolute opposite of the Occident.

What Was Really So Different about the Orient?

"Life differs from death in the matter of movement," wrote Roderick McKenzie.[3] The Chicago sociologists saw everything through the lens of migration. Migration and change were the great constants in the study of sociology. Sociologists might look at the history of a city by considering how the transportation technologies connecting it to other cities had changed. For example, San Francisco had been 80 days from Hong Kong by clipper in 1849. At the same time, the western port had been nearly 120 days by wagon train away from the East Coast. By 1880, steamships had cut the time between San Francisco and Hong Kong to 21 days, but the transcontinental railroad had slashed travel time from the East Coast to only 14 days. This explained why the West Coast had initially been populated by Asian migrant laborers coming eastward instead of white laborers coming westward. It had been faster and cheaper in the mid–nineteenth century to transport people by water from Asia than to bring white workers overland. By the end of the nineteenth century, this situation had reversed. The irony was that Asian workers had helped build the very transportation network that undercut the value of their labor. Roderick McKenzie and other Chicago-trained sociologists elaborated on the global interconnections between places and regions in a series of articles dealing with "time distance" and "spatial distance"; their great accomplishment was to outline the dynamic relationship between movement, location, and social change.[4]

The sociologists were enthralled by the new transportation and communication technologies that had transformed the world and saw them as the genie that had allowed world dominance by what they often labeled "Occidental societies." Echoing centuries of stereotypes, they saw the "Orient," in contrast, as perpetually stagnant. Fifteen years earlier, William I. Thomas had held a forum, "The Significance of the Orient for the Occident," and his conclusions still structured the way many of the Chicago social scientists saw relations between the East and West in 1924.[5] Thomas mapped what he understood as the differences between Occident and Orient, pairing traits of the one as the diametric opposites of the other. So, too, did Chicago sociologists who followed his theories. "The secret of environmental control lies in the ability to conquer distance," McKenzie wrote, and the "great difference between the East and the West at the present time is in the matter of movement." In comparison with the West, "the East is sluggish, stagnant, immobile." Although Asia possessed over half the world's population, it had "less than nine per cent of the world's motor cars, less than three per cent of the world's telephone instruments, and sends about one per cent per year of the world's telegraph messages."[6]

The Chicago sociologists had rejected racial superiority based on biology, but they did generalize about the hierarchy of different forms of civilization. The progress from "primitive," stagnant society to "modern" life, like the change from small-town life to urban society, was the product of movement and migration.[7] The West was modern because it was in constant flux and conflict. Contacts between different peoples had created cosmopolitan outlooks and the ability to quickly adapt. In contrast, the East had long been stagnant and peaceful, with rigid social hierarchies and well-defined social relationships marking a largely rural world.

The Chicago sociologists' emphasis on conflict as a force for progressive change marked their greatest difference from the missionaries with whom they were allied. The missionaries believed in lessening conflict and bringing harmony to social relations; the sociologists thought such a goal might be undesirable. Slavery, after all, was a peaceful accommodation, and racial segregation the epitome of spatial equilibrium. For the sociologists, conflict was not simply inevitable; for subordinate groups, it sometimes brought about change for the better.

In many ways, the sociologists' conception of the Occidental West was similar to Frederick Jackson Turner's portrayal of the mythical American West, a place of mobility and freedom.[8] Turner's view of America was a civilizing frontier moving across the wilderness, producing among European Americans traits of individuality, self-reliance, and democracy. In contrast, Chicago sociologists emphasized the frontier as the place where people came into contact. The Pacific Coast was the zone of contact between a stagnant Orient and a modern, mobile Occident.

Seeing the United States as a global melting pot, the place where all the world met, the sociologists envisioned America itself as the site of modern progress. The great global movements of laborers and immigrants from Europe and Asia had transformed the United States in the late nineteenth century. It had created overlapping diasporas, and urban sites such as Los Angeles, San Francisco, Seattle, Honolulu, and Chicago were ideal locations—"laboratories"—for studying the contact between migrating populations. Modern America represented the boundary zone between the civilizations of the Orient and the Occident, and Park repeatedly referred to "racial frontiers" in discussing the American West.

The physical distance between the East and West had shrunk. Changes in transportation had allowed for mass migrations that had implanted people from each place into the soil of the other. Contacts between Orientals and Occidentals were on the increase, and for the Chicago sociologists, the important question was whether the two groups would continue to fight each other or instead would draw closer as they huddled together in the cities of western America.

Measuring Racial and Cultural Difference: The Social Distance Scale

After years of observing racial segregation and Jim Crow laws while at Tuskegee Institute in Alabama and in the city of Chicago, Robert Park recognized segregation as the spatial expression of race relations. "The Negro is 'all right in his place' and the same is probably true of every other race, class or category of persons," Park observed. Physical separation and boundaries marked the American landscape as the seemingly tranquil accommodation to white supremacy. "Every one, it seems, is capable of getting on with every one else, provided each preserves his proper distance," Park wrote with a note of irony.[9]

Underlying the metaphor of keeping a proper distance was the paradox that physical relations between races were in fact commonly intimate. Why, for example, could a white woman in the South in 1924 casually undress in front of Negro servants as if they were not even there? If cultural difference as a theory was to be taken seriously, then this entwining of physical intimacy with cultural separation needed to be explained.

To the Chicago sociologists, culture and space were tied together, and the theory of social distance completed the linkage. Social distance started as a simple metaphor, alluding to how a lack of feeling for someone standing right beside you was, symbolically, equal to their standing on the other side of the moon. As an engaging metaphor, it was illuminating precisely in its difference from actual physical distance. Park explained to Emory Bogardus in 1924 that social distance was not about physical distance. If you just ignore the existence of a person, your social distance from her is great.[10] The key to the paradox was the lack of empathy. Personal attitudes were the scale for social distance—whether a person cared about another, or could imagine the other's point of view.[11]

Social distance brought together culture and physical space and made them interchangeable. It reinforced the splitting of culture from the physical body, yet it still provided a tangible measure that described the practices of racial segregation. The idea was simple and elegant. People were asked in questionnaires, for example, to rank on a scale from 1 to 5 how they felt about another racial group. If they wanted them driven from the country, their answer would be 5. Allowing them into your home as friends would be a 2, and actually marrying someone and living with them was a 1 or even a zero.[12]

With this survey, the Chicago sociologists created a simple way of measuring how much two groups disliked each other. They did this by quantifying racial prejudice through spatial metaphors—living in the same country, in the same city, in the same neighborhood, in the same house, in the same bed. By adding up and averaging all the responses of European Americans to Chinese Americans, for instance, the sociologists could say that the social distance between these groups was 4.28. In comparison, the social distance between European Americans and the British was only 0.27.

The measurements quantified racial hatred and conflict but also put cultural difference and physical space into a tenuous relationship.[13] Why was sex and intermarriage to be the ground zero of social distance? Would a racist white man marrying an Oriental woman and treating her like a prostitute really show close social distance in a way more preferable to someone making a racist joke about a coworker at the office? Or how about a slave owner who had sex with enslaved women under the cover of night? The possibility that someone could at the same moment abhor and desire a person of another race was counted an impossibility by the equations of social distance.

The strangest result was that in objectifying racial prejudice as a quasi-physical quantity that could be measured, the categories of race became fixed. Chinese and Japanese each existed as a race, and the only question was to find out how much each was disliked. Emory Bogardus, who used social distance questionnaires extensively in Los Angeles during the Survey of Race Relations, concluded: "Race prejudice is measurable in terms of social distance, and racial goodwill expands to the degree that social distance shrinks."[14] How race awareness arose, or the factors that caused it to ebb and wane—all these considerations were left aside. Strangely, this ran counter to the emphasis on the formation of group consciousness that so much of Chicago sociology preached. It also revealed how dependent the Chicago sociologists were on allusions to physical bodies and spatial boundaries within their theories of culture.

In this way, social distance as a metaphor snuck in the physical categories of difference that cultural theories tried to erase. The allure of social distance reflected the Chicago sociologists' strong emphasis on spatial relations and their desire to make physical their conceptions of cultural difference. The world was becoming a smaller place. The increasing animosity and growing social distance that were apparent on the West Coast were the result of the actual decrease in physical distance between different peoples, as mass migration brought into close contact people who would have lived an ocean apart twenty years earlier.

Park believed that the lessening of physical distance could only lead to a decline in social distance. This was why, without any supporting evidence, he was so optimistic about the eventual disappearance of exclusionary laws and other prejudicial legislation. Park asserted that it was "vain to underestimate the character and force of the tendencies that are drawing the races and peoples about the Pacific into the ever narrowing circle of a common life. Rising tides of color and Oriental exclusion laws are merely incidental evidences of these diminishing distances."[15]

Mapping techniques and the theory of social distance gave a spatial component to social research, and an explosion of maps and diagrams resulted. The sociologists from Chicago became avid practitioners of human geography, mapping and measuring the racial and cultural communities of America, plotting where Orientals and Negroes lived and how far away they were from each other and from whites. A map that was produced at USC for the Survey of Race Relations (see figure) shows most clearly how Bogardus and his colleagues plotted physical locations in order to understand social relations.[16] The spot map ostensibly charted the "race" of households in a neighborhood to the west of USC.

It is interesting to note how the boundary line maintained the purity of the white zone—areas with a black resident were defined as part of the

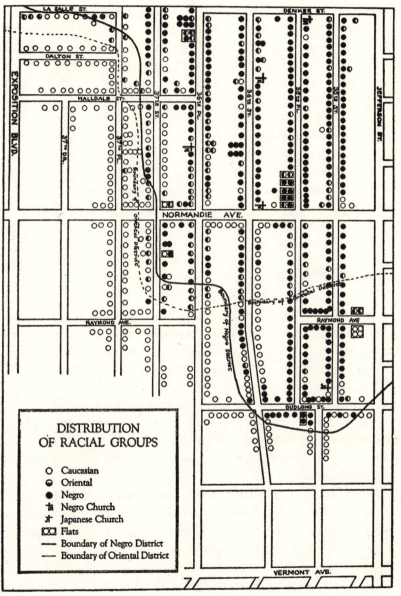

Map produced at the University of Southern California for the Survey of Race Relations. From Emory Bogardus, *The New Social Research* (Los Angeles: Jesse Ray Miller, 1926), 37.

"Negro District." Geographic space and racial or cultural identity were represented as interchangeable. In addition, the uncertain place of the Oriental as a bridge between black and white was reflected even in the symbols used for representing the different races: a black spot for "Negro," a white spot for "Caucasian," and a half-white, half-black spot for "Orientals."

The spatialization of social interaction was one of the most powerful intellectual moves made by the Chicago sociologists in their study of race relations on the West Coast. It structured their understanding of the Oriental Problem like a well-surveyed map. The link between culture and physical sites forged in the 1920s by social scientists in western cities such as Seattle and Los Angeles has had important ramifications. Spatial metaphors mapped exotic cultures into physical space.

The metaphorical linking of racial identity and physical location was a road that went both ways. It gave rise on the one side to notions of place that were highly racialized, and on the other to notions of ethnic, racial, and cultural identity that adopted the tangible, physical features of land. Cultures became self-contained objects with clear physical boundaries. Culture was bounded, with a borderline demarcating the difference between one culture and another.

A Wedding

On June 19, 1897, the Reverend Walter Ngon Fong, pastor of the Methodist Mission of San Jose and a recent graduate of Stanford University, was married. He and his bride, the new Mrs. Emma Fong, exchanged their vows in a small, quiet ceremony in Denver, Colorado.

Walter Fong had been an exceptional student at Stanford. He had served as the president of Stanford's Nestorian Debating Society and had consistently received high grades. It was not, however, his academic achievements that had distinguished him. While studying in Palo Alto, Walter Fong had been the only Chinese student in the whole community of Stanford University.

A year after Fong graduated, his life would continue to be marked by distinction. He became a lawyer in San Francisco and the head of the Chinese Revolutionary Party in the United States. Fong's professional status marked him as a rare, educated elite at a time when most Chinese in America were merchants, laborers, or servants.

Fong's shining public status, however, was overshadowed by an even greater personal achievement. For a Chinese male in the United States in 1897, just being able to marry was an accomplishment. An overwhelming number of the Chinese in America at the turn of the century were men—

about eighty-five thousand compared with a little more than forty-five hundred women. This situation had arisen because of the dominance of labor migration as the initial impetus for Chinese immigration to America in the 1860s and 1870s. Like much labor migration of Europeans to the East Coast at the same time, the predominance of young, single males resulted from the need for mobile workers.

This demographic pattern had been frozen by exclusionary federal legislation in the 1870s and 1880s that had been designed to keep Chinese women out of the United States. American legislators believed that without Chinese women, Chinese men would be unable to establish families and therefore would not permanently settle in America.

Unlike Japanese Americans during the early 1900s, who were able to bring wives and establish families in the United States, the only choice for most Chinese Americans was a family that spanned the Pacific, with wife and children unable by law to join the men in America. Some Chinese migrants had established families in their home villages in China, to whom they regularly sent money, providing them with comfortable lives. Most Chinese American men, even if they had wives in China, lived the lives of lonely bachelors in the United States.[17]

There was even more that was exceptional about Walter Fong besides his ability to live with a wife in the United States, Although living and working in the Bay Area, Fong had not been able to marry in his home state, for California law prohibited him and his new bride from receiving a marriage license.

The reason? Emma Fong was "white."[18]

In 1880, California's Civil Code had been amended to prohibit the issuance of any marriage license to a white person and a "Negro, Mulatto, or Mongolian." "Miscegenation" was the pseudotechnical and legal term for "sex between races," and by the 1920s, antimiscegenation laws forbidding marriage between "Orientals" and "whites" had been enacted in almost every western state: California, Washington, Oregon, Nevada, Montana, Idaho. The Fongs had been forced to travel all the way to Colorado, one of the few western states without such laws, to sanction their union.

By 1922, even if a "mixed-race" couple traveled to a state that would issue them a marriage license, there were additional legal problems. One of the provisions of the Congressional Cable Act of 1922 specified that American women who married aliens "ineligible to citizenship" (in effect this meant "Mongolians" or Orientals) would cease to be citizens themselves. By law, Chinese, Japanese, Filipino, East Indian, and other Asian Americans were ineligible to become citizens through naturalization. Therefore, the recently passed Cable Act stripped any woman who was an American citizen ("white" or American-born "Oriental") of her citizenship if she married a foreign-born "Oriental." In practice, the Cable Act was much more damaging for Asian American women than "white" women, since Asian American women were more likely to have their citizenship stripped, and it was much more difficult for them to regain their lost legal status.[19]

This was the world in which Walter and Emma Fong lived, and it was a world with which Chicago sociologists became absolutely fascinated.

Social Distance at Its Most Intimate:
The Fascination with Interracial Sex and the
Meanings of Intermarriage

There were two outstanding examples for both the social scientists and the missionaries of how the imagined physical boundary between Oriental and white cultures could be crossed. The first was interracial sex and intermarriage, where the physical separation between the two cultures was erased through sexual contact. The second route for border crossing was embodied in religious conversion and the associated process for sociologists, cultural assimilation. The fascination of American Orientalism with sex, conversion, and assimilation resulted from sociologists' denial of the relevance of the biological and physical.

In sociological theories about culture, the physical difference between Oriental and white was visually marked by skin color. It was also spatially mapped in the geographic distance between the "Orient" and "America." Such physical differences and distances, according to the Chicago sociologists, could be traversed and overcome by a process of purely mental change such as cultural assimilation. Interracial sex and marriage, the most intimate contact that resulted from population migration and contact, provided the perfect site for investigating such processes.

The marital history of Emma Fong (later Emma Fong Kuno) is an illustration of the peculiar interest that many Americans had in marriage between Orientals and whites. Between May 24 and June 14, 1922, a series of articles appeared in the San Francisco Bulletin, with a title like a headline from a tabloid magazine: "My Oriental Husbands—The story of a San Francisco girl, who married a Chinese graduate of Stanford University, and a year after his death became the wife of his lifelong friend, a Japanese instructor of the University of California, by Emma Fong Kuno."

Published in installments to take maximum advantage of the anticipated readership, the story of Canadian-born Emma Howse's marriages first to a Chinese American and then to a Japanese American caused a great stir. The day after her series ended, the Bulletin itself published an editorial attack on intermarriage between races. Such vehement condemnation had marked Emma Fong Kuno's life for a quarter of a century, and her autobiography described the angry denunciations she had suffered because of her spousal choices. Most of all, however, she detailed what it had been like to live with her two Oriental husbands: what the differences were between Chinese men and Japanese men, how they treated her, and how different they were both from each other and from white men.

The fascination of Protestant missionaries and Chicago sociologists with sexual relations between Oriental men and white women was out of proportion with the small number of publicly reported cases.[20] Almost as soon as it was published, Emma Fong Kuno's narrative began a long life as textual documentation for Chicago sociologists of intermarriage between Orientals and whites.[21] Her story and a handful of other documented cases of intermarriage between Orientals and white Americans became the focus of a fascination of Chicago social scientists with sexual relations across racial lines. How can we explain this?

The intellectual interest of the sociologists and missionaries in the subject of intermarriage must be placed within a wider fascination with sexual relations between Orientals and whites. Social scientific knowledge was created in the context of widespread curiosity about miscegenation, and the social scientists' interest in the love lives of Oriental and white couples takes on additional meaning when understood in relation to more popular conceptions. Without taking into account the obsession and abhorrence that could be invoked by public discussions of interracial sex, the sociological examination of intermarriage cannot be properly understood.

When Emma Fong Kuno's marital history was first published in 1922, the text and the subsequent attacks on it plugged into a larger arena of debates over racial competition and fears about the long-term survival of the "white race." Racial death and the end of white supremacy and Western civilization had been prophesied in popular works such as Madison Grant's book *The Passing of the Great Race* (1916) and Lothrop Stoddard's tract *The Rising Tide of Color against White World-Supremacy* (1920).[22] In the competition between the races, whites were being warned in newspapers, magazines, and books to fear the alleged reproductive advantage of Mongolians, who, although purported to be intellectually and physically inferior, were believed to be more fertile.

Academic interest in the sexual relations of Asian American men with white women was inextricably tied to a widespread fear of the sexual behavior of Oriental men. No matter how upset or emotional West Coast anti-Asian activists became over the issue of Oriental immigration in general, they became even more enraged over the subject of interracial sex—the idea of "mongrelization" and of "dirty Orientals" lewdly fondling white women. The Yellow Peril rhetoric that inhabited pulp magazines and dime novels was not based on rationalizations of unfair labor competition and overly efficient farming practices; it dwelled instead upon Oriental men preying upon helpless white women. Perhaps best realized in Sax Rohmer's fictional character Fu Manchu, the depiction of Orientals was of scheming, sinister men with long fingernails, waiting to ambush and kidnap white women into sexual slavery.[23] Just as lurid was the denunciation of and obsession with Oriental women, as expressed through descriptions of them as prostitutes and sex slaves.

The sexual threat of individual Oriental men and women was used as an icon to represent the larger threat of the Oriental race. Anti-Asian newspaper cartoons, for instance, often portrayed lewd Oriental men harassing white women.[24] Interracial sex was a taboo subject that seemingly everyone—white and Oriental—wanted to think about and read about, yet only pornographic novels or pulp fiction dared to explore. Would America be purely white in the future, or would the sexual threat of the Yellow Peril turn Americans into a mongrel race? It is hard to recover just how obsessed and incensed people were with the subject of interracial marriage and sex. Despite the sociologists' self-conscious attempts to write rhetorically neutral texts during the Survey of Race Relations, the wider context of prurient interest in interracial sex could not be separated out.

Early on in the survey, J. Merle Davis asked Park to produce a sample questionnaire to pass around in an effort to drum up interest and financing for the project. In response, Park gave him an extensive document on interracial marriage. Davis distributed hundreds of copies in order to elicit interest and donations for the survey. The missionaries did not pass on the opportunity to capitalize on interracial marriage as the technique to retool their fund-raising efforts. Davis raved about the public response to the questionnaire. He gave copies of the document to people in Seattle and noted that "practically everyone is crazy to get a copy." There was a great deal of interest in the topic, and the document had already "revived the drooping interest of some of our leaders here in Seattle." Davis further remarked that Park had "certainly made a happy choice" in the subject matter of the questionnaire, noting: "From the way folks act or react to it, one would be led to believe that most of these good people at one time or another had had serious thoughts about marrying a Chinese or Japanese."[25]

What was this amazing document that could revive "drooping interest" in the survey? What questions would warrant such a response from inquiring minds up and down the Pacific Coast? What did people want to know about interracial marriage and sex? In fact, the questionnaire seems quite sedate, and it never probed very deeply into the roots of sexual attraction between races.

Several of the questions inquired what kind of white woman would marry an Oriental. Of what "height and coloring" was she? Did she herself look like an Oriental woman? What kind of "Oriental man" did the "American woman" marry? Was he "American in appearance"? What seemed to have been the "basis of the physical attraction"? Such questions resonated with the curiosity of white Americans.

But it is also important to consider the different perspectives that anti-Asian activists brought to their readings of the questionnaire. They focused on the provocative aspects of interracial sex. Some of the questions intimated that the white woman must have been abnormal in some way. The questionnaire asked: "Are the American women who have married Orientals wholesome and conventional people? Do any of them belong to marked psychological types, the romantic, the neurotic, etc.?" Anyone and everyone who wanted to know why white women would ever be attracted to Oriental men could identify with these questions. Women of the "romantic" type or the "neurotic" type who were suggested as possible marriage partners were obviously not the same as "wholesome and conventional people."[26]

Park and the sociologists were also very interested in the class aspects of interracial marriage, asking if the woman was of the same economic or social level as the man, and if her status was raised or lowered by the union. Again, such an interest from the point of view of the sociologists was a neutral and seemingly dispassionate inquiry into the social and economic background of the lovers. Yet coupled with the question about whether the American woman was of a "conventional" and "wholesome" type, the inquiring mind of the reader could quickly tour the slums and ghettos of urban America. Was she "white trash" or perhaps a prostitute? Was she somehow gaining status by marrying an Oriental of a better class when no white man would marry her? These possibilities were hinted at by the line of questioning.

The assumption that it would be an Oriental man marrying a white woman was revealing. The question refracted the Yellow Peril fears that most Orientals in the United States were men who posed a sexual threat to white women, and that the few Oriental women were prostitutes believed unfit for marriage. However, even though the number of women compared to men in the Chinese American population was still unbalanced, among Japanese Americans it was nearly equal. The basis for the questionnaire's assumption of a white woman marrying an Oriental man thus had more to do with popular preconceptions of protecting white womanhood, and of the sexual availability of Oriental women to white men, than it did with demographics.

People obsessed with the question of interracial sexual relations could find hints of their own erotic fantasies within the text of the interracial marriage questionnaire, as there was a great range between Robert Park's intended meanings and the meanings people could read into it. The interracial marriage document was deliberately provocative, and Park was aware of the potential ways in which it could be read. Having been a newspaper reporter and a public relations director at Tuskegee Institute, Park considered himself an expert on the range of receptions a text could invoke. Prior to writing the questionnaire, he had responded coolly to Davis's request for a public relations release concerning the survey. Park believed that it was better to keep the survey's exact nature under wraps so that people could come to their own understandings of its purpose.[27] He believed in the technique of generating public interest through the hype of secrecy. Davis, however, convinced Park that there was a danger that anti-Asian agitators would assume that the survey would be pro-Oriental and thus refuse to cooperate. Instead of a press release, Park wrote the questionnaire.

The questionnaire was a masterful text designed to arouse everyone's desire for more information about interracial marriage. It appealed to the sociologists' and the missionaries' need for enlightened knowledge, while at the same time stimulating the darkest obsessions of anti-Asian agitators. The interest of Chinese Americans and Japanese Americans was also piqued. Much like the intense interest of nativists in the threat of Oriental men to white women, Asian Americans responded to the surveyors' questions about intermarriage with a clarity that revealed long reflection on the matter.

Ironically, the Survey of Race Relations had actually begun with little intention of addressing intermarriage. During the formative stages of the survey in 1923, long before Park became involved, Sidney Gulick, the prominent American missionary to Japan, had questioned Davis about the survey's apparent lack of interest in intermarriage. "I am a little surprised," he wrote, that "so slight a reference is made to the question of intermarriage." Gulick admitted that at that moment it had not become a "burning question" because considerable numbers of American-born Japanese were not yet of marriageable age. But, Gulick warned, in ten years the situation would change, and he feared it would become one of the "burning questions which politicians will capitalize and make the basis of much trouble." Gulick was "not sure however that it will be wise for your survey group to touch it." If the scientific experts could conduct a "distinct study of the question" and then "deliberately exclude the subject" from the actual survey, he added, "it might be wise."[28]

Gulick's odd combination of curiosity and reticence is telling. He was being disingenuous when he remarked that intermarriage was not a "burning question" at that time; his warning to Davis to keep the investigation of intermarriage quiet or even separate indicated that he recognized the subject's current volatility.[29] What he really meant was that, for the missionaries, intermarriage had not yet become the solution to the Oriental Problem which they hoped to find. In ten years' time, as more Japanese Americans reached the age of marriage, the issue would really ignite.

Intermarriage for both the missionaries and the sociologists served as a focused example of what interracial and intercultural relations meant. Intermarriage sat as the crucial crossing point along the boundaries between social groups. Sexual relations and reproduction came to represent the most intimate of social relations, equated with the shortest measurable distance (both physical and social) between two races or cultures. Racial intermarriage was thus the truly successful end of American assimilation. The missionaries saw intermarriage as the last hurdle in proving that Orientals were being Americanized. If white women were accepting Oriental men as spouses, then America was truly a melting pot. Robert Park agreed with the missionaries' understanding of intermarriage as the ultimate proof of American assimilation. "If the Japanese are not permitted to intermarry in the United States," he wrote, "we will always have a race problem as long as they are here."[30]

Park was interested in intermarriage for two reasons, as a focal point of cultural contact and as a relationship that produced racially mixed offspring. Intermarriage stood for all race relations, the distillation and symbol of two different cultures coming into intimate contact. Whatever tensions there were between two groups' cultures and social attitudes, he believed that marriage between individuals from each of those groups would be the most intimate place to explore those tensions. The relationship between a man and a woman of two different races was the perfect experiment for discovering how different cultures and races could coexist. What changes in attitude were required? How was race consciousness overcome?

Park was not interested in whether the children of such "hybrid" relationships would be biologically inferior or superior, as he was certain that there would be no genetic inferiority among such children. He was, however, interested in the children of intermarriages as cultural products, as the embodiment of two social groups in contact. Did either community ignore the children or ostracize them? Did either community cut off ties with the married couple? What about the families of the couple?

Like the missionaries, Park was interested in intermarriage as the ultimate solution to the problem of race prejudice. If physical markers such as skin color allowed people to create an awareness of different races, then physical "amalgamation" might eventually remove these racial markers. This interest in intermarriage as a biological homogenizer, however, was purely theoretical, and Park never advocated it as a solution.

Park remained convinced that cultural assimilation would be a sufficient end to the melting pot. Could this belief have reflected his personal distaste for interracial marriage? It was more likely derived from his emphasis on the validity of cultural assimilation as a purely social phenomenon, devoid of biology. The fact that the Japanese and Chinese in America were not permitted to intermarry with whites disturbed him—not primarily because hybrid children would never be produced, but because the prohibition indicated that the social interaction between the races was not intimate. Social distance was still too great, and assimilation in the cultural sense was obviously not taking place.

For Park, the intimate contact of intermarriage was synonymous with close communication. Racial prejudice and discrimination could be overcome without eliminating the physical characteristics that marked racial difference. Actual sex, and the possibly deracialized biological products of sexual union, remained for Park interesting but unnecessary.[31]

Both missionaries and social scientists during the 1920s explored the possibilities of intermarriage as the ultimate solution to the racial conflicts of the United States. Carefully using the "burning" interest in this topic as a way to provoke interest and raise funds for the survey, the missionaries and sociologists of the survey placed intermarriage at the center of the Oriental Problem. It became one of the largest and most intensely scrutinized aspects of the Survey of Race Relations, occupying a significant portion of the research. In files coded "IM" for "intermarriage," documents related to sex between Oriental and white Americans made up about 10 percent of the approximately four hundred life histories and interviews collected by the surveyors. Even after the survey ended in 1926, interracial marriage and sex remained a key subject of interest for American social scientists.[32]

The explanation for why the sociologists became so fascinated by intermarriage lay in its richness of meaning. As a relative rarity, it shed light on the "extreme types" of individuals who engaged in it. It could also represent the distillation of "normal" race relations between two groups. For many people, intermarriage offered hope as the ultimate solution to so-called race problems and prejudice. Intermarriage also provoked the most extreme and emotional reactions, and thus it could function as the ultimate red flag to gauge people's reaction to another race. As the social distance scale showed, Chicago sociologists hoped that by charting different attitudes toward intermarriage, they could measure the social distance between two groups.

Because of the multivalent uses of intermarriage, the sociologists' curiosity about intermarriage between Orientals and whites connected all their ideas of culture, assimilation, space, and distance. Sexuality and sexual reproduction between individuals became the focal point for concerns about the metaphorical reproduction of American society as a whole. Could interracial couples live in harmony? And, by analogy, could different races truly mix? Examining intermarriage seemingly provided an answer.

The possibility inherent in intermarriage for the erasure of cultural differences gave the conception of intermarriage an enormous range of meaning. There was, however, a constant tension between intermarriage as the amalgamator of difference and intermarriage as the most visible representation of difference. Why did Orientals become such a focal point of interest? The answer was that they were the ultimate symbol of exotic difference.

Exoticism and the Split between Mind and Body: Cultural Assimilation, Spiritual Conversion, and the Ocean between Traversed

Whereas "Oriental American" was a phrase that needed both words to have meaning, "white American" was semantically redundant. Newspaper accounts in both 1897 and 1922 understood Emma Fong to represent the American within her interracial relationship with Walter Fong, yet she was not American by birth. Born Ellen Howse in Port Dalhousie, Ontario, she is a perfect example of how easy it was for white immigrants to the United States, particularly those from Canada or Great Britain, to instantly become identified as Americans. In contrast, Asian immigrants were by legal and cultural definition foreign and exotic, no matter how long they had resided in the United States. Within discussions of intermarriage, there was an assumption that the white woman was American and that the Oriental man began as not American. Social scientists, along with almost everybody else in the 1920s, equated white with American and treated the terms as interchangeable.

The Chicago sociologists' definitions of the Oriental began with the simple assumption that Orientals were different. The sociologists' emphasis on intermarriage as an interesting phenomenon theoretically reinforced rather than erased the boundary between Oriental and white. The very conception of intermarriage between races and cultures depended on the acceptance of a boundary that marked the stark difference between one group and another. Without accepting the validity of this boundary as actually marking meaningful difference (in contrast to the idea, for instance, that such a boundary is arbitrary and that the people on either side are much more similar than different), any interest in interracial or intercultural contact would be pointless and devoid of meaning. In other words, only in positing that there is a difference between two sets of people, and that this difference has great meaning, does someone come to be interested in examining the relations between those two people.

The Chicago sociologists' conception of Oriental culture was dependent on an assumption about its foreign origins and its opposition to native and white American culture. The cultural divide between Orientals and whites relied on this conception of the alien nature of immigrant ghettos. Roderick McKenzie described the Chinese and Japanese in Seattle as transplanted patches of foreign communities, displacing native flora and fauna. William Smith and Emory Bogardus saw the Japantown and Chinatown of Los Angeles as little pieces of the Orient in America.

As much as a community tried to become rooted within the landscape, it also embodied the foreign land from which it had been originally transplanted. Plant metaphors reinforced the organic affinity that racial groups seemingly had for their original lands. Despite the emphasis within cultural theory on consciousness and social attitudes, the spatial dynamic of Chicago theories of culture retained this association of ethnic culture with exotic foreign origin. For instance, although most white Angelenos were also new migrants to Los Angeles, this fact did not make them as foreign to the city as Orientals and Mexicans.

Although the missionaries argued for the acceptance of Asian immigrants in the United States, they also replicated the idea that Orientals represented foreign origins. Having themselves spread the gospel in the Orient, they connected Asian immigrants in the United States with Asians they had known in Asia. Conceiving a vast gulf between America and the Orient, the missionaries seized upon visible signs that marked the difference between the two poles.

The missionaries involved in the Survey of Race Relations saw great symbolism in the wearing of American versus traditional Asian-style clothing. Stylish use of American clothes, as opposed to the traditional dress of the immigrant community, was an outward sign of assimilation purportedly equal to successful Americanization. For them, clothing was a semiotic marker that held great meaning; it could represent not only the difference but also the vast distance between American and non-American.

A somewhat strange event that occurred three years before the survey began highlights the symbolic importance of clothing. Since 1895, Donaldina Cameron, a Presbyterian missionary in San Francisco's Chinatown, had run a famous mission home for "rescued Chinese slave girls." For well-publicized raids on brothels in Chinatown, Cameron had enlisted the help of the police to release young Chinese girls from "slavery" and prostitution. Some of the rescued girls eventually returned to Chinatown, but many remained and converted to Christianity, serving as helpers in the mission or eventually marrying Chinese Christians around the United States. The fact that the crusade targeted only Chinese girls in Chinatown brothels, ignoring the white prostitutes literally down the road, was an initial indicator of the missionaries' specific interests. A scene, typical of Cameron and the mission, that occurred in 1920 at a conference of mission workers is particularly revealing. As described in a pamphlet published later, while Cameron spoke to the audience about "Chinese slavery" and the danger of Chinatown tongs: "Enter six rescued Chinese slave girls dressed in native costume who sing in their own language 'Out of my bondage, Sorrow and Night, Jesus I come.'" The meaning of the "native dress" was unmistakable: Cameron shrewdly used the symbol of the foreign "heathen Chinese" to show just how great a divide Christian conversion could traverse, how even Chinese "slave girls," the embodiment of the most depraved practices of the exotic Orient, could and should be saved by Christ.[33]

Missionaries were not the only people who were interested in the Oriental as a symbol of the exotic and the foreign. When Robert Park used the phrase "racial uniform" to describe the skin color of Orientals and Negroes, he recognized the connection between clothing, costumes, and skin color in creating a sense of exotic difference.[34] The sociologists' fascination with the Oriental Problem revealed the heavy load of meaning that the Oriental could bear. Donaldina Cameron had cleverly used the juxtaposition between exotic native costumes (one wonders whether the racial costume of Oriental skin color and physical features might have been enough) and Christian hymns to display the striking difference between heathen and saved, and thus the success of her mission. The sociologists found in the Oriental the same extreme example of the great gap that could be bridged by assimilation. Possessing a permanent racial costume that was distinct and different from that of white Americans, the Oriental was nonetheless capable of cultural assimilation through social interaction.

Missionary conceptions of assimilation as Christian Americanization and sociologists' theories of cultural assimilation were similar. Each required outward physical signs to show the gap that subjective changes such as spiritual or cultural conversion could traverse. The link between missionary conversion and social scientific assimilation also revealed the sociologists' reliance on the validity of spiritual conversion as a working model for cultural assimilation. Modern conceptions of culture, following the Chicago school and anthropological theorists such as Franz Boas, are predicated on the importance of consciousness rather than biology as the primary domain of culture. Such a focus away from the body came from the repudiation of biological justifications for racism, but it also arose from a historical context in which social reformers' faith in spiritual conversion served as a blueprint for the social scientists' belief in cultural assimilation.

The emphasis that sociologists put on intermarriage as a cultural phenomenon, and the consequent de-emphasis on any physical components, paralleled the missionaries' emphasis on conversion as a matter of the spirit and not of the body. Protestant missionaries, in their desire to convert and Americanize Orientals and other people who were racially different from Anglo-Saxon whites, emphasized the idea of assimilation in a spiritual sense. As a matter of conscious faith and acts of piety, the missionaries' version of American assimilation had little to do with the physical body. Social scientists paralleled this separation of the physical body from the definition of assimilation by promoting the concept of culture, which they defined as divorced from the biology of the body. Intermarriage, for Park and the sociologists, was more interesting as a social phenomenon than as a biological act. Indeed, if the concept of assimilation was to be a purely cultural interaction, then it was improper to discuss the body as anything except the site of cultural mixture.

Looking for signs of religious conversion or cultural assimilation became a shell game. Faced with bodies that were merely vessels for the significant but virtually invisible changes inside, both missionaries and sociologists needed to look for exterior signs of change that indicated what was going on underneath the outer shell. Since both the starting points and the ending points of spiritual and mental processes were contained within the interior of bodies, indeed were somehow separable from the body, the dilemma was how to measure such changes from the outside. Outward signs that might be but were not necessarily equivalent to interior changes became the key. In practice, all kinds of surface manifestation became identifying markers for spiritual or cultural processes.

This was why clothing was such a powerful metaphor. Changes in the outer shell became tied to changes within, and clothing could measure the starting point (native dress) or ending point (American-style clothing) of such changes. When the body itself came to be seen as a uniform or a piece of clothing, then it, too, could mark the starting point for measurements of spiritual or cultural change. Robert Park brought the metaphor of clothing to its fruition. Expanding upon skin color and other signs of physical difference as a "racial uniform," Park connected these outward markers to the highly mutable world of the theater. Clothing could be a costume and thus also a disguise.

To the study of seemingly inscrutable Orientals, theatrical metaphors contributed the powerful notion of race as a disguise. Following from the idea that the face was a mask, the Oriental face became a disguise that could hide inner thoughts and feelings from the gaze of outsiders. At the conclusion of the Survey of Race Relations, Park wrote about an incident that echoed Donaldina Cameron's display of her saved Chinese slave girls. "I recently had the curious experience," Park described, "of talking with a young Japanese woman who was not only born in the United States, but was brought up in an American family, in an American college town, where she had almost no association with members of her own race." This Japanese American woman fascinated Park and provided an ideal example of how the white sociologists thought of Orientals: "I found myself watching her expectantly for some slight accent, some gesture or intonation that would betray her racial origin," Park wrote. The woman's Asian features seemed like a Halloween mask, hiding her true identity as an American. "When I was not able, by the slightest expression, to detect the Oriental mentality behind the Oriental mask, I was still not able to escape the impression that I was listening to an American woman in a Japanese disguise."[35]

The racial uniform of the young woman, a "Japanese disguise" not unlike the native dress of the Chinese slave girls, marked her as different and foreign, but everything else about her said American. If such assimilated Orientals, so obviously different from "normal" Americans, could fool Park into thinking they were actually Americans in Oriental disguise, then obviously the amount of cultural assimilation that an Oriental could undergo was enormous. Based on the presumption of a great difference between Orientals and Americans, the missionaries and sociologists chose to use the example of Orientals to prove the validity of their theories about cultural assimilation.

Missionaries and sociologists were looking for a good way to show the great spiritual and mental changes involved in conversion and assimilation. According to them, these changes were in no way physical. However, it is difficult to measure the difference between the consciousness of two human beings. Orientals, because they had been physically marked as the most different from white Americans, were the ideal bodies by which a purely cultural process of assimilation could be proven. Assimilated Orientals possessed proof of the universal nature of spirit/mind/culture while at the same time displaying physical bodies that showed the differences that cultural assimilation could erase. Thus, Oriental bodies became the perfect measuring devices.

During the Survey of Race Relations, individual Orientals became examples to be displayed. Political arguments over the assimilability of foreigners and over Americanization and Christianization all used Orientals as symbols of both otherness and the potential for sameness. Flora Belle

Original caption reads: "[*Left*] Mrs. Dr. Matsuye Suzuki of Florin, California, who treats both Japanese and American patients. [*Center*] This young man's father is a Japanese and his mother an American. He can speak no Japanese. He took his college course at Yale. [*Right*] Mr. and Mrs. Nojiri, both born in Japan and educated in America. Their courtship, engagement, and wedding followed approved American customs."

American missionary fascination with Japanese American assimilation and intermarriage can be seen in this and the following photographs. Notice the meaning placed upon the statements that Dr. Suzuki "can speak no Japanese" and that he went to college at "Yale." Photograph and text courtesy of Sidney L. Gulick, *The American Japanese Problem: A Study of the Racial Relations of the East and the West* (New York: Scribner's Sons, 1914): 220.

Jan served as a walking and talking symbol of the possibility of cultural assimilation. Robert Park's interest in the young American woman in a Japanese disguise, just like his interest in Jan, had to do with her being the embodiment of successful assimilation at its extreme, a perfectly "normal" American wearing an exotic Halloween mask. At the same time that Park argued for the sameness of Orientals and whites, he was also asserting their exotic difference, their perpetual foreignness.

The separation of mental or spiritual processes from the physical body was partially hidden by the sociologists' focus on the spatial movements of physical bodies. Because Oriental bodies came from such a long distance away, the metaphorical distance covered by spiritual change from Oriental to Christian American was mapped onto the physical distance between Asia and the United States. The distance traversed by spiritual or cultural conversion was literally as immense as the ocean that physically separated America from the Orient.

For Park and his colleagues, the Survey of Race Relations was an opportunity to test the validity of their ideas about cultural assimilation. It is unlikely, however, that the sociologists were going to abandon their theo-

Mr. Otto Fukushima.   Mrs. Otto Fukushima (American)

Original caption reads: "Mr. Otto Fukushima [*top left*]. Mrs. Otto Fukushima [*top right*]. The four daughters of Mr. and Mrs. Fukushima [*bottom*]: a typical American-Japanese family."

Note how "Mrs. Otto Fukushima" is designated as "American" (the equivalent of white) and that their daughters are defined as "typical American-Japanese children." It is uncertain whether Sidney Gulick, in using the term "typical," was trying to assert that the Fukushimas were representative of the majority of Japanese American families in America (clearly they were not) Rev. Gulick's emphasis upon the Fukushima children as exemplars of the "American-Japanese" reflected his belief that children of such unions were the only solution to the "race problem" in America. Only when such marriages were commonplace would the United States live up to its ideals. Photograph and text courtesy of Sidney L. Gulick, *The American Japanese Problem: A Study of the Racial Relations of the East and the West* (New York: Scribner's Sons, 1914): 130.

Original caption reads: "The mother on the left is half American and half Japanese. The daughter is three-quarters American and one-quarter Japanese. The mother and son on the right are pure Japanese. The mother came as a young girl to California, where the son was born. The photograph illustrates the contention of Professor Boas in regard to children born in this country."

The "contention" of Franz Boas, professor of anthropology at Columbia University, was that children of immigrants would begin to assume the "bodily form" of other Americans because of the influence of the "American environment." In 1912, "environment" for Boas included the effects of intermarriage. For Robert Park in 1924, intermarriage would be interesting less for its physical effects, but for changes in consciousness. Culture would be uncoupled from biology. Notice how Gulick calculates racial purity, trying to determine by comparison the difference between bodies which are "half American and half Japanese," "three-quarters American and one-quarter Japanese" and "pure Japanese." Photograph and text courtesy of Sidney L. Gulick, *The American Japanese Problem: A Study of the Racial Relations of the East and the West* (New York: Scribner's Sons, 1914): 150. Franz Boas is quoted in Gulick, *American Japanese Problem*, page 136; original discussion from F. Boas, "Changes in Bodily Form of Descendents of Immigrants," published by the Immigration Commission, 1912.

ries. In a way, the ideological implications of the assimilation cycle were too great, promising an inclusive, coherent America that would transform every immigrant that came to it. The survey was an opportunity to prove the validity of the Chicago theories. Park concluded at the end of the Survey of Race Relations, just as he had concluded before the survey began: "The race relations cycle—contact, competition, accommodation and eventual assimilation—is apparently progressive and irreversible."[36]

Significantly, Robert Park was talking about more than Orientals in America becoming assimilated to American culture; he was also making a point that America was beginning to seep into the Orient itself. "American films, with their realistic and thrilling pictures of American life, have transmitted to the Orient some of the restlessness and romanticism of the Occident." Park was not an American exceptionalist. He truly believed that the world as a whole was becoming a melting pot and that the future of the world lay in some Americanized version of change and exchange

Original caption reads: "The father of the little girl on the left is Japanese, her mother a Chinese woman with an American and later a Japanese education. The child herself, born in California, had only American training and is proving herself highly gifted. The father of the children on the right is Japanese, and their mother American."

Sidney Gulick's calculus of race did not focus exclusively on the biological content of bodies. Calculations of racial composition conflated the effects of education with biology, creating a connection between the two that was subsumed under the category of "American environment." For Gulick, America as a place and location was the cause of both behavioral and physical change. The Chicago sociologists removed biological and physical change from their focus of study; nevertheless, they kept a strong sense of spatial location as a determinant of "cultural difference." Photograph and text courtesy of Sidney L. Gulick, *The American Japanese Problem: A Study of the Racial Relations of the East and the West* (New York: Scribner's Sons, 1914): 170.

between peoples and cultures. "If America was once in any exclusive sense the melting pot of races, it is so no longer. The melting pot is the world."[37]

All of this hope for a better world, however, began and ended with the presupposition that Orientals were by definition not Occidental. Chicago sociologists used the idea of the sluggish Orient as the foil for their description of an Occident full of movement and change. The Orient was the unmoving object against which they could literally orient the direction in which Western civilization was traveling. The Pacific Ocean, arching from Asia to America, encompassed the journey from one extreme to the other.

Americanization as a cultural process became equivalent to the process of travel, containing within it the movements of migration from a stagnant Orient to a modern America. In spatializing cultural difference with their theories, the sociologists had made the distance traversed literal. The Orient was a world away, but Orientals could still be made into Americans. Perhaps surprisingly, the question of whether white Americans would ever become Orientals was never a major concern of the sociologists.

4

The Survey's Ends

The Survey of Race Relations on the Pacific Coast marked the beginning of American social science's long-term interest in Orientals. Originally defined by the outlook and concerns of Protestant missionaries and reliant upon their social networks, the survey's construction of the Oriental Problem was eventually built upon the needs of the sociologists. Their understandings of Orientals in America would structure the way American intellectuals thought about Asian immigrants for most of the twentieth century. The goal of the missionaries was to reeducate the public about Asian immigrants and therefore lessen anti-Asian hostility; the sociologists' ambitions ended with their acquisition of knowledge about Orientals. What they learned would serve less to enlighten Americans than to elaborate and validate their own theories. This disagreement over the survey's purpose would fracture the alliance between the missionaries and sociologists and lead to the survey's premature end.

The Missionaries and the Sociologists Disagree: Enlightenment and Changing Attitudes as the End of Racism

In 1925, as Park was ending his tenure as research director of the Survey of Race Relations, a discussion took place at a meeting of the Research Council over the end goals of the survey.[1] Some argued for the importance of "just getting the facts," while others wanted to change social attitudes.

Emory Bogardus and Roderick McKenzie, though sympathetic to the goal of education, both believed that the sociologist's role was restricted to acquiring and interpreting facts. They felt the objective of gathering information "should be kept entirely apart" from its dissemination. The missionaries disagreed. George Gleason, the Japanese missionary from the Los Angeles YMCA who had been one of the prime instigators of the survey, spoke of the "desirability of organizing the application of the results of the Survey in the life of the people," combining research and education. Eventually, this argument over whether to combine the goals of gathering and disseminating information was decided in favor of the sociologists, but the different goals of the two groups led to an irreconcilable disagreement.

In 1925, the release of tentative research conclusions illustrated this argument between missionaries and sociologists. In March, a large findings conference was held at Stanford University, where the early accomplishments of the survey were detailed and displayed. Major findings included the declining population of Chinese and Japanese on the West Coast and the successful assimilation of American culture by American-born Orientals. These were accepted with great enthusiasm by the audience of academics and interested Progressive elites. The survey had also found that the "feeling on the Pacific Coast toward the Chinese has been a tolerant one for many years." During the nineteenth century, "any Chinese walking on the streets was in some danger of being molested. This is no longer the case." The Chinese in the United States, the sociologists concluded, were "no longer feared."[2] The missionaries supported the second conclusion, that the Chinese were now more accepted by whites. Indeed, they had been trying to lessen hostility toward the Chinese ever since the early days of exclusion.

One of the other findings, however, sparked a major controversy between the missionaries and the sociologists. After the discriminatory Alien Land Laws had made it illegal for Asians to own land, and the recent Immigration Acts of 1924 had cut off further Japanese immigration, the missionaries felt a sense of failure and political defeat. Therefore, when the sociologists concluded that the laws had in fact created on the West Coast "a kindlier feeling towards its Japanese population," the missionaries were incredulous. Such a statement undermined everything the ministers had been trying to accomplish politically and was especially offensive in light of the timing. They had been fighting anti-Japanese legislation for decades, and the announcement of "kindlier feelings" after the passage of the recent laws seemed to vindicate the actions of the missionaries' political foes. Galen Fisher of the Institute of Social and Religious Research wired the secretary of the survey two weeks after the findings conference and warned that "further grants [were] doubtful," since the institute found the "findings on public opinion dubious and misleading."[3]

The sociologists' conviction that there had been a lessening of ill feeling toward Orientals was a direct result of their theories concerning the interaction cycle and social distance. They believed that less economic conflict led to a more stable overall situation and a reduction in harsh feelings. In a 1926 issue of the *Journal of Applied Sociology* that contained several articles on the survey's results, Roderick McKenzie concluded that the lynch mob violence that had driven the Chinese into Chinatown ghettos during the nineteenth century actually had contributed to the increased "friendly" feeling toward them. "Instead of being considered as a disturbing element in our communal life, the Chinatown, in some cities at least, is looked upon as a commercial asset—a sort of human zoo—which becomes a point of attraction for tourists."[4]

The missionaries were left wondering about such "friendlier" feelings toward the Chinese. With friends like these, had the Chinese ever needed enemies? For missionaries who had fought politically for fair treatment of Chinese and Japanese immigrants in the United States and considered themselves true friends of Orientals, the social scientists' conclusions were politically and morally unbearable. The missionaries at the Institute of Social and Religious Research questioned the value of the sociologists' "indirect, uncontroversial, factual approach."[5]

For the missionaries, the survey served a larger political purpose, as a step toward better treatment of Orientals in the United States; in their eyes, the information gathered should have moved toward this goal, not undermined it. The "factual" conclusions of the social scientists were acceptable as long as they did not support the political aims of their opponents. The sociologists stuck to their conclusions. According to them, they simply gathered and interpreted the facts, and it was not their business to give their findings the proper persuasion and political impact.

Much of this disagreement stemmed from the sociologists' emphasis on attitudes as the subject of their research. Along with the social scientists' interest in spatializing their studies through their theories of human ecology and social distance, they also engaged in the extensive collection of life histories. The life history was a narrative that contained the origin of an individual's attitude. Park and his colleagues tried to formulate a precise definition for attitudes as a "tendency to action" toward a specific thing, person, or group of persons, differentiating attitudes from mere opinion.[6] Attitudes provided the hypothetical link between race consciousness and acts of racial discrimination and prejudice that characterized social interaction on the West Coast. Park also hoped to discover situations in which these attitudes were changed or eliminated. His desire to discover the economic and social conditions that reduced discriminatory attitudes toward Orientals had led the sociologists to emphasize the recent anti-Asian exclusion laws.

Japanese Americans revealed an ability to see through the rhetoric of the anti-Asian organizations—an ability which the sociologists seemed to have lost in their emphasis on attitudes. Roy H. Akagi, a member of the Japan Association (a mutual aid society organized by Japanese American immigrants) was asked by the missionaries for his response to the survey's conclusions. Akagi stated that he did not believe that attitudes toward Orientals had become "kindlier" since the enactment of discriminatory laws. The sympathetic feelings of some Americans toward the Japanese may have grown stronger, Akagi remarked, but so had the discriminatory feelings of anti-Japanese groups and organizations. "I saw and heard many instances to prove this during my last trip along the Pacific Coast," he observed. "Residential troubles, anti-Japanese uprisings, expulsion of Japanese groups, so-called K.K.K. outrages, and the like are becoming more common happenings." In a forceful, incisive, and damning conclusion, Akagi dismissed the survey sociologists: "In other words, what the anti-Japanese leaders and organizations say in statements and interviews are quite different from what they actually do; and they never place anti-Japanese motive in some of the very discriminatory activities occurring during the recent dates."[7]

In decoupling stated attitudes from actual actions, Akagi pointed to the weakest link in Park's conception of racial attitudes and race relations. First of all, the techniques the sociologists employed to discover attitudes— questionnaires, opinion surveys, interviews, and life histories—relied on the perceptiveness of both subjects and researchers. The amount of insight contained within the life histories depended on the subject's degree of self-revelation and the researcher's interpretive ability. Even though the relationship between attitudes and actions could be approached with more sophistication—taking into account empty rhetoric and self-justifications— the degree of nuance recognized still depended on the subtlety of the particular researcher, and not all of the researchers were, or would be, equally perceptive. For instance, a Ku Klux Klansman could say that he had no problems with Asians, but the assessment of whether this attitude was or was not the origin of his tendency to act to the detriment of Asian immigrants depended on the insight of the researcher.

Another crucial weakness with the conception of attitudes was the tendency to focus on consciousness. Defining attitudes as the cause of actions de-emphasized the importance of acts that did not flow from a stated intention. Actions that defied the conscious self-understandings of people interviewed, which were poorly understood even by themselves, were difficult for the sociologists to track. Another way of analyzing attitude theory is to compare it to Freud's psychoanalytic theories, for which the Chicago theorists on the whole found little use; attitudes did not explain what Freud had labeled as unconscious. If a person was not aware of how he treated Negroes or Orientals differently, how could an attitude be explicated? In addition, attitude theory had a hard time explaining paradoxical behaviors, for instance, how some white Americans could abhor the presence of Orientals in principle yet also find Asian women attractive and sexually desirable. In the end, the inability of many white Americans to articulate clearly the reasons they disliked Orientals made the sociologists' emphasis on conscious attitudes a problem.

Most important, however, an emphasis on attitudes and consciousness ignored any historical legacy of inequality that had begun with an intentional act yet was being maintained without any conscious intent. As an example, imagine two people who were considered for a business loan, with one of them denied the loan because of racial discrimination. Three generations down the line, the white family had become financially stable because of the exclusive economic opportunity granted to them by racial privilege. They did not need to maintain a racial attitude in order to justify actions that maintained or furthered the wealth they had amassed. Their financial comfort was enough to continue and reinforce a hierarchical, racialized order that had been founded on conscious acts of racial inequity.

The Oriental Problem as an intellectual construction would retain as one of its foundations an emphasis on the formation of racial attitudes. Enshrined as one of the main components of Chicago theories of race consciousness and prejudice, it reinforced the assumption that a person's actions began with a conscious idea. Social acts could thus be studied by understanding the ideas behind actions. This proved a partial, and thus flawed, approach to race relations. And though this was not the only mode of social analysis employed by the Chicago sociologists, it would be their greatest and longest-lasting legacy for race relations theory.

This focus on attitudes and consciousness as the interesting subject for race relations has continued to bedevil American understandings of race. Attitude theory reiterated the split between the mind and body that had marked cultural theory. Just as Chicago theorists had separated culture from the physical body, they separated attitudes, originating from the mind, from actions, carried out by the body.

The emphasis on ideas as the origin of social actions stemmed from the belief of both missionaries and social scientists in the ultimate value of knowledge. Society's enlightenment depended on knowledge for transformation. But the splitting off of the physical from the spiritual or mental also tended to devalue the physical, so that there was a strong denial of the importance of the physical body. Arguments by the missionaries and the social scientists against biological racism contained this tendency toward the abnegation of the physical. The most moral world for the missionaries would be one in which bodily differences such as race did not matter, and the most powerful social analysis, from the sociologists' perspective, would emphasize the importance of culture and not the body. The Chicago sociologists, following their missionary allies, tried to make the theory of culture into an emancipatory vision denying the relevance of biological differences for understanding race relations. By moving racial consciousness and all cultural phenomena into the realm of the mind or spirit instead of the physical body, the sociologists created the possibility that anyone could share knowledge. Men and women of all physical types could share the same culture.

Cultural theory defined enlightenment—the possession of new knowledge—as inherently antiracist. This was the visionary hope of the theory of the cultural assimilation cycle. Coming to know the unknown, in particular how other people might see the world in a different manner, led toward a single shared world civilization. Cultural theory assumed that once everyone shared the same knowledge, then consciousness of physical difference would disappear.

From a current-day perspective, this assumption seems naïve and wrong. But it is wrong in a way that many people today still do not clearly understand. The reiteration of an age-old Platonic split between the body and the mind/spirit had many consequences. In the context of rampant racism based on theories of biological racial hierarchy, the removal of considerations of the physical body from group difference was a progressive move. But in the end, the false distinction between body and mind would lead to idealized and utopian politics. In making social phenomena first and foremost a matter of consciousness, theories that centered on culture shifted the relevance of physical differences to a matter of mere perception.

But changing peoples' *ideas* about race was only a partial change. Race as a way of defining some human bodies as privileged and more deserving than other bodies has been an inextricable part of virtually every legal and economic practice since the founding of the United States. These racial practices continue, with or without conscious intent. In the dark shadows cast by the structures of such a world, the enlightenment goal of changing a few ideas remains a pale flicker.[8]

In divorcing cultural knowledge from the concerns of the body, the Chicago sociologists reenacted a denial of the physical as an element of intellectual enlightenment. If this theory of culture created problems, perhaps they are difficult to recognize because physical denial remains so ubiquitous an ideal. A strong spirit is associated with a freedom from the body's weaknesses, so that the ultimate triumph is to overcome the limitations of physical infirmity. We praise those who can think clearly despite bodily pain. We admire those who are intelligent and brave despite physical handicaps.

Such distinctions place our hopes on a spirit of intelligence racing to escape the body. Yet the ideal has always depended on underlying definitions of what the body is to mean, even if that meaning is pure abnegation. The missionaries and sociologists sought within bodies marked by racial disfigurement the triumph of their own theories of pure culture.

The missionaries and sociologists were putting forth an ideal of Americanization that limited the process to a matter of the mind and spirit, but we are continually seduced by this vision into thinking that an end to racism is nigh. If we accept the theoretical validity of the split of the mind and the body, then racism is just a matter of attitude, of prejudicial thoughts and bigoted remarks. Therefore, if we all just stopped thinking about race, then racial conflict would disappear. But there are crucial problems with these cultural definitions of racism.

First and most simply, the missionaries and sociologists needed physical bodies that they imagined to be different in order to prove the validity of cultural change. Indeed, in searching for the mental changes that accompanied cultural assimilation, the missionaries and sociologists themselves continually used the body to define the extent of such changes. Orientals were used as the test case to prove these theories because their bodies and those of Negroes showed the greatest physical difference from white bodies. They reinscribed race as a product of visible physical difference in bodies at the same time that they were seemingly repudiating its effects on mind and spirit. From the point of view of their own theories, the Chicago sociologists brought into practical use the categories of race.

Ever since, the twin claims that race as a biological difference does not exist and that culture has nothing to do with bodies have in practice reinforced the importance of perceptions of bodily differences. If, according to the missionaries and sociologists, American culture is a matter of ideas, a mental attribute, then the body is seemingly superfluous. But to stop being aware of bodies was impossible. The metaphor of racial uniforms, of skin color as clothing, snuck the body back into a system of meaning that was supposedly nonphysical and led to the curious image of thinking about Asian Americans as somehow real Americans in an Oriental body.

The sociologists were forced to identify the difference between cultures with the differences between bodies because they defined the origins of exotic cultures with the migration of bodies from somewhere else. An awareness of bodies and their origins was everywhere in the Chicago sociologists theories of culture. Thinking about their own bodies' travels created the questions that led to the theories they produced. They were aware of their own origins in small towns across the Midwest, and this awareness was everywhere displayed in their ideas about rural and urban, traditional and modern, gemeinschaft and gesellschaft. They were also aware of the origins of the Oriental bodies that fascinated them. Asian immigrants had somehow embodied an exotic Oriental culture in moving from Asia to North America, and so, even as the sociologists tried to prove that Orientals were American in culture, they were continually fascinated by their own belief in the essential foreignness of Oriental bodies.

Using bodies that were starkly different to prove that the culture was the same, Chicago sociologists continually linked supposedly mental differences to particular physical bodies. The sociologists were professional thinkers whose theories resided on the foundation that culture was not about bodies, but the culture concept itself was flawed by the ways in which the Chicago sociologists searched for and defined cultural difference. They could not have done otherwise, since the distinction they made between the mind and the body was false from the start.

We cannot fault the white sociologists for their inability to leave behind a fascination with bodies. It was a product of the very split between minds and bodies that they were trying to promote. The idea that being American was a matter of the mind, a spiritual and cultural conversion separate from the human body, was politically progressive in the context of the times. But being American cannot be a matter of culture. You cannot split off a person's consciousness from the physical history of his or her body. There was no *real* American inside the racial uniforms, no true American spirit stuck in an Oriental body, trying desperately to escape. Individual Oriental Americans might struggle to understand themselves in such a way, but to do so is already to deny the relevance of one's own skin color in a manner that a white person is seldom forced to undergo.

During the 1920s, social scientists and missionary social reformers created the institutional practices that defined Orientals, drew Chinese Americans and Japanese Americans into an elite white social world, and further created new knowledge about Orientals in the United States. These institutional practices, which I emphasize in labeling the institutional construction of the Oriental Problem in America, were at the heart of American Orientalism as a structure that constrained the lives of Asians in the United States.

The Final Racial Frontier: Hawaii and the
Institution of American Orientalism in the Pacific

The Survey of Race Relations dissolved in disagreement, amid the disheartening immigration legislation of 1924 that ended an era in American history. However, the difficult alliance between the missionaries and the sociologists continued.[9] This partnership produced the longest-lasting institutional legacy of the survey at the western extreme of the United States. Hawaii was to become the site of everything the Survey of Race Relations had hoped for and left unrealized. In 1924, J. Merle Davis began shifting his energies away from the Survey of Race Relations toward organizing a new project for the YMCA International, a gathering of experts from North American and Asian countries to talk about the common concerns of Pacific nations.

Davis and his missionary allies created the Institute of Pacific Relations (IPR) and the East-West Institute, places where representatives of the Occident and the Orient could meet peaceably and discuss their differences in an enlightened manner. Yearly conferences paid for by the YMCA and the Rockefeller Foundation brought together educated elites from around the Pacific Rim to confer about international relations and to promote peace and understanding. The sociologists joined in the discussions, but for them, the more important institution was the sociology department at the University of Hawaii, a place where Chicago sociology and the theories developed to study the Oriental Problem would dominate as they did nowhere else.

The missionaries had picked Hawaii as the base for the IPR because of its central geographic position between East and West and its long history as a way station in the middle of the Pacific Ocean. It had served as the halfway base for their missions to the Orient for the last century. They recognized that more than any other place, Hawaii was the meeting ground for all the different races and nationalities of the Pacific Rim. The Hawaiian Islands had been a territory of the United States since their annexation in 1898, but New England traders, plantation owners, and missionaries had been active there since the 1830s.

Outside observers in the 1920s marveled at the islands' diverse populations of native Hawaiians, Chinese, Japanese, Filipinos, Portuguese, and Yankee overlords. Although often portrayed as a tropical paradise because of its seemingly peaceful mix of peoples, Hawaii contained a myriad of racial tensions and labor conflicts. American plantation owners had created a racially divided economy that grew sugar, coffee, and pineapples. By recruiting successive waves of laborers from different Asian countries to work in the fields, undercutting each other's wages, they had actively sought to keep their workforce divided. To top it off, they used only white Portuguese or Americans to direct the Asian laborers.

The editor of *Survey Graphic*, a periodical published for social workers, reformers, and other interested elites, pointed to the "racial drama" occurring in Hawaii. The 1926 issue of *Survey Graphic* was devoted to the Survey of Race Relations, summing up what the sociologists and missionaries had found on the West Coast. The contributors also outlined their hopes for Hawaii. Robert Park remarked that in the "Hawaiian Islands, where all the races of the Pacific meet and mingle on more liberal terms than they do elsewhere, the native races are disappearing and new peoples are coming into existence."[10]

Hawaii became the fantasy island of the surveyors, the place where all the ends and goals they had imagined during the Survey of Race Relations would be realized. To the missionaries, it would be the meeting ground for racial harmony. To the sociologists, it was the ultimate racial laboratory, a place where the formation of the cultural melting pot they had predicted for the West Coast was already taking place. That Hawaii was a series of islands was significant to the sociologists, who saw them as the natural laboratory for making observations just as Charles Darwin had used the Galápagos Islands.[11]

As the point in the farthest west of America, Hawaii could be seen as the extreme frontier, the future of America. If it could be proven that the races were getting along in Hawaii, then there was hope for the rest of the United States. The frontier symbolized the unfolding of America through time, and therefore the farther west one traveled, the more one delved into the future stages of American development. Unlike Frederick Jackson Turner, who saw the western frontier as a representation of earlier, pioneer stages of America that would pass into higher forms as the frontier continued westward, the sociologists saw the "racial frontier" out west as the future of America and the world, a glimpse of the millennium.

The Pacific Ocean and the Orient were to be America's future, and Hawaii was to be the site for a reorienting of that future. Punning on the word "Orient," editor Paul Kellogg proclaimed: "On the Pacific Coast Americans encounter a new orientation—in both meanings of the world. Confronted with the Orient at the seam of the hemispheres we must get our bearings afresh: in the course of time this process amounts to a reversal of our point of view." Announcing a new center to American civilization, Kellogg concluded: "We were looking east, toward the Atlantic. Now we are looking west, toward the Pacific."[12]

The emphasis on the vast expanse of the Pacific Ocean as the central locus for such encounters was reinforced by descriptions of a new stage in civilization taking place around the "whole rim of the Pacific." The Pacific Rim became a descriptive label that connected Asia to the Americas as the new center of world civilization, replacing the ancient Mediterranean and the recent Atlantic rim. Connecting disparate events around the Pacific, Park concluded: "The present ferment in Asia and the racial conflict on the Pacific Coast of America are but different manifestations of what is, broadly speaking, a single process."[13] The Orient was the opposite of everything American, but it would be the collision and interpenetration of the two that would define future civilization. The new stage of progress was the Pacific, and it would center on Hawaii, where whites and Orientals mixed to the greatest degree.

The island fantasy of Hawaii in which the missionaries and sociologists indulged paid homage to the booster mythology propagated by the white planter class—a Hawaii supposedly dominated by the old native Hawaiian aloha mentality of hospitality and tolerance. The sociologists saw through the myth, however. They described the waves of labor that had characterized Hawaiian history, from the Chinese to the Japanese to the Filipino and the Portuguese, and the plantation economy that pitted racial groups against each other. Hawaii was dominated politically and economically by a few elite haoles (a Hawaiian term for whites), while the various Oriental races constituted an overwhelming majority. Explaining how such a racial hierarchy was progressing became the work of the Chicago sociologists.

Hawaii became a locus for research as a direct result of the same alliance between missionaries and sociologists that had produced the survey. Organizers had wanted Hawaii to be involved with the Survey of Race Relations in 1923 but could not make arrangements in time. Nevertheless, Hawaii would end up inheriting the survey's research agenda.

Chicago sociologists began to come to Hawaii as if it was a pilgrimage site. Beginning with Chicago-trained sociologist Romanzo Colfax Adams, who had come from Nevada and founded the sociology department in 1919, and continuing until the 1970s, sociology at the University of Hawaii would be dominated by Chicago graduates. In the years after the survey had ended on the West Coast, research continued in Honolulu as Chicago sociologists such as Robert Park, William Smith, Andrew Lind, and Edward Byron (E. B.) Reuters came to the islands to conduct research. Reuters, who had completed his 1919 dissertation under Park on the mulatto as a marginal broker between blacks and whites, taught at the University of Iowa. After spending a research sabbatical in Hawaii, he recruited a pair of students from Hawaii, Jitsuichi Masuoka and Doris Lorden, to study with him. Both conducted research on Orientals in Hawaii while receiving their degrees in the middle of Iowa. Reuters's bringing of students from Honolulu to Iowa City was just one instance in an overall pattern.

From Honolulu, Hawaii, and from various locations all around the Pacific, Chicago sociologists would meet and recruit students of Asian and non-Asian background to help them study the Oriental Problem. The Survey of Race Relations had set up a series of sites—Seattle, Los Angeles, San Francisco—where a unique two-way exchange would take place. Chicago sociologists could come to these sites to study race relations and apply the theories developed during the survey; Chinese, Japanese, Chinese American, and Japanese American students, as well as white students interested in the Oriental Problem, could go through the local institutions on their way to earning higher degrees in Chicago and Chicago-dominated sociology departments. The locations became both destinations and feeder sites for researchers, and Honolulu eventually became the place where the exchange with Chicago happened most frequently.

If there was a unique feature of American Orientalism in the 1920s that distinguished it from earlier American and European versions, it was the connection of Orientals at home with those in the Orient. The institution of Orientalism in the research universities of the United States occurred within a social network of missionaries and social scientists who combined their definitions of Asians in Asia with an understanding of Asians in the Americas. Hawaii was the gateway to Asia and, at the same time, the gateway for Asians to America. Park himself used Hawaii as a halfway point in several trips to Asia, including one immediately after the first meeting of the IPR in 1925. Just as the missionaries had done before him, he set sail to China to spread the gospel, carrying in his case his and Ernest Burgess's Green Bible of sociology. Several years later, he spent several months teaching sociology to Chinese students, including a young Fei Xiaotong, who would go on to become the most famous sociologist in China.[14]

It is in social institutions, particularly academic institutions of higher learning, that knowledge is reproduced the most effectively and efficiently. Social science was more than the network of sociologists and missionaries who produced knowledge about exotic Orientals. Social science as an academic discipline also reproduced these ideas and disseminated them in journals, conferences, and classrooms. Scholarship involved disciplining students to understand the world in the proper way, and the legitimization conferred by elite institutions of higher learning transformed the travelers' knowledge of missionaries and sociologists into scientific theory.

The belief that the Orient was fundamentally different from America laid the foundation for Orientalism. It defined the desire for the exotic that drove merchants, missionaries, and amateur scholars to travel great distances around the globe. American Orientalism began when the first Yankee traders set sail for China in 1784, eager to buy tea, silk, porcelain, and other exotic goods. Missionaries followed in the 1820s, wanting to prove that they could convert such obviously different people.[15] American Orientalist writings arose, therefore, long before the 1920s, narrated in the amateur ethnographies of China and Japan produced by merchants, missionaries, and travelers, as well as in the lurid pulp fiction and Yellow Peril tracts of anti-Asian nativists.

The knowledge of Orientals produced by missionaries and social scientists in the 1920s, however, had powerful long-term effects because of its discursive life in academia. What distinguished the work of the survey and the IPR from earlier scholarly studies was the systematic institutional framework that generated research. For instance, *Chinese Immigration* (1909), a seminal study by Progressive California academic and social activist Mary Roberts Coolidge, anticipated many of the themes and conclusions of the Chicago sociologists. But it was an isolated study written by a singularly gifted woman.[16] In contrast, the Orientalist discourse coming out of the survey was coherent and self-replicating.

United by a few key theories, the Oriental Problem as a set of research questions reproduced itself in study after study for the next forty years. Tied to the University of Chicago, such research had a powerful effect on academic and popular knowledge about Asians in America. Key assumptions and claims about race and culture spread from teacher to student in graduate seminars, in undergraduate lectures, and in popular education programs. Disseminated by the Chicago sociologists as they themselves spread across the nation and the world, Chicago theories about race, culture, and the Oriental were set to convert the world.

Exoticism, Modernity, and Cosmopolitan Whiteness

"Races and cultures die—it has always been so—but civilization lives on." Robert Park wrote these words in 1926 in the article "Our Racial Frontier on the Pacific."[17] What could he have meant by such a cryptic statement? What was the difference between race, culture, and civilization? It was within the distinctions between these terms that Park and the other Chicago sociologists built the Oriental Problem into a set of theories about civilized whiteness.

Each of the legacies of the Survey of Race Relations in Hawaii—the Institute of Pacific Relations and the sociological research program dominated by Chicago theories of the Oriental Problem—combined a hope in the transforming effects of knowledge with a focus on international connections. The elite white men who set up both believed themselves to be the embodiment of such transnational, transformative knowledge. While organizing the Survey of Race Relations on the Pacific Coast, the missionaries had seen themselves as observant travelers whose knowledge of Orientals abroad provided them with expertise about Orientals at home. In a related way, the sociologists believed that their knowledge of Orientals in America told them something about Orientals in Asia. This belief in the validity of a traveler's expertise had some powerful consequences for understandings of the place of elite white Americans in the world.

The missionaries and sociologists saw their own journeys back and forth between two continents as acts that could bridge two utterly different worlds. The more knowledge of the exotic Orient they collected and possessed, either by traveling in Asia or by studying Asian immigrants in the United States, the more they came to understand themselves as worldly, cosmopolitan experts. Their knowledge made them important, qualified to speak on behalf of Americans to Asian audiences, and in many instances on behalf of Orientals to American audiences.

Here was the answer to the question about why white Americans never felt that learning more about the Orient made them more Oriental. If theories of cultural assimilation ran both ways equally, then there should have been a theoretical parallel to the process of Orientals becoming more American by acquiring knowledge about whites. Assimilation should have been a two-way street. White Americans should have wondered what all this knowledge about Orientals was doing to them. But, of course, the possession of cultural knowledge by whites had utterly different meanings.

Exotic knowledge was exciting, something to be collected and objectified. What made such knowledge a fetish for elite white men and women was that it represented the adventure of the exotic. The Orient was the opposite of everything that was uninteresting in their own lives. As Winifred Raushenbush, Robert Park's assistant, explained while lecturing white American audiences on the social mores of Oriental immigrant communities in North America: "In meeting persons of another race there is also a certain amount of adventure involved."[18]

Along with the adventure involved in encountering the strange, Raushenbush revealed in her lectures the collector's value of the knowledge of the strange. Having learned enough about Orientals to render them familiar to herself, she could tell an audience about Japanese communities in California, or about the Chinatown in Vancouver. Part of the satisfaction of getting to know the exotic and strange was the sense of mastery and expertise that this knowledge imparted, particularly when it was revealed to those for whom it was still inscrutable. In the end, the process of fetishizing and collecting knowledge about the Orient was also an attempt by elite whites to render themselves as connoisseurs of the strange. At the same time that they searched for and produced knowledge about the Orient, they also produced themselves as cosmopolitan travelers, expert purveyors of the exotic.

American Orientalism was the product of the migrations of elite whites. The knowledge produced about Asians in the United States and Asia came out of the journeys of Protestant missionaries and sociologists to Asia and the West Coast of the United States. Within the large-scale population shifts back and forth across the Pacific, they were but a few of the multitude of migrants, but they wielded the power to produce and evaluate knowledge. In their self-appointed roles as seekers of the unknown, they saw themselves as embodying modern civilization.

Progressive social scientists from the Chicago school came to understand America as a *modern* nation through the construction of the primitive or premodern other against which it was differentiated. Research on Orientals in America contributed to a sense of difference between home and foreign, between native and ethnic, between white and colored. Descriptions of Oriental stagnation were easily aligned with the tribal primitivism imputed to Africa and Pacific Polynesia by American anthropologists, and a vast array of racial and cultural oppositions situated modern, progressive, white, Protestant America (and the intellectuals who embodied such perspectives) as different from the premodern, traditional, stagnant others who were being left behind in the progress of history.

Ostensibly, modernity for the social scientists concerned new ways of thinking that arose from contacts between previous strangers. Park's sense of a new universal consciousness was marked by his training in Hegelian philosophies of history while he was pursuing his doctorate in Germany. In Park's view on modernity, increasing cultural contact had created a newfound sense of one's own particularity. At the same time, cultural contact offered a new enlightenment through understanding the universal that encompassed everybody. Particular societies that had lived in isolation were no longer able to believe that their way of understanding the world was all that was necessary to know.

According to Park, people in the contemporary world were forced to interact with others who saw the world in utterly different ways. Such contacts made them realize that their own perspective was only one among many. This, for Park, was the essence of modern consciousness, and it was the end point of historical development in social relations. All the world's people were being brought into a singular, universal history in which they understood themselves in relation to everyone else.

For Robert Park, this was the difference between civilization and mere culture. Cultures were particular ways of seeing the world. Races and cultures "died" when their members realized the narrow perspective they held within a wider world. The result was a modern civilization that lived onward, built upon a consciousness that encompassed all cultures.

It is important to note that the consciousness of culture itself was possible in two ways. First of all, at the moment of contact with strangers, members of an isolated society begin to understand that they have a culture. Culture is a creation of the awareness that how you think makes you different from someone else. The second possibility was that an enlightened thinker could imagine a number of cultures, each with a different way of life. Within the consciousness of this universal perspective, particular cultures could exist as imagined entities. From this universal point of view, any culture that did not understand its place relative to other cultures, indeed, did not even realize it had a particular culture, was by definition premodern. Such an exotic culture, however, could still be brought into modernity.

Social science played a central role in this process of bringing the gospel of modernity to the world. Sociology was the perspective that best understood the relationships between the particular and the universal; if a sociologist could understand a particular culture's position relative to all others, then that culture was embraced within an ever-growing universal consciousness. Sociology itself, as a universal perspective on all peoples, was the encapsulation of modernity.

The ultimate enlightenment goal of gathering knowledge about unknown cultures paralleled the salvage operation of anthropology, with one important distinction. Anthropologists were interested in "savages" as representatives of the beginning of the spectrum from primitive to modern. Uninterested in changes wrought by cultural contacts with whites, they suppressed mentioning any deviations from the pristine stage of traditional primitive life that they were trying to save for posterity. In contrast, sociologists were fascinated by the progress of cultures along the spectrum between traditional and modern. They focused on processes such as assimilation and all the imagined and actual physical movements from one end of the spectrum to the other.

Native Americans and native Pacific Islanders intrigued anthropologists as representatives of the primitive, and they were most interesting if they remained at the beginning of an imagined spectrum of progress. Anthropologists kept their subjects at a distance metaphorically and physically, fixing them in faraway locales to which the ethnographer was forced to travel. Within the imagined danger of "going native," of becoming too much like the people studied, was the evaluation of the native as all that was opposite to white civilization. Studying the primitive nature of the native reflected on the anthropologist as white and civilized.

Although sociologists were also intrigued by the exotic nature of the unknown other, they were much more interested in the possibilities of traversing the divide, of a progress across the spectrum. They valued the exotic other for showing the distance encompassed by modernity as a process.[19] A new modern civilization was brought about by whites understanding exotic natives, but it also happened when the natives became like whites. Thus, the melting pot civilization of America, the end goal of a culturally assimilated United States, was modernity itself.

Like anthropologists, however, Park's definitions of modernity highlighted the exotic and the strange. Such xenophilia seemingly countered the Eurocentrism of enlightenment knowledge and paralleled the widespread sense in the 1920s within philosophy and the arts of the dissolution of a single universal order. The realization that other cultures and peoples saw the world in different and incommensurable ways was coupled with a fascination with the strange, the exotic, and the primitive.

The term "modernity" may have been impossible to define in a singular fashion, since it was used in almost every conceivable context during the 1920s, but extolations of it were invariably opposed to something premodern, primitive, or traditional. What is interesting is how objects and people were defined as exotic and interesting, embraced for their supposed primitive or traditional qualities, and often valued as being relics outside of modernity. The issue of *Survey Graphic* that preceded the one on the "Orient" was a special edition examining the flourishing Harlem Renaissance. Both issues reflected the perspective of a white progressive evaluation of the exotic cultures of Negro Americans and Oriental Americans. In canvassing the cultural differences between white and black, American and Oriental, the sociologists' contributions to *Survey Graphic* drew the line between white self and racial other, categorizing and ordering their differences systematically and giving them meaning and importance.

In this way, the Chicago sociologists were aligning the definitions of modernity produced in their race relations studies with the aesthetic modernism becoming popular at that time among many elite whites. In both cases, the necessary economic base was either the wherewithal to travel and seek the unknown or the privilege of purchasing the exotic and bringing it closer. Whether it was the supposedly primitive, primeval rhythms and symbols of African music and art or the mystical, mysterious religions and philosophies of the Orient, a fascination with the exotic was essential to definitions of the modern, especially to those whites who imagined themselves rebelling against or fleeing from modernity.

The outsider's perspective, cosmopolitan and interested in all cultures, was an illusion founded upon a denial of the one perspective that sat at the center of definitions of modernity. The deracinated, universal perspective removed from all points in space was imagined by elite white intellectuals as the embrace of all. In fact, it was an extolment of elite whiteness, a collection of the exotic, while it denied the relevance of the privilege and power of the collector. According to the sociologists, their studies reflected the point of view of knowledge itself.

The goal of enlightenment was to gather all that was unknown. But, in the end, what was unknown was defined by the men who were doing the studying, and it was the terrain of their own ignorance that drew a map of the world. Despite their claims to the contrary, the knowledge they produced betrayed its origins in a curiosity that was peculiar to them. White sociologists from small midwestern towns were interested in Orientals and Negroes in a very particular manner.

Grounded in the position of white elites in U.S. society, sociological interest in Orientals also depended on the national power and privilege of Americans along the travel routes that crossed the Pacific Ocean. For the white missionaries and sociologists who were fascinated by the Orient during the 1920s, their affirmation of themselves as cosmopolitan coincided with their own expanding possibilities as consumers of the exotic. Able to travel long distances because of new transportation technologies and the ever-growing protection that American military and economic power afforded them in foreign countries, academics from universities in the United States built white knowledge as a hungry appetite that sampled exotic delicacies.[20]

In entwining American definitions of race and culture with international migration and modernity, Chicago sociologists built the foundation for a nationally defined study of race relations and immigration. At the base has been an intellectual practice that has emphasized and valued exoticism, even as it demanded its ultimate erasure. The end result has been a structure for the production of knowledge of the exotic that has endured, founded on the tremendous privilege that white American academics held in the project of enlightenment.

To the credit of the white Protestant missionaries and Chicago sociologists, they welcomed Asian Americans into the circle of elite society in which they traveled. This was no small gesture, and their ideal of a progressive change in the racial structure of the United States is a positive legacy that lives on. If there is a heroic narrative that could be told about the Chicago sociologists (and it has been told by others), it would describe how they created institutional openings for intellectuals of color at a time when such openings were rare. Moreover, they created a way of understanding race that de-emphasized the physical body, a change that on the whole benefited racial minorities.[21] But there have also been problems within their legacy.

At the very moment that American intellectuals constructed social theories de-emphasizing the physical body, they embodied their ideas with the perspectives and social positions of elite white men in the United States. By the time Chinese, Japanese, Chinese American, and Japanese American intellectuals joined the profession of sociology, the ground had already been broken, and they came to build upon a foundation not of their own making. Their presence was essential within Chicago theories about race relations, but their perspectives were seen by the white academics as adornment on the walls. In reality, the existence of racial others such as Asian Americans and African Americans in the United States supplied the necessary supporting beams of the entire structure of white supremacy.

If power corresponds to the possibilities for action that are available to an individual within a larger structure, then, in comparison to those whites who defined American Orientalism, those treated in practice as Orientals faced a myriad of restrictions. Asian American intellectuals were not powerless as they searched for their own answers to the Oriental Problem, but as they struggled to find a voice within an academia dominated by the questions of others, they were certainly constrained. The nature of these constraints is the subject of the rest of this book.

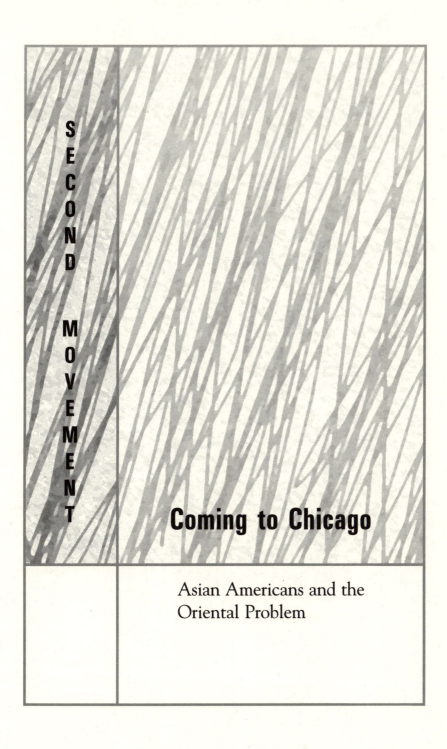

SECOND MOVEMENT

Coming to Chicago

Asian Americans and the
Oriental Problem

5

Wanted:
Interpreters and Informants—
Orientals, Please Apply

"Chicago is the city from which the most incisive and radical Negro Thought has come; there is an open and raw beauty about that city that seems either to kill or endow one with the spirit of life." So wrote novelist Richard Wright in his 1945 foreword to St. Clair Drake and Horace Cayton's *Black Metropolis*, a study of Chicago's African American community. In his essay, Wright asserted that Chicago sociology had helped him understand what it had meant to be a Negro in the United States:

> I felt those extremes of possibility, death and hope, while I lived half hungry and afraid in a city to which I had fled with the dumb yearning to write, to tell my story. But I did not know what my story was, and it was not until I stumbled upon science that I discovered some of the meanings of the environment that battered and taunted me.[1]

What did Wright mean that he had "stumbled upon science"? In the twenty years between the Survey of Race Relations in 1924 and Wright's statement, Chicago sociologists took the knowledge they had collected from Orientals and Negroes and made it into scientific theory. When Asian Americans and African Americans such as Richard Wright came upon these theories, they fell into a whole new way of understanding themselves and their place in U.S. society.

What was it to be an Oriental in modern America? What was it to be thought an Oriental, and how did being thought an Oriental affect the way people thought of themselves? How did ideas about being Oriental get mediated through certain sociological theories? How did these theories provide a language for self-understanding, a means of translating the past into a sensible present, a foreseeable future? What were the connections between this sociological language and an institutional practice that reinforced the Oriental identity of the people who were the objects of its study?

The following chapters will explore how a number of young men and women, intellectuals who were immigrants or whose parents or grandparents were immigrants from China and Japan, thought of themselves before encountering Chicago social science. In a circular route, their thinking entered into Chicago sociology's theories, and Chicago social theories transformed the young intellectuals' understandings of themselves and their place in American society. At the same time that the theories explained the world, they also diagnosed "problems," giving answers to questions that bothered many of the Chinese American and Japanese American students during their lives. The Chicago analyses enlightened the students as to why and how they had suffered in the past.

In many ways, the social scientific theories of the Oriental Problem served as a language for expressing hope and discontent, naming woes and defining problems by giving them larger meanings. Social science placed personal dilemmas within the framework of larger social processes, so that the problems not only made sense theoretically but also were stripped of moral turmoil on an individual level. In a manner similar to that of the white sociologists and yet also very different, Chinese American and Japanese American sociologists used the ideal of the detached point of view. In particular, the sociological perspective gave them the freedom to distance themselves from the pain, anger, and emotion wrought by discrimination against Orientals. Social science allowed them to survey the problem of being Oriental from a vantage point outside of themselves, a much more secure location than the turbulent place occupied by Japanese Americans and Chinese Americans in the United States.

The intellectual construction of the Oriental Problem involved more than the delineation of a set of theories, questions, and problems deemed to be interesting and worthy of research. It was also about a proper method of investigation and a particular language for presenting both the questions and the findings. The most important step toward achieving a coherent research program was rigid adherence to a consistent language of terms and definitions by multiple researchers. Emory Bogardus later described the problems the sociologists had with maintaining definitions and with disciplining research workers into the Chicago school's understandings of social interaction. The Survey of Race Relations had "not proceeded far before it was evident that different research workers were using even common terms, such as race, community, competition, in different ways, and hence were misunderstanding each other." Worse still, the way in which "laymen" understood terms such as "racial invasion" was potentially catastrophic. "Thus," Bogardus concluded, "the determination of a careful, accurate, and basic usage of terms is a minimum essential."[2]

For Robert Park and his Chicago-trained colleagues, the Green Bible and a shared journey through graduate school had helped in keeping terms straight. However, for those under their direction who were actually researching and collecting the materials for the survey, and who had not yet been exposed to the good words of the Green Bible, the disparate conceptions of sociological terms became a methodological Babel. This confusion of tongues highlighted the need for researchers who were trained in the language of Chicago sociology's theories and research methodology to carry out the Survey of Race Relations.

University students, open to instruction and direction from their professors (and unpaid for their services), proved to be the most amenable and easily disciplined research workers. Many research surveys, such as the massive Pittsburgh survey of industrial workers a decade earlier, had relied on social workers or church networks to supply volunteer researchers, but the sociologists in 1924 took advantage of an abundance of university students. Emory Bogardus, as head of the sociology department at USC, and Roderick McKenzie at the University of Washington both had undergraduate and graduate students write research papers on various aspects of the Oriental Problem. While the young students gathered information and data about the Chinese, Japanese, East Indians, and Filipinos on the West Coast, they also learned proper methods of inquiry, relevant research techniques, and the exact usage of Chicago's sociological language and terms.

Emory Bogardus was a well-meaning and methodologically rigorous thinker; he derived many of his own theories from Park, and his great contribution to the field was to apply the theories of his Chicago colleagues. Bogardus might not have had the same flair as Park and McKenzie for supplying a global context to the social interactions he measured, but he had a powerful gift—the ability to manage and produce social research. Bogardus was able to organize students and assign them research topics and methodologies appropriate to their own interests.

During more than three decades at the University of Southern California, Bogardus directed and advised, encouraged and supported, overseeing an astonishing number of student master's theses and doctoral dissertations. Most of them were relatively unremarkable, consigned to collect dust on library shelves, but some were fascinating works, and their sheer volume and methodological consistency are amazing.[3] Because of Bogardus's gifts as a research director, Los Angeles was second only to Chicago as a location mapped and surveyed by Chicago-style sociology students.

The survey's emphasis on life histories, based on written questionnaires and oral interviews, meant that the gathering of relevant data was a labor-intensive activity. The hundreds of interviews needed for the survey involved dozens of university students; most important, they created a need for translators to bridge the linguistic gap between the researchers and the many non-English-speaking subjects. In June 1924, during the early stages of the survey, both William Smith and Robert Park requested more money to hire people to translate Japanese, Chinese, and Filipino texts, as well as to interview for life histories.

The need for this kind of help was revealed by such instances as the project of a Stanford undergraduate named Ruth M. Fowler, who for an economics course tried to conduct a study of Japanese immigrants' food consumption patterns in San Jose and Santa Clara Counties. The intrepid surveyor designed an elaborate form that asked the subjects to report what they had eaten for each meal over a month, as well as an inventory of weekly food purchases and grocery costs. The amazing thing is not the paltry number of Fowler's forms that were sent back but the fact that any were returned at all, considering the language barriers and the amount of work her survey entailed. Not surprisingly, most of the forms that were returned were from households with American-born schoolchildren who had the time and linguistic expertise to answer such detailed questionnaires.[4]

The strategic position of Americanized Oriental students became a defining characteristic of the Survey of Race Relations. Young Chinese American and Japanese American students combined the qualities of amenable researchers with the linguistic and cultural advantages of inside informants, and thus were at a premium. These students helped translate and gather life histories, and invariably, they themselves gave some of the longest and most detailed life histories.[5]

Histories of a Life: Kazuo Kawai, the Second Generation, and Marginality in the Modern World

There is a childhood game called telephone or grapevine in which someone whispers a sentence or a phrase into the ear of the next person. That person then whispers it into the ear of another person, and so on. When the original sentence is revealed, it has often been comically transformed by its passage through the grapevine, and, like the rumors and stories that pass through gossip networks, it can be changed beyond recognition.[6] The game encapsulates a social process of which we are all aware, in which listeners translate what they hear into something very different. One of the fascinating aspects of the institutional network of the sociologists who worked on the Oriental Problem is how they, in a similar manner, transformed the stories and life histories they gathered during the Survey of Race Relations into very different narratives.

In searching for racial minorities in the United States and collecting stories about their lives, social scientists organized the experiences into generic narrative forms. They then retold to other social scientists the stories they had collected, in the process transforming the stories into another type of narration altogether. The sociologists flattened stories involving memories of personal history into narratives based on categories. They changed stories that had emphasized dynamic personal and historical change into ones that emphasized the importance of belonging in a category, whether that category was a racial group or a culture. These sociological narratives of category became a specific genre for the expression of ethnicity. At the same time that the sociologists collected these stories in the 1920s and popularized their own retellings of them within academia, they also structured the way that Americans would later come to understand race and ethnicity.

For example, Kazuo Kawai, a twenty-year-old student at the Southern Branch of the University of California (later renamed UCLA), became one of the most fascinating figures of the Survey of Race Relations. He serves as a good example of how young Orientals, recruited from either missionary networks or university classes, played a prominent role in the survey research. Along with the young Chinese American journalism student Flora Belle Jan, Kawai became both an informant and a researcher during the survey. Their ideas and stories about their place in America were essential to the Chicago sociologists' theories and descriptions of the Oriental Problem.

Kawai and Jan's strategic position as both informants and researchers gathering life histories meant that their understandings of their own personal experiences contributed more to the sociologists' understanding of Orientals than practically anything or anyone else involved in the project. In March 1925, Kawai wrote a twenty-page life history for the sociologists of the survey. It was a remarkable literary document, a striving for self-understanding combined with an open attempt at recognition. Compared with most of the other life histories gathered by the Survey of Race Relations, Kawai's stands out in his sense of the importance of his own life. He clearly reveled in recounting the tale of himself.

Kawai was not alone in believing his tale was exceptional; Robert Park and the other survey sociologists seized upon Kawai as representative of the Oriental Problem on the West Coast. In the 1926 issue of *Survey Graphic*, which served as the primary published result of the survey, Kawai was given a whole article to write, equal billing with Robert Park, Emory

Bogardus, William Smith, and the other major surveyors. The only other Asian American given such star billing was Flora Belle Jan, who had several of her poems included in the issue.

Kazuo Kawai regarded himself a writer and began his life history with a flourish lacking in most of the other autobiographical statements:

> There are times when one feels like unburdening the story of all the hopes and dreams of one's life into somebody's sympathetic ear. There are times when one longs to confide vague fears and doubts to someone whom one can trust. There are times when one grows reminiscent, and one glories in the telling of one's past. But such times don't come when one is confronted by a business-like questionnaire with a command to turn out "a narrative, concise, vivid, personal, with all the inflections and accents of the individual," embodying within it the answers to all the questions in the questionnaire, and to have it in the mail by such and a such a time, so that a commission of sociologists might dissect and analyze it.[7]

Despite opening his life history with such a disclaimer, Kawai went on to enthusiastically unburden precisely such a personal narrative. More than answering all the questions that the sociologists had asked of him, Kawai supplied extensive meditations on how tough it had been to be him. He told how he had spent his life tacking back and forth between his Japanese and his American heritages. His father, the son of a long line of prominent Japanese statesmen and officials, had become a converted Christian during college in Japan and had come to the United States for theological training and to proselytize to the Japanese in California. Although born in Japan, Kawai had accompanied his father to America at the age of six. Recalling nothing of his early childhood in Japan, and remembering only a few embarrassed snippets of Japanese, Kawai was nonetheless forced to confront his Oriental race.

The Chicago sociologists were fascinated by Kazuo Kawai's narration of a confusing journey between Japanese and American identities. At one time, Kawai identified strongly with white America and against the "Japanesy" high school students who made him feel self-conscious. However, Kawai related how, upon entering college, "for the first time, I felt myself becoming identified with Japan, and began to realize that I was Japanese." But was he really Japanese? "What would I be able to do in Japan?" he asked, "I couldn't speak the language except for a silly babytalk. I couldn't read or write Japanese. I didn't know any of the customs or traditions of Japan."

Ironically, the experience of being labeled by whites as Japanese forced him at the same time to realize that he was not Japanese. "Where did I belong?" Kawai asked himself, as he felt "with a pang" that he was a "man without a country." He wrote that "in language, in thought, in ideals, in custom, in everything, I was American. But America wouldn't have me." Detailing this moment of self-identification, Kawai stated: "Once I was American, but America made a foreigner out of me—Not a Japanese, but a foreigner—a foreigner to any country, for I am just as much a foreigner to Japan as to America."[8]

Becoming "identified with Japan" was crucial for Kawai, a moment of self-realization that he described using purple prose and literary quotes. "Breathes there the man with soul so dead / Who never to himself has said: / This is my own, my native land," Kawai quoted, before going on to gush, "I realized then that I had never been able to say that. My soul wasn't dead, though. I knew it lived, for it hurt." Clearly, the style in which Kawai chose to write his life history reflected his literary aspirations.

The literary crafting of Kawai's narrative was understandable. Robert Park's life history questionnaires had explicitly asked for illuminating moments of self-awareness concerning the consciousness of race, and Kawai had self-consciously structured his narrative to provide them. Robert Park appreciated Kazuo Kawai's written responses precisely because Kawai had learned writing techniques well enough to provide exactly what Park had been searching for—short stories narrating biographies of epiphany. Like an O. Henry story or a journalist's sketch, the life history was meant to illustrate larger truths through laden moments of clarity.

The types of stories told by Chinese Americans and Japanese Americans and the kinds of things deemed interesting by sociologists were inextricably linked. The sociologists' very act of drawing statements from Oriental Americans affected how these narratives were structured, because in their questionnaires the sociologists emphasized certain aspects of a person's story as interesting while considering other parts of their lives uninteresting or unproblematic. Sociologists shaped the narratives of ethnic and racial informants in their roles as collector and audience.

According to Robert Park, a single succinct description of what a person felt when he came to a realization of his own race was more powerful than books full of numbers and facts supposedly detailing race relations. The desired effect of the life history narrative was to evoke and relate some moment of recognition, when a person came to understand herself, or her situation, or another person, in some new light. The flash of poignant enlightenment created by the narrative was highly dependent on the insight of both the writer and the reader. The smallest narrative details and descriptions, chosen and placed correctly by the writer, could evoke the sympathy of a reader. On the other hand, a bad storyteller or dull reader could make life histories seem a worthless technique.[9]

The match between the needs of Park the sociologist and Kawai the aspiring writer was absolutely perfect. Kawai was given an appreciative audience, and Park obtained the ideal informant to articulate the problems of being an Oriental in America. Kawai's life history became an exemplary text for a number of the sociologists' theories about the place of Orientals in American society, and his moments of epiphany provided them with illustrative examples.

The contours of the ideal narrative for the sociologists were more than what might be called the classic assimilation story of someone with Old World traits transforming into the New American. Although Robert Park was testing the theoretical validity of the assimilation cycle, the story he wanted to hear from Oriental Americans involved marginality. Having begun the survey with the assumption that the Orient was different from America, Park and the other sociologists saw in Kawai's tale a story of existence in between two opposites, neither one nor the other. Chinese Americans and Japanese Americans were marginal, permanently foreign because the Orient was by definition foreign, but also half American because of their life in the United States.

For Robert Park and for William Carlson Smith of USC, Kawai's story was ideal for illustrating the category of so-called second-generation Orientals. As Chinese Americans and Japanese Americans born or raised in the United States, the second generation was a unique subject for study. Unlike second-generation European immigrants, who were merely divided from their parents by an attitude of cultural repudiation of the Old World, second-generation Orientals were also repudiated by white Americans and thus were caught in a no-man's-land. These individuals did not belong to their immigrant communities, and at the same time they were unable to find employment or social acceptance outside of these communities.

William Smith concluded that the main problem for Orientals of the second generation was that they felt like strangers in all countries. According to him, the difficulties encountered by American-born Japanese and Chinese when trying to obtain jobs, housing, and entry into non-Asian social groups produced alienation and marginality. Smith emphasized the young students' feelings of not belonging and not being valued, describing them as a "lost generation" of wasted, unappreciated talent.

The second-generation Orientals who wrote life histories for the sociologists often employed contemporary literary metaphors to describe their own feelings. It is not surprising, therefore, that Smith would have found echoes of Ernest Hemingway and F. Scott Fitzgerald in the budding writers' narratives. Literary metaphors of modernity that described being exiled from one's own country, or of wandering aimlessly within a world shorn of the possibility for believing its pieties, appealed to both the students and the sociologists. Such descriptions of loss and confusion informed the former's life histories as well as the latter's social theories. William Smith focused on the portions of Oriental life histories that described feelings of marginality. During the survey and during a year of research in Hawaii in 1926–1927, Smith culled snippets from his collection of life stories. He then pasted these extensive quotes together as his evidence in a series of papers on the second-generation Oriental.[10]

Kazuo Kawai's narrative serves as an example of how the Chicago sociologists used individual experiences and particular points in a narrative to produce general categories of analysis. Specific segments of a life history were used to evoke the whole of a person's life, and a single moment in Kawai's life was taken as the representation of the existence experienced by similar Oriental Americans. By taking moments out of individual life histories and displaying them one after another within his articles, Smith framed them as holistic representations of the life of second-generation Orientals, turning what were narrations of singular moments in a person's life into epigrams for their whole existence. In this way, the narrative climaxes of Kawai's life history, those points where his self-understanding changed radically, became embedded in the schematic structure of a series of sociological categories.

Smith put an enormous emphasis on the marginality of Orientals, echoing Park's emphasis on marginality as the essence of racial and ethnic experience in America. The feelings of being "caught between two worlds" became the most common and the most valuable way of describing the problem of second-generation Orientals. Narratives emphasizing moments of marginality as a category of consciousness became the device for describing the attitudes of Oriental Americans and, by extension, all racial and ethnic types in America. Marginality was thus transformed from an epiphany within a narrative into a defining characteristic of racialized existence in America.

Kawai's narrative was not somehow representative of all the other second-generation Orientals who gave life histories to the sociologists. In fact, it could be argued that the life histories varied wildly and the only reason they resembled each other at all was because they were produced in response to the same set of questionnaires. The sociologists, however, did argue that Kawai was representative and that he approached what they labeled an ideal type (following Max Weber's formulation of a conceptual ideal that did not exist in reality but that clarified analysis by providing an extreme example of a hypothesis). Therefore, Kawai's narrative became a representative example of how the sociologists themselves retold life histories.

Sociologists used moments of epiphany within life history narratives as representative examples for their own narratives of category. What might be called the naturalization of these narrative moments—the conversion of them from literary epiphanies into universal categories of sociological analysis—is best illustrated by the use of generational difference as a category. By creating a narrative in which cycles of change revolved around a procession of generational units—first, second, third—the sociologists created a powerful story to explain cultural change in America.

Issei, Nisei, Sansei:
Assimilation and the Narrative of Generations

The narrative of a first generation coming to America, followed by a second generation born in America, was popularized by novels and plays of the Americanization movement, such as Israel Zangwill's popular play *The Melting Pot* (1909). By always beginning the story with the arrival of the immigrant, the narrative of generations was a cycle outside of time, a recurring structure that was used to order experiences and conflicts within immigrant communities and families regardless of any specific historical period. Whether an immigrant or group of immigrants arrived in 1870 or 1920, the narrative of generations began with the first immigrant and cycled through their children and grandchildren.[11]

The first consequence of this ahistorical construction was that its categories were based on perceived signs of the assimilation of American characteristics. The opposition between old country traits and American traits was an inherently self-defining set of categories—without the first generation, there was no second generation, and vice versa. Any trait that was deemed Old World and thus a quality of the first generation found its opposite within the second generation, since the second generation was the repudiation of the characteristics of the first. The traits associated with either generation could be highly arbitrary, changing according to who was doing the defining and varying for different people at different historical times. What was retained, however, was the essential opposition between the traits of the first and second generations.

The categories of generational conflict and of ethnicity were linked in the sociologists' narratives of American history. Within the Chicago sociologists' stories about America, the causal role of ethnic or Old World culture was evident in the conflict between immigrant parents and children. For instance, the sociologists might describe the conflict between a first-generation immigrant father and his second-generation daughter over the control of her wages, or they might describe an argument between them about how late she was allowed to stay out at night. The sociologists understood such conflicts within the context of generational difference in an immigrant family and defined them as stemming from the traditional beliefs of first-generation immigrants and the Americanized beliefs of second-generation immigrants.

But there were other ways of defining the same circumstances. A family of twentieth-generation Americans could experience similar conflicts over wages or staying out at night; in this instance the conflict would not be defined as an immigrant issue. Or we might see that over a myriad of issues within an immigrant family, there was no disagreement at all, and that only when there was a conflict would a sociologist begin to define the disagreement as a result of opposing traditional and American values. By so defining such conflict, the sociologists' analysis of generational conflict set both the families and their conflicts into a different category of analysis from those of nonimmigrant families. And for the Chicago sociologists, cultural differences between an ethnic culture and American culture created the dividing line fracturing immigrant families. Thus, ethnicity and culture became causal explanations within American social theory.

As William Smith and other sociologists took life histories such as Kawai's and converted certain elements into a sociological narrative of categories, they emphasized the power of ethnicity and culture as explanations of family conflict among immigrants. The conflict between immigrant culture and American culture became the analytical explanation within a story that emphasized the role of categories such as ethnic culture and generational conflict in *generating* change. Culture, rather than being a mere description of the mores or folkways of a certain group of people, assumed causal force in the sociologists' narratives of category.

The members of an immigrant family themselves might also understand the conflict between parents and children as one between the Old World and the New World. But even if the idea of generational difference as the cause of conflicts between parent and child was popular, its resonance could be circumstantial. For instance, first generation Japanese immigrants (Issei) in particular felt their own history as a community was riven by generational categories, but this was based on an accident of history. Partly because of labor recruitment, Japanese Americans all came to the United States at the same historical moment in the late 1890s and early 1900s. "Nisei," the term for second-generation Japanese Americans, were almost all born around the same years of the early twentieth century and spent their formative childhood years in lockstep with each other. By the time Japanese were legally cut off from migrating to the United States in 1924, there was a sizable group of immigrants with American-born children. Therefore, in the case of Japanese Americans, the generational labels fit actual groups of people who were of the same age and living through the identical moment in history. The situation was very different for Chinese or Filipino immigrants. Generational theory had much less resonance for Chinese Americans and Filipino Americans because their children often did not grow up with the same historical experiences. Because they came to the United States over very different historical periods, and thus married and had children at different times, their children never existed in history as neat generational units.

Chicago theories about second-generation Orientals converted historical contingency into a sociological generalization that claimed some uniquely Oriental American cultural consciousness. As a story of problems between immigrant parents and their children, the narrative of generational difference had much greater meaning among Japanese Americans. However, it became an "Oriental" problem.

Ultimately, the resonance of a narrative of generations relied on its appeal as a story in and of itself. The narrative of immigrant generations could be spun in many ways as a moral tale. It could illustrate, for instance, the desirability of or the horror over the loss of traditional values among the second generation. Or it could describe the ironic poignancy of second-generation immigrants too eager to give up their parents' beliefs yet trapped in marginality by their inability to enter American society. It was the story's power as a moral fable making sense of immigrant life that provided much of its resonance to both immigrants and sociologists.

Because the schema of generations carved up the world along a spectrum of Oriental and American traits, it easily entered the sociologists' categories of analysis. They laid the distinction between first generation and second generation alongside their theories about other social transformations in the modern world—Old World/New World, traditional/modern, tight social control/individual freedom, rural/urban. All these binary pairs could be brought in to make the opposition deeper and more nuanced.

The narrative itself, however, was a literary product, an elaborate story to make sense of life in modern America. There was something uniquely American about the generational story, and the American context for such narratives and metaphors cannot be overlooked. When Asian American consciousness movements appeared decades later, the moral resonance of the generational narrative again became apparent, echoed in the rhetoric of many third-generation Japanese Americans (Sansei) "rediscovering our grandfathers" and redeeming the lost "authentic culture" that Americanization and assimilation had taken from American-born Chinese and Japanese. Moral tales warning against the perils of "complete assimilation" and "culture loss" were mapped onto the cautionary fables about the problems of "second-generation Orientals" told years earlier.

Modernity and the Rise of Ethnic and Racial Identity

What did the sociologists' narratives of category have to do with subsequent narratives of ethnic self-identity? Ethnic and racial identity as a manner of existential understanding, as narratives of self-description, owed much to the Chicago sociologists' retelling of life histories. Identity as a mode of consciousness was based on a certain way of understanding the connection of the past to the present. This connection had everything to do with a historical narrative that explained the personality and behavior of the present as the product of key events in the past.

As a short story of self-understanding, the life history took excerpts from a life full of events and emphasized some as the most important. The form and genre of the life history contained a genealogy of significant events. Behavior in the present and in the future was explained as the product of particular events in the past. For Orientals in America, these events were most significant to the sociologists if they had to do with racial consciousness. The sociologists emphasized in their questionnaires the moments of epiphany that came about when someone realized his own race or ethnicity. The sociologists' concern with such epiphanies was connected to their ideas about the nature of modernity. They looked for ways in which human empathy and understanding were still being produced in superficial social encounters. Thus, the social scientists' interest in the short, quick, yet poignant empathy of short stories was connected to their own concern with the problem of human community in a fragmented and individuated world.

The time-intensive and repeated interactions that the sociologists defined as the traditional, small-town way to get to know someone had to be replaced by the quick encounters of mass urban society. According to the sociologists, there was little time in the modern world to explore a person's past, but the necessity for building mutual trust and understanding was as strong as ever, perhaps even more so. Therefore, any kind of information and knowledge was vital and valuable, but it had to be acquired quickly. The constraints of time and mobility created a situation in which wasted information was wasted time, and so certain kinds of knowledge were adjudged more significant and valuable: place of origin, cultural and racial background, family history.

The importance of abstractions such as race, place, nation, or culture marked how identity as a concept and a set of categories acted as a way of symbolically and imaginatively sharing memories and experiences. The labels were seemingly static—I am from China, or I am a midwesterner—

but each bespoke an implied history that could lead to identification and empathy. In other words, the categories through which we now understand ethnicity and identity are telescoped from narratives of geographic origin and migrational history.

An intellectual could react to the rise of modern societies by either bemoaning or embracing the passing of traditional communities. Both narratives were a common trope in modern American literature and social science.[12] Anthropology, for instance, commonly used the narrative of incipient loss to describe traditional or primitive culture. Anthropologists of the late nineteenth and early twentieth centuries often portrayed their enterprise as an attempt to save a textual representation of "savage" cultures that modern civilization was threatening to sweep away.[13] In contrast, the Chicago sociologists did not lament the passing of the good old days. The traditional world was no more desirable, nor was the modern world to be disdained.[14]

The Chicago sociologists' understanding of cultural identity reflected their sense that modern identity, particularly national and racial identity, was perhaps even more powerful than traditional forms of community. Modern identity was not superficial, even if the flash of identification it relied on was quick in time. The passions that ethnic and national identity evoked were hardly shallow. Ethnic identity had the power to remake the world because a person barely met could seem like a brother or sister. It was powerful precisely because it could build a collective sense with so little and in such a short time. It did not require a novel or an epic but could be contained in the insights of a moment, the amount of time it takes to share an experience, to tell a story.[15]

The Chicago sociologists' descriptions of modernity captured much of social life into the category of marginality, of feeling like an outsider. More important, in using metaphors of the theater to narrate the quick moments of modern life, the Chicago sociologists also gave marginality its most powerful language of description. Men and women who suffered racial discrimination within the United States would find a deep resonance within the Chicago theories of race and ethnicity, and in particular the metaphors of masks, roles, and dramatic performance.

Finding a Role in Life:
From Interpreter to Marginal Man

Kazuo Kawai described how he had come to see himself as belonging to neither Japan nor America, and how this had led to feelings of confusion and alienation. These were the moments William Smith used to flesh out his category of second-generational marginality. This moment of marginalization did not stand by itself in Kawai's narrative, however. The difficulties of being a stranger in one's own country became the setup in his story for a later revelation that was much more powerful. Within the structure of his tale, the darkness of his days wandering in confusion was transcended by his realization that he could be a valuable interpreter.

By embracing his liabilities as a marginal Oriental, Kawai could transform himself into someone useful. "If I can learn Oriental history and become able to teach Oriental history to Americans, I would be rendering a service as an interpreter of the East to the West." Robert Park seized upon this point. "My present intention is to study the history of the Orient," Kawai wrote, "especially the history of the relations between the Occident and the Orient." Park supported Kawai's desire to explain Oriental culture to non-Orientals even though Kawai had none of the language skills and little of the expertise. Kawai realized that although his "knowledge of things Oriental" was limited, the knowledge of "the mass of the American people about things Oriental" was even "more limited." The fact that this credibility had little to do with how much Kawai actually knew about the Orient did not seem to bother him, for he expected to simply learn the knowledge that was expected of him.[16]

Kawai suddenly had a role in life, and this was an epiphany as thorough and powerful as Christian conversion. Having emphasized how dark his days had been earlier, he now described the wonderful rewards of having seen the light. Being between cultures was a liability only if he did not utilize his unique status. He was finally at peace with his position of marginality between the two races.

Kazuo Kawai was so thoroughly a product of racial exclusion that happiness involved mere social acceptance. Noting that his decision to be an interpreter "has improved my relations with both races," Kawai admitted that he was now "happy because I don't try to be a poor imitation of an American." He was also happy that he was not trying "vainly" to be a poor imitation of a "genuine Japanese." Kawai could be "simply who I am." He pointed out that his happiness existed because he was "never disappointed" and no longer found himself "excluded from either side." He believed he was now "more of an American, and also more of a Japanese than in those junior high days when I was only an American, or in those high school days when I was only a Japanese."[17] Kawai was now "more American" because whites who had excluded him socially found that he might be interesting after all.

The biggest payoff of being valued as an interpreter of East to West was that Kawai no longer felt inferior to white Americans. He had something they needed, and his very difference from them, his exoticism, which they would never let him forget, was in fact directly responsible for his value as the bridge between Oriental and American. "I am never disappointed when I am not treated just like the other Americans," Kawai asserted, arguing now that his history of being excluded was the very thing that made him useful. It was "the very fact of not becoming swallowed up and losing my identity in the mass of Americans" that enabled him to carry on his "peculiar work" as an interpreter.

Instead of being ashamed of his difference, Kawai could now wear it proudly as a badge of expertise. He was no longer trying "to imitate Americans against their desire," and thus he felt a measure of self-respect. Kawai could receive recognition as an "ambassador, a representative, an interpreter"; he concluded: "I can be proud of my position."[18] Kawai's newfound sense of mission had changed his life, and he wanted to impart his zeal to all his generational cohorts: "Because I believe that I have found my mission as a member of the second generation, I am anxious to have all other young people of the second generation come to realize their mission as interpreters, also."[19] It also happened to be a mission that the sociologists wanted students such as Kawai to follow. They took his realization of his value as a translator between two worlds and created the role of the "marginal man."[20]

Kawai's story of how he came to realize his goal in life highlighted two major epiphanies: the first one in college, when he was struck by his marginal existence between two worlds, and the second, much later moment when he came to see that this position was actually valuable. What is fascinating about the Chicago sociologists' transformation of Kawai's narrative is how they used these two moments of self-realization. They focused on the first epiphany and turned it into the existential dilemma of all second-generation Orientals.

But the sociologists also took both points and collapsed them into a single analytical category. Two separate moments in Kazuo Kawai's narrative of self-understanding, different stages of his story of a life changing over time, were plucked out of their respective places and embedded in a singular description of the traits of the marginal man. The gap in time and in understanding between the two was erased, and thus the realization of being caught between two worlds and the realization of having an important role as a translator became equivalent within the description of the marginal man.

This collapsing of Kawai's narrative of change into a single analytical point contributed to the enormous explanatory power and personal appeal of the marginal man theory. By making the two moments of epiphany theoretically equivalent, the sociologists created a language of hope for many Oriental intellectuals who may have understood themselves as being caught between two worlds. An instantaneous and evangelical hope was offered to those who felt marginal and confused. They now had a valuable role to play in life.

In creating a theoretical opposition between old and new, traditional and modern, the Chicago sociologists also invented a new category to describe the position in the middle. But since their descriptions of ethnicity and race were founded upon the same oppositions, racial consciousness was theoretically the same as the consciousness of marginality in general. In between and in transition, neither one nor the other, belonging neither here nor there, always in motion and in migration—these became the metaphors of both modernity and race for Chicago social theorists.

In his article "Human Migration and the Marginal Man," published soon after the end of the Survey of Race Relations, Robert Park gave his fullest description of the ramifications of marginality. Increased migration and cultural contact broke down traditional societies and produced a new type of person. Park celebrated this new social type, the marginal man, as being freer and more creative, released from the bonds of custom, tradition, and the social control of the group. Although a price was to be paid in confusion from lack of direction and control, Park had no doubt that the attendant gains in freedom and empathy, a cosmopolitan ability to move among and understand different cultures, were more than compensatory.[21]

In many ways, the marginal man signaled the future for Park. He agreed with Kawai's self-assessment that he had an important role to play in racial and cultural relations. The outlook of the stranger, which Park and his colleagues tried so hard to emulate, and which they asserted was the ideal perspective for the sociologist, was a natural and functional product of the daily life of the marginal man. It is ironic that this higher order of sensibility was to be found in individuals who had been marked as outcasts or outsiders by society, and not among members of the Anglo-Saxon native stock who were so often depicted as the acme of civilization.

The theoretical concept of the marginal man had a special resonance for many University of Chicago intellectuals with immigrant backgrounds—Asian, Jewish, eastern and southern European—because it seemed to mirror their perceptions of being estranged both from their immigrant pasts and from American society. The theory served as a language of hope that named and reified internal conflicts between perceived traditional and American worlds. The concept of the marginal man served the scholars as a descriptive expression of personal situations; more than that, however, it helped to embed these situations in a larger theoretical framework that suggested greater ramifications and possible solutions.

Many of the Asian American intellectuals who would be deeply touched by the marginal man theory came from the same background as the students who contributed to the theory's conception. One of the fascinating aspects of the intellectual and institutional construction of the Oriental Problem in the United States was that American-born Oriental students were drawn into an estranged relationship both with each other and with themselves. As part of the Chicago sociologists' map of the Oriental Problem in America, the marginal man theory provided a shortcut for Oriental sociologists in their own intellectual journeys of self-understanding. This shorter path, however, went through the abstraction and estrangement of sociological theory.

The sociologists took individual experiences and removed them to an abstract terrain. Research into the Oriental Problem was not a mutual support group where people with similar experiences traded stories and helped each other understand themselves. The understanding acquired traveled through a network of intervening texts and theories, passing the experiences through a strange filter that removed them from the contexts that gave them individuality—time, place, their point in a personal narrative. The Chicago sociologists' construction of the Oriental Problem created categories for understanding Oriental existence in America by taking individual stories, universalizing them, and reapplying them as objective laws. Knowledge of what it was like to be an Oriental in America was thus alienated from Orientals and returned to them in the form of esoteric theories, wrapped in the language of social science.

This objectification and analysis through categorization could be both an enlightening and an oppressive process. By depersonalizing the experiences of Orientals and embedding them within larger theoretical frameworks, sociology could provide an emotional buffer between everyday life and the world of theory, providing Chinese American and Japanese American intellectuals with a place of refuge from the difficulties of quotidian existence. The intellectual categories and institutional demands created by the Oriental Problem could also be limiting and even debilitating, but sociology provided a powerful language for expressing moral and political concerns without the rhetorical drawbacks of personal advocacy. As products of an objective, neutral science, texts that used the rhetoric of sociology could be much more persuasive and convincing than texts written from a seemingly more political perspective. The gains in self-understanding and rhetorical power that the Oriental Problem provided could be extremely valuable, and many Chinese American and Japanese American students became very aware of the utility of a career in sociology.

Language of Hope:
The Oriental as Marginal Man

Why did a number of Asian American intellectuals between the years 1924 and 1960 become committed to the profession of sociology? For what reason did social science, and Chicago sociology in particular, become more welcome to Asian American intellectuals than other academic disciplines? At the end of the nineteenth century, social science had been associated with the same racial barriers that all of American academia held for nonwhite intellectuals. In fact, the close historical connection between scientific theories of race and the support of racial hierarchy in the United States would seem to have made social science an unattractive place for nonwhites.

Explaining why Asian American intellectuals were drawn to social science tells a great deal about the parallel processes that also drew African American intellectuals to Chicago sociology. Robert Park taught a number of prominent African American sociologists. Charles S. Johnson, author of the famous report on the 1919 Chicago race riots and later president of Fisk University, was a student of Park's at Chicago. E. Franklin Frazier, who became known for his studies on the Negro family, and St. Claire Drake and Horace Cayton, the authors of *Black Metropolis* (the study for which Richard Wright wrote the foreword), all studied with Park.[1]

Racialized intellectuals created within Chicago sociology a powerful language for articulating the problems of racial discrimination and marginalization within America. They narrated their self-identities through sociological theories such as that of the marginal man. The powerful hold that such theories had on their definitions of self goes a long way toward explaining the appeal that social science held for intellectuals of color within the United States.

Between 1924 and 1960, around twenty graduate students in the departments of sociology and anthropology at the University of Chicago worked on topics dealing with Orientals in the United States and Hawaii. Most were of Chinese or Japanese background, either having come from China or Japan to attend American colleges or having been born in America to immigrant parents. They came from a variety of social, family, and economic backgrounds: several were from landed gentry in China or Japan, one was the son of a laundryman in the United States, another the daughter of a merchant importing Chinese goods to Montana. There were five women among the group, one of whom, Rose Hum Lee, became the first woman in the country to head a sociology department. The students went on to a variety of careers after completing their doctoral dissertations or master's theses. Some entered academia, others undertook social work, and one even became a movie actress. But they all had one thing in common when they were at Chicago: they researched some aspect of Orientals in America. Even though the specific actors changed, while they were working on the Oriental Problem they inhabited and performed specified roles. Their utterances were presented in a strictly structured genre, an academic form and style pitched to an audience of fellow social scientists.

For researchers who were non-Asian, their work on the Oriental Problem was ostensibly limited to the role of researcher. They may have had a deep interest in their research for personal reasons, but rhetorically their self-identities remained separate from their research. Indeed, the social scientists' ideal of neutral, detached analysis encouraged the furthest emotional distance between the object of study and the researcher. For Chinese American and Japanese American students, the ideal of detachment from the subject was similar, but, for many of them, the role of studier was often intimately connected with their sense of self-identity, since they were also being asked to play the role of the studied, to be an Oriental. The position of the Oriental researcher as both studier and studied provides an example of how the social science project of investigating the Oriental Problem constructed dual, and sometimes dueling, roles for the Oriental researchers involved. In their roles as researchers, they could identify, and be identified, with their other role as Orientals in ways that non-Oriental researchers could not.

Of course, non-Asian researchers may have identified strongly with Orientals for personal reasons, such as similar feelings of being marginalized from American culture or society. In addition to the white sociologists already mentioned, there were many other examples of non-Asians who researched the Oriental Problem. For instance, a self-described "sixth-generation Pennsylvania Dutch," Clarence Elmer Glick, whose 1938 Chicago dissertation was entitled "The Chinese Migrant in Hawaii," taught at the University of Hawaii. He and his Hawaii colleague Andrew Lind were among Park's favored students, and both went on to empathize strongly with the Asian Hawaiians they studied.[2] Each of these white sociologists deeply desired to understand Asian Americans, but as deep as their empathy ran, they still performed a singular role as researchers.

In contrast, as both researchers and informants, Oriental sociologists found themselves performing two roles. They performed on a stage not of their own making, and they acted in front of an audience that asked them for two very different presentations. The following chapters describe how individual Asian American intellectuals dealt with the demands of being a performer on the stage of the Oriental Problem. Many saw their roles as emancipatory, and the rewards and accolades they received made them famous. Others garnered less promising reviews. Only by taking all their performances together can the overall history of the Oriental Problem as an institutional practice be examined as a whole.

All the World's a Stage: Race and Theatrical Metaphors

The stage as a metaphor for social life was a powerful device that Chicago sociologists used to describe the world. Robert Park wrote in 1926 that "everyone is always and everywhere, more or less consciously, playing a role. We are parents and children, masters and servants, teachers and students, clients and professional men, Gentiles and Jews. It is in these roles that we know each other; it is in these roles that we know ourselves. Our very faces are living masks."[3] From the earliest days of the University of Chicago, philosopher George Herbert Mead had used theatrical metaphors in his theories on social psychology, and social performance became a serious analytical model. The social analyses of Park, and those of later Chicago sociologists such as Erving Goffman, echoed with terms such as roles, masks, and audience.[4]

Life was likened to a drama, and social interactions therefore demanded the assumption of prescribed roles and proper performances.[5] In describing the Oriental Problem as a staged performance, we can see just how compelling an image such metaphors suggested. The Chicago sociologists often described the world and themselves in terms of social performance, and theatrical metaphors also provided a descriptive language for race and ethnicity. Earlier I examined the Chicago sociologists' use of clothing and mask metaphors to describe racial and cultural difference. A uniform, or mask, in being treated by the sociologists as separable from the real person, allowed for racial or cultural identity to be defined as an object.

In linking race to removable masks or disguises, the sociologists suggested that race was merely a performance. But if American society was a theater, racial minorities had little choice in their roles. Playing an Oriental or a Negro was not a matter of putting on a disguise every morning. Unlike white actors, there were virtually no other roles open to racial minorities. To picture the Oriental Problem as a dramatic production is to highlight at first the aptness of the sociologists' histrionic analogies, but it is also to point to how the language of the theater obscured the limitations of race. Many Orientals would have jumped at the chance to remove their masks and play another role.

The role of the marginal man seemed to be potentially free of racial constraints. It was both racial and yet not purely a matter of race. By celebrating young Oriental students for their marginality, Chicago sociologists created a value for their racial identity. In using the metaphors of theater to describe such a valuable role, however, they obscured the way they transformed race and exotic ethnicity into an object, a thing that could have value and could be exchanged in a market transaction.[6]

Ching Chao Wu:
Chinese Americans as Marginal Men

If Chinese Americans and Japanese Americans were valued by social science for being Oriental, Asian Americans also discovered within sociology a powerful way of naming their own place in American society. Almost immediately after Park had formulated the role of the marginal man, Oriental students began to apply it to Chinese and Japanese in the United States. In a 1928 Chicago sociology dissertation, a young student from northern China named Ching Chao Wu used the theory to understand American Chinatowns. According to Wu, when a Chinese immigrant was subjected to such American influences as Sunday schools, public schools, and missionary efforts, "he is, sooner or later, transformed into a marginal man, a new personality which is the subjective aspect of the fusion of cultures." Following Park's formulation almost to the word, Wu noted: "The conflict of cultures which is inevitable when incompatible ideas and practices are brought together goes on just in the mind of the marginal man. His mind is the real melting pot of cultures."[7]

Discussing how the marginal man was often thought by white Americans to be a detriment to society, Wu tried to explain Chinese immigrants' reputation for "immoral" behavior such as opium smoking, gambling, and prostitution. "A man who has been under the influence of two cultures is often described in an unfavorable light," Wu wrote; "The marginal man is not only described by others as confused and lost, but he himself often feels the conflict of two cultures in himself." "Pulled by two forces," he often did not know the "right way to follow." His behavior was thus unconventional and strange. This was why Chinese immigrants did things that seemed immoral to others.

Using the formula that Kazuo Kawai had provided, and that Robert Park had turned into the marginal man theory, Wu then transformed the negative aspects of marginal life into the dramatic role that Kawai imagined for himself. The "unfavorable aspect of the marginal man does not need any further elaboration," Wu stated, dismissing it as uninteresting. What needed to be understood about the marginal man was that "few people know the important role that he has played, or will play in the future. In the modern days of racial and cultural contact, we need some people to interpret the other group for us." Again following Kawai and Park, Wu asserted: "No one is more qualified to be an interpreter than is the marginal man."[8]

Ching Chao Wu was an astute thinker and quickly picked up on the concepts of Chicago sociology. He began work on the problem of Chinese immigration in the Pacific region at the same time the Survey of Race Relations began, and he used materials gathered from the survey for his doctoral dissertation on Chinatowns. At first glance, it would seem to be no surprise that Park and Burgess would have recruited Wu to study Chinese immigrant communities in the United States. He was, after all, Chinese. But Wu was not as natural a choice as he might seem.

There were many China-born students such as Wu at the University of Chicago. Most had ended up there through the same social network of missionary contacts that had created the Survey of Race Relations. After the failed Boxer Rebellion against foreigners in China at the turn of the century, the Chinese were forced to pay foreign nations an annual indemnity. The United States used these funds for scholarships to send Chinese students to America. Most of the students who were chosen for these scholarships, and were actually willing to use them, were connected in some way to American Protestant missions in China. Many had attended missionary schools such as Saint Johns University in Peking and Jinling University in Nanking. Some, but not all, were converted Christians.[9]

Because so many of the American foreign missions were in northern China, the Chinese students usually spoke Mandarin and often came from a very different background than most Chinese immigrants to the United

States. The students tended to be from elite or educated families and usually were from urban areas. In contrast, Chinese immigrant laborers in the United States were overwhelmingly Cantonese-speaking peasant farmers from poor rural areas of Guangdong Province in southern China. Mandarin was so unfamiliar to the Cantonese immigrants that they sometimes mistook Mandarin speakers as Japanese.[10] The linguistic and class differences were extreme and proved to be quite a problem for most of the Chinese college students who had not come from the south of China. Few of the China-born students at Chicago had much connection to the Chinese communities in the United States, and most researched topics dealing with China. Almost all of the China-born students returned to China after they finished their degrees. Some of them, Wu in particular, became prominent intellectuals there.

Ching Chao Wu viewed himself as Chinese, treating his American training as an interlude. He applied the theories of Chicago sociology to Chinese immigrants but not to himself. Wu saw Chinese immigrants in America as marginal men, able to mediate between the two different worlds of China and America, but he himself did not fit the description. Although an insightful and conscientious observer, Wu had only come to the United States as a college student, and he was non-Cantonese in an immigrant world dominated by Cantonese.

Rather than conducting personal interviews, Ching Chao Wu gleaned his insights on the marginal man from the hundreds of life histories in document form gathered during the Survey of Race Relations. The studies of Wu and other China-born students also relied heavily on the translation services of Chinatown elites, who were sometimes able to speak Mandarin in addition to Cantonese. The work of Ting-chiu Fan, who completed his master's thesis ("Chinese Residents in Chicago") in 1926, and Yuan Liang, who completed his master's thesis ("The Chinese Family in Chicago") in 1951, was marked by a near-total lack of interviews conducted in person. Wu and Fan seldom left the University of Chicago while researching their theses; when they did venture into the Chicago Chinatown, they rarely interviewed anyone except community leaders. In the end, they were as much foreigners to the Chinatowns of America as were the white sociologists.

The identification of Wu, Fan, and Liang as having valuable insights into Orientals in America was due more to the needs of researching the Oriental Problem than to the expertise of the actual informants. Many of the Chicago sociologists recognized the shortcomings of using China-born students for research; one of their dissatisfactions was that the students did not write or speak English well enough. Whenever American-born students were available, the sociologists actively recruited them.

S. Frank Miyamoto: Self-Identity and Playing the Role of Marginal Man

Many American-born Oriental students explicitly saw themselves as marginal men and seized upon the powerful description of the role of cultural interpreters. In a 1938 master's thesis in sociology at the University of Washington, Shotaru Frank Miyamoto explored what was widely regarded as the extraordinary "social solidarity" of the Japanese community in Seattle. Ever since the Survey of Race Relations, Park and other sociologists had become deeply interested in what seemed like the strong social control exerted by Japanese American and Chinese American communities over individuals. The tight social organization of Oriental communities in America was one of the staple topics for investigation within the Oriental Problem. This interest stemmed from the perception of Oriental communities as clannish and insular, a phenomenon that the sociologists speculated might have retarded the assimilation of Orientals in America.

Interestingly, the strong social solidarity within the Japanese community in Seattle was a phenomenon that Frank Miyamoto's family had tried to escape. Miyamoto was born in Seattle in 1912 to Japanese immigrants. His father, who operated a furniture business, had tried hard to move his family away from the bounds of the tight-knit community composed of approximately six thousand Japanese Americans. Although Frank Miyamoto knew many Japanese Americans in Seattle, he was raised outside the immediate geographic and social territory of Japantown. He attended the University of Washington as an undergraduate and stayed on to earn a master's degree in sociology.

The University of Washington's sociology department had been dominated by its Chicago connections from the days of the Survey of Race Relations and maintained its strong research interest in the Japanese community.[11] Replacing Roderick McKenzie as departmental chair was Jesse Steiner, a former mission teacher in Japan. Steiner had written his doctoral dissertation at the University of Chicago about the Japanese in the United States, and he quickly became Frank Miyamoto's academic adviser and mentor.[12] Steiner encouraged Miyamoto to go on to pursue a doctorate at the University of Chicago. In 1939, soon after completing his master's degree, Miyamoto made his pilgrimage.

When Frank Miyamoto arrived in Chicago, he presented a background paper in Ernest Burgess's introductory seminar, explaining how his desire to become a sociologist had much to do with his racial background. "The strongest criticism of American society which I felt as a child was concerning the matter of race prejudice," Miyamoto wrote. Using the perspectives of sociology that he had learned at the University of Washington, Miyamoto explained that "because of my father's desire of finding a better home than those offered in the Japanese community, our family rode at the forefront of an ecological invasion, and we took the brunt of white-American disapproval." The profound scars Miyamoto had received from white prejudice led him to try to understand what had happened to him and his family. "I felt deeply the injustice of the whole affair, and naturally began searching for means by which these injustices might be removed. Thus, the problems of Japanese-American relations came to take on personal meaning for me."[13]

Learning the science of sociology allowed Miyamoto to understand the social forces that had affected his youth and to reinterpret his past. Race prejudice resulted from the Japanese "ecological invasion" (a technical term in human ecology defined by McKenzie twenty years earlier) of which his family was just a small part. The marginal man theory had a deep effect on Miyamoto's self-identity and memory. He remarked how it was the "circumstance of the Japanese culture being superimposed upon the American culture, vividly contrasting the two, that further stimulated my interest in social problems." Such a contrast led him "to be critical of the one or the other of the cultures, for from my particular perspective, I felt a step removed from both and no strong subjective attachment to either." Finally, recognizing the links between racial marginality, detachment, and good sociology, Miyamoto stated: "In this way I was developing the attitude of detachment fundamental to the sociologist—I was becoming, in a sense, a 'marginal man.'"[14]

Miyamoto came to understand during his training as a sociologist that he had some personality traits that were important antecedents for becoming a social scientist. He had always felt aloof and apart from the world around him, even as a child, and this emotional and intellectual detachment made him feel that he was constantly observing social interactions from the outside. At times Miyamoto attributed this sense of estrangement to his personality and family background, but each of these became subsumed under the category of culture.[15]

Miyamoto believed that the attitude of the marginal Nisei was the ideal viewpoint for a sociologist, and he saw his pursuit of sociology as a profession as integrally connected to his Japanese background. Miyamoto categorized his feelings of self-consciousness and personal detachment as character traits of the second-generation Nisei. "In the case of Americanized nisei," Miyamoto wrote, "there is always that trace of Japanese influence . . . in the personality of the individual, or perhaps one might say his psychology." Miyamoto insisted that Nisei might be "thoroughly American" in culture, but their "psychology" differed from that of most Americans.

There were varying degrees of "reservation, inhibition about saying things directly to others, and self consciousness that distinguish us from other Americans of our class." Miyamoto attributed these to "Japanese" family influences that were never "erased" by contact with whites.[16]

Miyamoto's autobiographical descriptions throughout his life reflected a growing but remarkably consistent self-awareness. In 1939, when he first arrived in Chicago to pursue his dissertation in sociology, in 1944, when he completed his graduate training and was applying it firsthand as a researcher, and in 1989, when he reminisced about a career spent observing social phenomena, Miyamoto maintained a remarkably coherent sense of his own place in the social world. And, not accidentally, Miyamoto's understanding of his own career path was configured in the language of sociology.

When Miyamoto was a teenage college student, his decision to become a sociology major seemed to him to be a whim. But as sociological training "increased [his] powers as a social analyst," he began to see a pattern. An array of factors in his background had determined his later interest.[17] Like Flora Belle Jan and Kazuo Kawai, Miyamoto had dreamed in his grammar school days of becoming a writer. But as for virtually all Japanese American and Chinese American students of that time, widespread racial discrimination meant there were no career prospects for an Oriental novelist. This led Miyamoto to study engineering, a "safer" major for career prospects. He disliked what he felt was the cold, inhuman nature of engineering, however, and, with his first exposure to sociology courses, his interests began to shift. As the science of human society, sociology appeared to be both analytical and humanist at the same time. Better yet, there seemed to be a genuine interest in Asian immigrants within the discipline.

Miyamoto's skills and his novelist's eye are evident in the second chapter of his study. His sketch of the Japanese American business district in Seattle opens with a description reminiscent of a short story or a novel:

> The business center is not today what it was in the heyday of the early nineteen-twenties, when Main Street teemed with the life of incoming immigrants and prosperous farmers visiting town. . . . The movement of life seems to have slowed to the pace of the "Skidroad" bum wandering up the hill, with a dollar rubbing his limb deep in his pocket, occasionally stopping uncertainly before a house where a rap on the window calls attention to the lewd wares of an illegitimate commerce.[18]

Miyamoto's prose reflected the possibilities for description allowed by the methods of Chicago sociology. Although the genre was strict in its emphasis on the detachment and objective viewpoint of the author's perspective, it also encouraged the realistic description of modern literature. In many ways, the eye of the sociologist resembled that of the investigative journalist. Following a lead, exposing to the reader a world unseen, Miyamoto used a third-person viewpoint that married the author and the reader together on a sightseeing journey through ghettos and vice dens.

Chicago sociology, then, despite its insistence on a neutral and objective point of view, was nonetheless receptive to those with literary ambitions. To Asian American students like Frank Miyamoto, the appeal of the Oriental Problem lay both in its interest in them and in its demand for written contributions. Unlike Kazuo Kawai, Frank Miyamoto's self-consciousness as a writer and social observer led him to dismiss the crafted narrative of adolescent epiphanies that marked so many life histories and that Park had encouraged with Kawai. "I cannot believe those who say that they suddenly became aware of their racial difference from the majority group through some striking experience after reaching adolescence," Miyamoto wrote, "for it seems to me that I was quite aware of the difference between a *hakujin* (Caucasian) and a *nihonjin* (Japanese) by the time I was in the kindergarten, although there had never been any special incident to bring the difference home to me."[19] Miyamoto instead narrated his life from the perspective of hindsight. His life history was not a story of distinct moments of self-realization but rather a continuous process of revelation. Despite his very different style, however, Miyamoto's self-identity reflected sensibilities very similar to Kazuo Kawai's. It was being excluded by both whites and Japanese Americans that created Miyamoto's and Kawai's perspectives.

The power that many of the Chinese American and Japanese American students found in sociology had to do with their abilities to analyze and explain the larger contexts for events in their personal lives. Miyamoto used the theories and concepts of sociology to understand portions of his youth. The theoretical descriptions of the marginal man also engaged strongly with Miyamoto's own understandings of himself and his role in the world. Recalling his own consciousness of being an outside observer unattached to any particular community, Miyamoto explained that he had always been a marginal man.

Many of the metaphors that Miyamoto used in writing up his life history were ones that had also resonated with Oriental students just like himself. The phrases "caught between two worlds," a "foreigner in one's own country," and "acting" as an "interpreter between two worlds" had originally come from life histories of students such as Kazuo Kawai. Such metaphors had then been used to construct the theory of the marginal man. That Miyamoto would then use the marginal man theory as the language to structure and order his own life history is a telling commentary on the Oriental Problem. Research into the Oriental Problem acted as the medium through which Chinese American and Japanese American students came to understand each other's experiences, at the same time that they tried to understand themselves.

This was the curious relationship that existed between Kazuo Kawai and Frank Miyamoto. The former's story about the epiphanies of his life was turned into a universal theory about sociological processes. The latter then came to a powerful new understanding of his own experiences after reading these theories. One of the wonders of the Oriental Problem lay in the way its conceptions came back to order the self-identities of Chinese American and Japanese American intellectuals, decades after its theories had been lifted from the experiences of other Oriental students.

Taking Note of Internment: The Japanese Evacuation and Resettlement Study

Relocation and internment during World War II had a profound effect on Japanese Americans, and Chicago sociology would frame those events for Frank Miyamoto and many other Japanese Americans. After taking courses in Chicago between 1939 and 1941, Miyamoto returned to Seattle to teach and to work on his doctoral dissertation. However, the Japanese attack on Pearl Harbor interrupted his career. Along with over 110,000 Japanese Americans, of whom two-thirds were American citizens by birth, Miyamoto spent most of the war in an internment camp.

Being interned did not put an end to Miyamoto's sociological work. He became one of the researchers for the Japanese Evacuation and Resettlement Study (JERS) organized by Berkeley sociologist Dorothy Swaine Thomas (who was married to Park's former colleague William I. Thomas). The study was designed to comprehensively record every aspect of Japanese internment and resettlement. It engaged a number of Japanese American researchers at each internment camp, and Miyamoto, because of his extensive training at Chicago, quickly became one of the head researchers.[20]

The interest that sociologists like Dorothy Thomas had in the social effects of mass relocation and internment added a new manifestation to the history of Orientals as objects of research.[21] In the same way that the Survey of Race Relations created a need for inside observers, the JERS again cast Japanese American students in the role of insiders. Again, it was among Park's putative marginal men from which the sociologists recruited their researchers. James Sakoda, one of the participant observers for the JERS, was a social psychology major at Berkeley before the war, and his research training had been informed extensively by the work of Chicago sociologists.

Sociological theories about the marginal status of the second-generation Oriental again resonated powerfully with the sociology students. Fifty years after internment, Sakoda described the group of marginal Nisei from which most of the JERS researchers were recruited. Even a half century later, Sakoda still used the same social psychology concepts he had first applied in 1941. "The Marginal Man," Sakoda explained, "described the dilemma of a person belonging to two cultures but not accepted by either one."[22] Sakoda broke down second-generation Japanese Americans into a "map with Nisei belonging to two different cultural spheres of influence, Issei on the one side and Caucasians on the other."[23] The "marginal" Nisei "disliked Japanese as a group and usually avoided belonging to Japanese students clubs or Japanese churches. They were most likely to adopt American ways and show few Japanese traits."

Echoing Kazuo Kawai's characterization of the social problems he had experienced, Sakoda explained that the Nisei's "marginal status was likely to leave them psychologically disturbed. They wanted to associate with Caucasians but often were not fully accepted by them."[24] Sakoda noted that marginal Nisei "often acted like Caucasians—more outspoken and forward in their behavior." Sakoda observed how more "acculturated" Nisei such as Miyamoto were better able "to pursue successful professional careers."[25] "Since they lived only on the fringe of the Japanese-American community, they were quite ready to leave if the opportunity arose. This willingness to leave and seek the help of Caucasian associates," he observed, benefited the more "acculturated" Nisei. Sakoda himself was less comfortable with the professional white sociologists who ran the JERS.

The loyalty of the acculturated Nisei to the United States was generally unquestioned, but they themselves saw other Japanese Americans as being "too clannish, and some believed that the community had brought the evacuation on itself." Sakoda's almost caricatured portrait of the marginal Nisei resulted from an emphasis within social psychology descriptions on extremes, but also from his own nonidentification with the marginal Nisei. Even though Sakoda placed most of his friends and fellow researchers within this group, he saw himself as having had a more "Japanesy" upbringing. He had lived in Japan for six years during high school and therefore was more able to get along with the less "Americanized" Issei and the more "Japanesy" of the Nisei.

Sakoda explicitly drew upon elements of the marginal man theory and the assimilation spectrum while describing his friends and fellow researchers as being in between two cultural worlds. As he put it, "The crux of marginality was the predicament of not being accepted fully by either the Japanese or Caucasian group."[26] Strangely, however, the region of marginality lay not in the exact middle of the spectrum, as the representation of the "marginal man caught between two worlds" suggested. Rather, feelings of marginality increased when the Nisei identified too closely with Caucasians. Moving toward being American did not remove the Nisei from the margins but only furthered their marginality by increasing their distance from the Japanese in-group. In the same way that the theoretical assimilation cycle used in the Survey of Race Relations proved to have a nonexistent ending for Orientals, one of the ends of Sakoda's spectrum—acceptance into Caucasian in-groups—seemed to be a dead end.

Orientals who identified themselves most strongly as American did not escape marginality. Marginal Nisei had done their best to master the American language and style of dress. Students such as Miyamoto were successful at entering an exclusive academic world, appearing to have successfully traversed the divide between Oriental and American and left behind their Oriental past. But these students found themselves continually told that they were in fact even more mired in the middle.

Ironically, many of the Oriental students often found that the most valuable aspects of their identity were in fact those that they had tried so hard to abandon. The role of the marginal man as a translator and middle man between two cultures actually undercut the spectrum of acculturation on which it was putatively based. The role of the marginal man demanded that those people who had escaped their racial enclaves and left behind their cultural heritage return to the cultural no-man's-land they had just crossed. For anybody who might have believed in the assimilation cycle and the possibility of becoming completely Americanized, the conception of the marginal man literally told them that their best hope was a sort of ethnic backsliding.

The marginal man theory as a language of hope was continually at odds with this less inspiring version of marginality. A negative, pathological definition of marginality resulted from the psychological problems stemming from disappointments of the assimilation cycle. This definition was in constant tension with a more positive, idealistic definition of the important social role of the marginal man. Not surprisingly, the contradiction between the two informed the professed self-identities of the students. As the examples of Rose Hum Lee, Tamotsu Shibutani, and Paul Siu in the next chapter show, the tension followed the same fault lines as the rift between the dual roles of Oriental sociologists as both researchers and research subjects.

7

Language of Discontent:
Using the Stranger's Perspective

Sociology provided a language for Asian American scholars to examine and understand their experiences in the United States. More important, it supplied a seemingly neutral perspective from which they could analyze extremely disturbing events. The ability to acquire analytical distance from the social world allowed many of the Oriental intellectuals the freedom to remove themselves to a place where the concerns of their personal existence took on more abstract meanings. The detached outsider's perspective of sociology, embodied in the outlook of the stranger, provided a means for intellectuals to extricate themselves from the entanglements of daily life. As it might be for a person who feels trapped in a small town, becoming an outsider could represent escape from the claustrophobic confinements of a life too well known.

The Oriental Problem valued Chinese Americans and Japanese Americans as marginal men between America and Asia, but it also offered them an intellectual perspective that seemingly had nothing to do with their racial identities. For those who had lived the difficult life of an Oriental in America, it was a powerful feeling to be known as a sociologist first and an Oriental second, to be estranged from the liabilities of one's racial and cultural identity while still being rewarded for one's knowledge of the unknown. The imagined distance contained within sociology's outsider perspective could serve very powerful functions. Moral arguments with a great amount of personal resonance could be made in a neutral and objective voice. Disturbing and emotional events could be examined in a therapeutic, cathartic manner. The standpoint of the detached observer gave

Asian American intellectuals the space to understand themselves and their communities in a new way, allowing them to map the difficult terrain of their lives from a distant perspective, far away from the pain, anger, or confusion of daily existence.

Rose Hum Lee, Paul Siu, and Tamotsu Shibutani each came to Chicago sociology from a different background, and each went on to use the theories they learned in divergent ways. All three used the rhetorical stance of objectivity to distance themselves from their subjects of study. Siu and Shibutani in particular used the technique of participant observation to achieve intellectual detachment from the social world surrounding them. A method borrowed from anthropology, participant observation was one of the common instruments of Chicago sociology. Oriental sociologists, however, utilized the technique in a unique manner.

Identified by fellow sociologists as Orientals just like the people being studied, Asian Americans found their status as detached outsiders continually challenged. The writings of Rose Hum Lee, Paul Siu, and Tamotsu Shibutani reveal interesting insights into the practices of modern social science and the relationship of a racialized intellectual's narrative of self-identity to the production of academic knowledge.

Returning the Body to Assimilation: Rose Hum Lee and the Utopia of Intermarriage

The tension between the difficulties of being an Oriental in America and the optimism of the marginal man theory was nowhere more apparent than in the life of the Chinese American sociologist Rose Hum Lee. Of all the Asian American students who became involved with the Oriental Problem, she spent the longest time studying Orientals in America and perhaps tried hardest to fulfill the role of cultural translator and marginal man.

In 1947, Rose Hum Lee finished her doctorate at the University of Chicago having written a dissertation entitled "The Growth and Decline of Rocky Mountain Chinatowns." By 1956, she had achieved the acme of a prolific career at Roosevelt University in Chicago by becoming the first woman, and the first Chinese American, to head a sociology department at an American university.[1] Throughout her career, she explored the progress of Chinese immigrants along the path of the assimilation cycle and, in a manner like no other Chinese American or Japanese American sociologist, accepted the ultimate validity of Americanization with an ideological fervor. Lee did not study Chinese immigrants exclusively. She was also a respected theorist in the field of urban sociology, and her work *The City: Urbanism and Urbanization in Major World Regions* (1955) was the

A 1950s publicity photo showing Rose Hum Lee, the "first Chinese American" and the "first woman" to chair a sociology department in an American university. Photograph is used with permission from Ralph Hum.

epitome of Chicago school urban theory. The study of Chinese in America, however, was the central focus of her life's work.

Lee often used her own family, and especially her mother, as examples of the successful assimilation of Chinese Americans. Her dissertation's appendix contained an extended life history of the Hums, and she often referred to her family's experiences to illustrate analytical points. Interestingly, however, all descriptions of her family and herself were cloaked in anonymity. Lee would quote from "Private Document No. 17, Life History No. 1" as if it was just another nameless, faceless piece of sociological data.

Lee maintained the rhetorical fiction of herself as the detached, unbiased sociologist using anonymous documents. This fiction is both an oddity and an absolute necessity, given the prominence of her family in Butte, Montana. The Hums were one of the richest landowners in the Chinese American community. Rose Hum was born in 1904, the second oldest of four girls and three boys. Her father had come from Guangdong Province in China in the 1870s and worked his way from California to Montana doing the manual labor typical of Chinese immigrants. By 1900, after working in laundries, in mines, and on ranches, he owned a Chinese merchandise store in what was then a thriving Butte. He was so successful that he was able to return to China and bring a wife to the United States, a considerable achievement given that Chinese women, with very few exceptions, were excluded by federal law.[2] Among the few Chinese American families in Butte, Rose Hum and her siblings were all honor students at Butte High School, and all went on to professional careers.

The need for Rose Hum Lee to erase her own identity within her study was more than the result of the particular demands of the genre of sociological monograph writing. Had she not pretended to be unrelated to the people mentioned in her dissertation, it would have become immediately apparent that she had close personal connections to every single person she was studying. Her ability to refer to her family in such a detached manner, to the point of referring to herself in the third person, serves as a wonderful example of how sociology as a discipline allowed its practitioners to distance themselves from their own lives.[3] Such a detachment was one of the rewards of a sociological perspective, but there were other ways in which marginality was not so desirable.

Robert Park and his fellow Chicago sociologists had constructed the basic framework of theories for understanding the Oriental Problem in the 1920s, and so it is amazing that when Rose Hum Lee reexamined the marginal man theory thirty years later, in 1956, her discussion still used the language and terms of 1926. Like James Sakoda in 1941, she was still trying to reconcile the marginal man with the assimilation cycle. Describing the negative aspects of marginality, Lee suggested that only assimilation could erase problems of the marginal man. As she asserted, "Culture conflict is responsible for his marginal feelings, composed of guilt, depression, instability, anxiety and frustration." Following earlier sociologists, Lee noted that these feelings were "more pronounced in the second, or marginal, generation of settlement in a new society than in the one preceding it and in the ones to follow." But when the "cultural gaps" were closed, she argued, the "cultural hybrid no longer poses a problem to himself and others." Closing the gap was brought about by the processes of acculturation and assimilation.[4]

Lee's analysis utterly transformed the assimilation theories of earlier Chicago sociologists. Robert Park had not offered any answers to the Oriental Problem other than to emphasize that, on a theoretical level, cultural assimilation was inevitable. Rose Hum Lee offered a more concrete prescription for its ultimate solution—universal intermingling of cultures and individuals. Lee added eradication of all physical evidence of foreignness to the standard definition of cultural assimilation. "Ideally," she wrote, "the completion of the processes includes the mixing of cultures and genes so that there are truly no 'dissimilar people.'"[5]

Lee's vision of the assimilation cycle went far beyond the cultural theories of the survey sociologists. Park had said that physical differences had nothing to do with differences between the races, except for their effects on self-consciousness, arguing that culture was a mental phenomenon. For him, the ultimate melting pot that lay at the end of the assimilation cycle was built purely out of shared memories and experiences; actual physical amalgamation was extraneous and unnecessary. Intermarriage was a cultural phenomenon to him. The physicality of sex indicated social intimacy, not the production of mixed children.

In Rose Hum Lee's early writings during the late 1940s and 1950s, she stayed well within the theoretical bounds of the Oriental Problem as discussed in earlier texts. During her fifteen years as a sociologist, and throughout her entire life, she had struggled to explain the failure of the Chinese in the United States to be accepted as completely American. By 1960, Lee was arguing for an absolute commitment to integration, a term that had never been important in the lexicon of the Oriental Problem. She also used the term in a completely different manner than was typical in the 1950s.

During that decade, "integration" had become a political banner word, invoking a debate and battle over racial segregation and civil rights, and so it comes as a surprise that Lee's use of it was completely removed from that context. Lee used "integration" as a shorthand for the whole Chicago description of the assimilation cycle and the race prejudice that blocked it. "The final objective of integration is a culturally homogeneous population," Lee wrote. "The barrier to complete integration is racial distinctiveness."[6]

If integration was the assimilation cycle encapsulated, to Lee it was no longer the value-neutral, natural process that Robert Park had described. Lee used the term "integration" in a highly political manner, and her commitment to the goal of achieving it engendered a personal advocacy that would have made Park cringe. Lee's vision was of a homogeneous America without a trace of foreignness or distinctiveness, a place where there were no "dissimilar people." In the context of 1950s America, when conformity was reinforced by cold war fears of subversion, this homogeneity may have been viewed in a positive light. But it was a utopian dream that revealed the difficult nature of Lee's struggles against those she saw as blocking the assimilation of Chinese.

By the time she published her summary work, *The Chinese in the United States of America* (1960), Lee saw the eradication of physical and cultural distinctiveness as the only way to eliminate both the racial prejudice of whites and the clannish tendencies of many Chinese in America.[7] Rhetorically, the book was uneven, at times switching from the analytical prose style that had characterized her earlier sociological work to a heated and often bitter invective. Lee railed against the Chinatown social institutions and organizations she blamed for hindering the unreserved integration of the Chinese in America.[8]

Lee's desire for the elimination of all traces of Chinese identity even extended beyond the shores of America. In the preface to her book, she opened the discussion of the Chinese in America by placing them within the global diaspora of "Overseas Chinese," extending the goal of total integration to them as well. "The Chinese in the United States of America are but a small segment of the Overseas Chinese," Lee wrote. Chinese emigrants lived "scattered throughout the world," and many of them have become so "integrated" in the societies where they or their ancestors settled that they were "indistinguishable" from the local population. That, according to Rose Hum Lee, was the "ultimate ideal" to which Chinese Americans should aspire.

Toward the Modern Woman: Americanization, Masculinity, and the Emancipation from Tradition

Rose Hum Lee's exaltation of total integration toward the end of her career must be seen within the context of a lifelong, highly gendered struggle to acquire a worthwhile identity in America. Her commitment to Americanization should be understood as part of her indeterminate identity as a Chinese American woman. The opposition between Chinese and American took on the additional aspect of traditional versus modern gender roles. For women like Rose Hum Lee and Flora Belle Jan, the struggle to escape what they felt were the restrictive roles of child bearers and homemakers was mapped onto the transitions of the assimilation spectrum.

Rose Hum Lee was so strongly committed to the desirability of personal deracination because she associated being Chinese with traditional domestic gender roles and being American with modern, educated roles for women. She equated the eradication of traditional notions of the Chinese family with the emancipation of women from oppressive roles. She pointed to the progress from her own mother, an uneducated and illiterate immigrant, to herself, the first Chinese American woman to head a sociology department, as a canonical example of the proper progress of immigrant women from traditional to American.

In her research Lee had seen the difficulties experienced by Chinese American women as they tried to break out of traditional Chinese gender roles. More important, she herself had lived the process. After graduating from high school in 1921 and briefly attending the local college in Butte, she married Ku Young Lee, a China-born engineering student at the University of Pennsylvania. She went with him to China after his graduation, living mainly in Canton for nearly a decade. The marriage eventually dissolved. In 1939, Rose Hum Lee returned to the United States with an adopted Chinese daughter, determined to pursue a career as a writer, teacher, and social worker. Supporting herself through odd jobs and the lecture circuit, she put herself through college and in 1942 graduated with a B.S. in social work from the Carnegie Institute of Technology in Pittsburgh. Lee then began graduate study at the University of Chicago's School of Social Work and Administration but soon switched to the sociology department.[9]

Lee's marriage and life in China had been a torment for her. She was unable to conceive a child, and her husband's family constantly criticized her failure to carry out what they felt was a woman's reproductive duty. Her final break with her husband and return to America can be seen not only as a repudiation of what she understood as the traditional roles of Chinese womanhood but also as an idiosyncratic attempt at Americanization. Lee's commitment to the assimilation cycle was reaffirmed as she left behind everything negative that she associated with China. The path from China to America, for Lee, was the same path from traditional women's work to a modern, emancipated womanhood.

In a way, living in China allowed Lee to discover the value of her American identity, and this identity was inextricably linked with her ambitions to be an educated, professional woman. Lee remained proud of her Chinese heritage but was selective in choosing which traits defined her own Chineseness. She denied those she considered negative, such as traditional gender relations, and emphasized those of which she could be proud in the context of America, such as Chinese art and philosophy or symbolic rituals like Chinese New Year.

The way that gender identity interacted with theories of assimilation and Americanization shows how a commitment to and identification with the assimilation cycle could intersect with a number of aspects of the Oriental students' narratives of self-identity. The role of marginal man was not restricted to men, and, as a woman trying hard to escape what she saw as the Chinese American community's strictures on the proper roles for women, Lee was very comfortable playing a translator of Chinese culture to Americans. Indeed, she found the role emancipatory.

The great irony of Rose Hum Lee's commitment to assimilation as a means of overcoming domestic gender roles is that she espoused such a connection during the 1950s, perhaps the high point of domestic ideology in twentieth-century America.[10] It is interesting to note how Lee associated all that she found restrictive about women's gender roles with traditional Chinese culture and completely associated American society with modern womanhood. Her ideas about what characterized a modern woman, however, were just as much at odds with the domesticity of American womanhood as they were with Chinese womanhood.

What Lee was advocating, in other words, had more to do with masculinity than femininity. Success within American society, for Rose Hum Lee and other Chinese American and Japanese American women, became equated with the need to become more masculine, not modern.[11] Lee's success in the profession of sociology depended on her ability to mimic the traits of masculine performance. She was the first woman to serve as chair*man* of a sociology department, an accomplishment that had little to do with the aspirations of the stereotypical ideal 1950s housewife, and everything to do with the aspirations of the professional American man.

The need for Chinese American and Japanese American women to act masculine in order to succeed also applied to Asian American men. In many ways, Oriental men had suffered in the late nineteenth and early twentieth centuries from a paradoxical opposition of stereotypes. Although often portrayed as sexual threats to white women, Asian men were also emasculated by stereotypes of passivity and weakness. The image of the Chinese laundryman and domestic worker or the Japanese flower gardener, willing to do the "women's work" that no self-respecting white man would perform, served to feminize the portrayal of Oriental men. The seeming paradox between the representations of sexual threat and asexuality did nothing to negate their simultaneous existence.

To succeed in the United States, Chinese American and Japanese American men, strangely enough, needed to assert their masculinity almost as much as Rose Hum Lee did as a woman. As the United States entered the war against Japan after Pearl Harbor, Japanese American men not only proved their loyalty to the United States by enlisting for service but also proved their masculinity and their fitness for male citizenship. Frank Miyamoto wrote in 1943 that his mentor, Professor Jesse Steiner at the University of Washington, had become "irked" by Miyamoto's "failure" to volunteer for the U.S. armed forces. Miyamoto related that "Dr. Steiner's view is that military service will be of infinite value to me when I seek a position in the post-war years, and that he will not be in a position to offer me the job at Washington again unless I have served in the Army."[12] Steiner judged Miyamoto's performance as an American male and worried about Miyamoto's future career prospects if he did not fight the war and perform his masculinity. Steiner would be unable, or perhaps unwilling, to broker Miyamoto's career in the face of the "failure" that not serving in the military symbolized to him and other American academics. Rose Hum Lee was not the only Asian American intellectual who had to prove her ability to succeed in a world of masculine roles.

Chicago sociologists welcomed Rose Hum Lee on stage as an interpreter of the Chinese American experience, but the subjects of her study often did not accept her role. In Lee's private and published writings, she repeatedly noted the negative reactions her work provoked among those she termed Chinese traditionalists.[13] The hostile reaction was partly due to her criticism of Chinatown organizations, but it also reflected the great divide she had created between herself and her background in Butte. By her choice of profession, Lee had consciously chosen to deny traditional Chinese values, repudiating those immigrant generations that would not embrace America. The rift between Lee and the traditionalists was brought about as much by her own movement toward the Chicago sociologists' definition of a modern, masculine America as it was by the intransigence of the Chinese in Chinatown.

Lee's strong advocacy of the assimilation process pointed to a personal story, one that encompassed the great gap between the Orient and America. Lee felt that she had crossed that divide, and, contrary to the theoretical marginal man who fulfilled the role of translator by remaining in the middle, Lee wanted everyone to cross over to the promised land with her. Lee's emphasis on removing the negative aspects of the marginal man through complete integration, so that he no longer "poses a problem to himself and others," reflected her discomfort with the position of the marginal man as a socially ostracized individual. Lee wanted to sever the link between the existential condition of the marginal man and his valuable role in a modern world of cultural contacts, the basis of the marginal man theory that had served as a powerful language of hope for thirty years. According to Lee, the assimilation problems of second-generation Orientals, as difficult as they were, could be solved by disconnecting the marginal man as outsider and the marginal man as interpreter.[14]

Rose Hum Lee's sociological outlook and career gave her a valuable intellectual and emotional distance from the Oriental community that she wanted so desperately to leave behind. She wrote in 1960 about the reactions of traditional Chinese to the education of women, giving an example of the slanderous gossip and criticism within a Chinese American community that had accompanied the news of one woman's college ambitions. Lee described how the woman's "desire to continue studying for her master's and Ph.D. degrees met with repeated censure from relatives":

> To retaliate for not heeding their wishes, they spread tales of her supposed misdeeds in the Midwest, where she attended a famous university. The Chinatowners of this prairie city were delighted to have a plum to pick. No native-born of this group had ever obtained a doctorate in philosophy, though some had received their master's and medical de-

grees. . . . The local Chinese, instead of being sympathetic to professional attainments, disparaged this girl's achievements. Her personal life was the subject of slander, gossip, envy and conspiracy. There were no congratulations when the doctorate was awarded.[15]

The case described was that of Rose Hum Lee herself.

Lee had analyzed the scandal of her own life by abstracting it through the theories of the Oriental Problem and had then acquired objectivity by referring to herself in the third person. But the estrangement provided by sociology did not completely eliminate Lee's emotions. Read in the proper context, a single line from her book—"In academic circles a medical degree is lower than a doctorate of philosophy"—contains perhaps more pain and pride than anything else Lee wrote.[16] Within this simple statement of fact was all of Lee's bitter resentment at being misunderstood by the Chinese American community, at not being able to exhibit the pride of accomplishment that was her and her family's due. A Ph.D. should be considered a higher achievement than a mere medical doctor, Lee asserted, a seemingly obvious hierarchy that the Chinese in their cruel obstinacy refused to acknowledge. She had made it in America, and the Chinese refused to recognize it. In a letter from Lee to her daughter Elaine, she noted:

> I shall never forget the faces of the women in Chinatown when they heard me say I got my Ph.D. The look of envy and greed came forth and instead of congratulating me for having arrived after years of struggle and sacrifice and malicious gossiping about my "loose ways," they smirked. I guess, too, they're mad because I don't socialize with them. . . . Well, I'll never do that now.[17]

The Demoralization of Oriental Men:
Paul Siu and the Chinese Laundryman

"The Chinese laundryman is not a marginal man as Park and Stonequist described," wrote Paul Siu; "he seems to be characteristically another type of stranger who represents a tendency toward isolation on the one hand and retardation of assimilation the other hand. It is another type, or deviant type, in the area of race and culture relations—'the sojourner.'"[18] In 1953, a doctoral dissertation entitled "The Chinese Laundryman: A Study of Social Isolation" was presented to the sociology department at the University of Chicago. Its author, Paul Chan Pang Siu, was forty-seven years old and had researched the bulk of his study during the 1930s. By the time he defended his dissertation, he had spent almost thirty years among Chinese American workers toiling in Chicago and Boston.

The lonely existence of Chinese immigrant bachelors in the United States was a phenomenon many white Americans had witnessed in small laundry shops and chop suey restaurants scattered across the country. It fell to Paul Siu to study the lives of these men. Using Chicago theories of social disorganization and personal demoralization to explain what he labeled the sojourner mentality of Chinese male immigrants, Siu created the richest and most detailed portrait of Chinese America that Chicago sociologists would ever produce.

Using an abundance of colorful excerpts from Chinese laundrymen chatting about their lives, Paul Siu described the immigrants' nonidentification with American life. The Chinese American men had responded to the prejudice and discrimination they encountered in the United States with the attitude of a sojourner, "an individual who clings to the heritage of his own ethnic group and lives in isolation."[19] When the Chinese laundrymen faced racial discrimination and were unable to form social relationships outside of the Chinese community, ethnocentrism became a defensive measure: "In leisure time and social events, the Chinese have a world of their own which is based upon the social solidarity of the families, the clans, and the kinship system."[20]

Laundry work in Chicago served as the point of entry for Paul Siu's understanding of the Oriental Problem in America. Siu agreed with Robert Park's earlier analysis of the Chinese as stuck in the assimilation cycle, unable to escape the dead-end result of social isolation. Male Chinese workers had been forced into jobs in which they did not compete with white workers, for instance, hand laundries and noodle restaurants. This had lessened the hostility whites felt toward the Chinese, but it also cut the Chinese off from communication with other social groups in America. What began, therefore, as an accommodation in response to racial discrimination and violence now served to maintain the isolation of the Chinese laundry worker. He was unable to "progress" to the final stages of the assimilation cycle.

The sojourner attitude was not inherent to the culture of Chinese immigrants; it was the result of the denial of the initial goals of migrant laborers and reinforcement by racial exclusion.[21] The devastating results of the Chinese Exclusion Act of 1882 had created a Chinese population in the United States that was overwhelmingly male. Unable to become citizens and unable to bring wives to the United States, Chinese men never felt at home in America. Home was China, where the laundryman could have a wife and family, and where he was known as an individual with his own name, not just "Charlie," a generic name derived from Hollywood movies depicting Charlie Chan, the Chinese detective who spouted cryptic pseudo-Confucian sayings.

No matter the immigrant's profession in China—teacher, doctor, scholar, playboy—in America his options were practically limited to work in laundries or chop suey restaurants. In an alien and hostile environment, these were safe options. Laundry work was an occupation by constraint, not by choice. In a wonderful piece of understated sarcasm, Siu remarked: "No Chinese laundryman, so far as I know, has ever seriously attempted to organize his life around the laundry, saying, 'I feel at home in this country and laundry work is my life, my career, and my ambition. I hope to be a prosperous laundryman.'"[22]

Eventually, laundry work became self-perpetuating. Those already established in America could help the newcomers, training them in all aspects of laundry work and setting them up with loans from relatives. Siu recognized that the Chinese laundry paralleled the experiences of many other immigrant groups to the United States. Like the Italian ice cream stand and the Jewish clothing store, the laundry was an example of an immigrant economy at work, providing a much needed haven of security from the economic world from which the Chinese were excluded.[23]

Denied a viable social life in America, Chinese laundrymen concentrated their lives around making enough money to become rich and return to China. According to Siu, this goal of a triumphant journey home was not a Chinese cultural trait. He referred in his dissertation to the work of fellow Chicago sociologist Clarence Glick, who had conducted his study of Chinese migrants in Hawaii at the same time that Siu had done his research on Chicago laundry workers. Glick asserted that, although the Chinese came to Hawaii as temporary migrants with a sojourner attitude, once they established families, they settled permanently in Hawaii.[24] Paul Siu and Clarence Glick's understanding of the Chinese immigrant worker as a sojourner extended from the Chicago conception of the marginal man. Although they both differentiated the sojourner outlook from that of the marginal man, both regarded the exclusion of the sojourner from a host society as analogous to the alienation suffered by the marginal man and second-generation Orientals. The main difference between the two types was that the sojourner responded to this exclusion by orienting himself even more strongly around his old society and culture. The sojourner, the marginal man, and the second-generation Oriental were all variations on the ideal type of the stranger, and thus each was a product of modern migrations and cultural contacts.

Paul Siu, however, went beyond Robert Park's initial analysis of the Oriental Problem as a potential but curable glitch in the assimilation and cultural interaction cycle. By applying Chicago theories of social disorganization, Siu analyzed the terrible effect that social isolation had upon the lives of his subjects.[25] This isolation was even more debilitating than the overall social isolation of the Chinese American community within "mainstream" American society. Communication with customers was perfunctory, and the long hours of difficult work, performed six days a week, often alone in the small confines of a laundry, created almost total social isolation. For the Chinese, the laundry served as an instrument for achieving their newly adopted goal of returning home rich, but, according to Siu, the intense isolation that the laundry perpetuated and even exacerbated led many of the laundrymen to "personal disorganization."[26] Siu defined personal disorganization as the process by which a laundryman stopped organizing his life around the return trip and his family at home.

The effects of disorganization on Chinese laundry workers involved gambling, prostitution, and what Siu termed "maladjusted" sexuality. The isolation of the individual laundryman from almost all communication with women, or even other laundrymen, was so extreme that adjustments to the situation, such as prostitution and gambling, were commonplace. Siu considered sex an appetite analogous to the need for food. Thus, the sheer boredom and sexual starvation of the laundry environment resulted in a frantic release every Sunday, when the laundrymen sought a week's worth of stimulation and excitement. Visiting brothels and prostitutes was not just for sexual release; it also provided for the adventure of doing anything besides washing and ironing. Laundrymen engaged in gambling and other vices such as drug use for the same reason they paid for sex: because they were so bored and isolated most of the time. Siu quoted a fascinating passage about four laundrymen who decided to go on a Sunday group outing, a daylong expedition to a series of brothels, a journey told in the form of an epic adventure.[27] All of the men's vices were adjustments to the same situation of extreme social isolation and boredom.[28]

Siu established that the group norm of the Chinese community in America was different than in China. Since morality was defined by the attitudes and beliefs of the majority of a social group, if the majority of the laundrymen agreed that visiting a prostitute was proper, then it was also deemed moral. Problems occurred only when sexual or gambling activities began to disorganize an individual, that is, if his activities began to clash with the goal of saving money for the eventual trip home.[29] The words "disorganized" and "demoralized" were in fact interchangeable. Anything that disorganized a laundryman, that distracted him from the goal of going home to China, also demoralized him.

Siu used the technical language of the Chicago sociologists to distance his analysis from blatant moral judgments of the laundry worker's behavior. Although he referred to the men's activities as vices, his overall point was to make their behavior understandable. Their vices were not evil or sinful but the natural result of social processes. The project of Chicago sociologists was to distance their analysis from moralistic language. The effect was to sublimate any political viewpoints into the structure of the analysis, ostensibly hiding them but actually making the moral claims systemic. Siu cited as an ideal example of the demoralization of Chinese laundrymen the case of a fifty-year-old bachelor immigrant who, after years of the hard life of laundry work, finally quit "without hope for the future, lonesome and discouraged."

> (S.Y.—age 50) . . . I lived in that hotel for almost a month after I sold my laundry. Yes, the hotel rent was twenty dollars a month, but could not I see any girl as I stayed right there? I had one almost every night and sometimes four or five times a night. In this way I spent almost one hundred dollars a week. . . . Money was spent like sand. I thought, sometimes, I better have some good times before I couldn't have it any more. What matter is money anyway? A person like me does not have much of a future. . . . I see very little chance for me to accumulate money to go back to China.[30]

Of all the sociology students who studied the Chinese in America, Paul Siu was undoubtedly the best field researcher, empathizing deeply with his subjects and probably understanding them best. The transcripts of laundry workers' conversations that he collected were intimate and highly revealing. The men trusted Siu and talked about intensely personal matters in front of him. Siu had been a social worker for over twenty-five years while completing his Ph.D., and he lived every day among the Chinese immigrants who were his subjects. For a time, he even worked as a delivery man to Chinese laundries, and thus was able to stop and chat with many of the laundrymen scattered throughout Chicago.

More than any other Chinese American or Japanese American researcher who worked on the Oriental Problem, Paul Siu satisfied the Chicago sociologists' desire for an insider. Born in 1906 in the Toysan district of Kwangtung Province and raised in China, he had attended an American missionary school in Canton. His father was a laundryman in St. Paul, Minnesota, and at age twenty-one Siu had managed to join him on a student visa. After studying in St. Paul for several years, he went to Chicago to further his schooling. One of Siu's professors, Louis Wirth, suggested that Siu study Chinese laundrymen, believing that he would make an ideal participant observer.

Siu himself recognized the factors that made him such a unique inside informant. Referring to himself in the third person, he noted: "The worker speaks the dialect spoken by most of the Chinese laundrymen. In fact, he was himself brought up in the same cultural heritage. He has friends and relatives among the laundrymen." This insider's ability "to comprehend the personal problems of the laundryman," however, also struck Siu as a possible liability. "The disadvantage is bias and loss of sight of some of the significant points."[31] Like Rose Hum Lee, the rhetorical fiction of referring to himself in the third person was closely connected to Siu's desire to distance himself from personal bias. What, however, did bias have to do with the other disadvantage Siu mentioned, the potential "loss of sight"?

Siu was pointing to the tension between researcher and subject of study that had always structured the participation of Asian American researchers in the Oriental Problem. Siu believed what his professors also believed, that the ideal vantage point of the sociologist was that of an outsider, and he worried that as an insider he might miss all kinds of interesting insights because they were too familiar to him. By identifying so closely with his subjects and by seeing the world from their point of view, Siu might be blinded to observations a stranger would immediately notice.

The tension between inside and outside perspectives was particularly apparent in the technique of participant observation. Chicago sociologists had used participant observation as a research method since the 1920s, and many of Chicago's most famous studies were based on it.[32] Cultural anthropologists had created the technique, and, fundamentally, the dynamic of participant observation was predicated on the struggle of an outsider trying to understand what was going on inside an alien place. Ethnographic descriptions were the written results of anthropologists explaining what was initially unfamiliar to them. A successful description of an exotic culture needed to create a bridge of understanding between outside and inside so that the actions and behavior of the natives made sense to the anthropologist.[33]

Just like the anthropologist in Africa or the South Pacific, the sociologist would write a description of a culture using the knowledge of an inside member. And, like the anthropologist, the sociologist translated this insider's knowledge for an audience of outsiders. In practice, however, Chicago sociologists differed greatly from anthropologists because they often trained insiders in the proper techniques of sociology. Anthropologists imagined themselves as outsiders coming to an exotic society, learning it to the point of being able to understand it as an insider, and then leaving to translate the knowledge for other outsiders. In contrast, Chicago sociologists actively recruited insiders to translate their native knowledge into sociological knowledge.

The technique of participant observation tended to exoticize certain aspects of American society. Chicago sociologists looked for and found social groups and communities within America that were unfamiliar to the professional white men who were sociologists. The everyday lives of hobos, or "street corner society," or "immigrant youth gangs" became the unfamiliar social worlds that social scientists could make understandable through participant observation.

Unlike anthropologists, sociologists produced knowledge of the unknown not by transporting it from exotic locales but by transforming the insiders themselves so that their knowledge was understandable to outsiders. Anthropologists devalued their native informants by treating them only as insiders giving information, which the anthropologists themselves transformed into valuable knowledge. Sociologists, however, valued insiders as the perfect participant observers who would themselves produce the knowledge sociologists desired. To the sociologists, both the informant and the information were valuable.

When Ernest Burgess and Louis Wirth discovered Paul Siu, they knew they had found the perfect insider. Siu produced voluminous transcripts of native laundrymen's conversation and speech. He wrote notes on everything about the Chinese in Chicago, their swear words, their gambling games, their jokes and bawdy stories. Siu had intimate access to conversations, and he possessed a wonderful ear for the caustic cursing of the male immigrants. Compared with the research of Rose Hum Lee and Ching Chao Wu, Siu's study was infinitely more colorful and inclusive. His portrait of individual laundrymen was never caricatured, and salty discussions about prostitutes and sex were commonplace.

Siu's analysis of his data, however, necessitated that he distance himself from his privileged access. Like Rose Hum Lee, he tried to erase his own presence from the sociological text, using the neutral language of the Oriental Problem to make a detached sociological analysis. Participant observation allowed Siu to describe the difficult lives of Chinese laundry workers from an insider perspective, but, in order to explain how they had developed their sojourner attitudes, he resorted to the detached, outsider analysis of Chicago sociology. By utilizing the seemingly objective, value-free language of sociology, Siu could make arguments with political ramifications using a language that claimed universal validity. The theories of the Oriental Problem allowed him to lay blame for the Chinese laundry workers' plight on the discriminatory legislation that excluded Chinese women and families. Siu did not have to make partisan claims or assertions; the detached outsider's perspective of social science was ostensibly above any particular moral or political standpoint. Despite the moral judgments that might have accompanied Siu's study, particularly in regard to gambling, prostitution, and "maladjusted sexuality," he could maintain distance by using the amoral language of sociology. The gains of sociological rhetoric were thus the result of the empathy of an insider perspective and the objective analysis of an outsider perspective.

In the end, the distance between the detached perspective of sociology and the feelings of Paul Siu was never so great as he claimed in the rhetoric of his dissertation. Siu had too much sympathy for his subjects; they were his friends, his relatives, and, ultimately, himself. Thirty years after Siu defended his dissertation, and almost fifty years after he conducted his research on the Chinese laundrymen, Siu's opinion of his own life remained tied to his subjects. "Given his experiences living in the United States for sixty of his eighty-one years," wrote historian John Kuo Wei Tchen, after interviewing an elderly Siu, "it may not be surprising to discover that Siu still thinks of himself as a sojourner. In this regard, his life parallels that of many Chinese laundry workers." In 1985, just a year before his death, Paul Siu wrote of his own life:

> I have finally settled down in Shadow Lake Village. The word "village" makes me think of my native village in my home country. Although the reality of my life lies only in New Jersey, I often reminisce about the native village where I grew up, my relatives in the old country, and my parents. All these memories now seem distant and irretrievable. They cause me to feel deeply the grief and loneliness of life.[34]

The Consolation of Sociology:
Tamotsu Shibutani and the Derelicts of Company K

"Detachment" is perhaps the perfect word to encapsulate the sociology and outlook of Tamotsu Shibutani. Recognized as a brilliant student during his high school and junior college days in California, he went on to a prominent career as a sociologist.[35] A keen social observer, dispassionate and probing in his insight, Shibutani showed a remarkable ability for applying sociological theories to social phenomena. He received both his M.A. (1944) and his Ph.D. (1948) from the University of Chicago, and his scholarly works reveal a skilled and engaging writer. As a researcher for the Japanese Evacuation and Resettlement Study, Shibutani took extensive notes of wartime internment; after he was drafted into the U.S. Army in 1944, he continued to keep detailed notebooks on his daily life.

Shibutani's experiences during relocation and his stint in the army became the central ground to which he would return repeatedly, reexamining what had happened to him from the detached viewpoint of the sociologist. Even more than for Rose Hum Lee, the emotional removal provided by the perspective of Chicago sociology allowed Tamotsu Shibutani to acquire analytical distance from the painful experiences and memories of his life. He gained enormous intellectual insight from his application of sociological theories, but he also acquired a therapeutic point of view.

Coming to see the world as a sociologist meant embarking on a personal odyssey that brought Shibutani to an understanding of himself as an individual enmeshed in complex social processes beyond his control.

Like Frank Miyamoto, Tamotsu Shibutani grew up outside of a Little Tokyo. Born on October 15, 1920, in Stockton, California, he attended school with Italian and Irish American children. According to him, his parents were not "typical" immigrants; his father was a Marxist intellectual who had come from Japan to study at Columbia University, and his mother was a well-educated daughter of a landlord in Japan. Also like Miyamoto, Shibutani had wanted as a child to become a writer and started college as an English major.[36]

Tamotsu Shibutani's work seems different from that of most of the other Chinese American and Japanese American sociologists who studied at the University of Chicago. His work was highly theoretical, examining aspects of collective behavior such as rumor circulation, group morale, and demoralization. Although he used the specific experiences of Japanese Americans for his studies, the fact that they were Oriental or Nisei was almost incidental for his purposes. He wrote in the introduction to his dissertation, "The Circulation of Rumor as a Form of Collective Behavior," that the fact that the "bulk of the field data deals with rumors among persons of Japanese ancestry" was not due to any "special propensity among Japanese to engage in such behavior." Rather, Shibutani explained it as a mere accident that a "student of rumor" had been "buffeted about by the fortunes of war from one situation to another, all congenial to rumor circulation."[37] In fact, Shibutani had been forced to observe only Japanese Americans because he, along with every other Japanese American in the United States, had been interned.

As a theorist, Tamotsu Shibutani emphasized the general import of the phenomena he had observed. Rather than taking Chinatown or Little Tokyo or the Chinese in America as his primary subject, Shibutani ordered his studies around social processes such as rumor circulation and social stratification. All of his writing was concerned with universal generalizations about social interaction.[38] Rhetorically, it seems very different from the monographic studies of Oriental communities and immigrants that other Chinese American and Japanese American sociologists wrote on the Oriental Problem. His book *Improvised News* (1966), based on his master's and doctoral work, explored how rumors were pragmatic attempts at making sense of the world during situations constrained by a lack of information. His study *The Derelicts of Company K* (1978) was based on his experiences in a segregated Nisei unit in the U.S. Army. In both books, the fact that his research subjects were virtually all Japanese Americans was almost incidental to the purposes of his study.

In *The Derelicts of Company K*, Shibutani examined how a group of men became demoralized, using the term in the same sense that Paul Siu had. Drafted in late 1944, Shibutani's army unit was formed after the all-Nisei 100th Battalion and 442d Regimental Combat Team had acquired heroic reputations fighting in Italy. In shocking contrast to the performance of the earlier Japanese American soldiers, however, Company K soon earned the reputation as one of the worst units in the U.S. Army, chronically unable to achieve its training objectives and riven with internal divisions and infighting. Shibutani set out to explain what had happened to Company K.[39] Just as for Paul Siu's laundrymen, Shibutani found that the demoralization of the Nisei men of Company K paralleled their social disorganization. The morale of a group was intrinsically connected to its degree of social cohesion; if everyone in a group was working toward the same goal, then the group's morale was high. In Company K, the Nisei soldiers came to perceive that the actions and policies of the U.S. Army were based on racial discrimination. These perceptions, reinforced by the segregation of the soldiers away from whites and the separation into groups of Hawaiian versus mainland Nisei, led to angry responses and breakdowns in authority. The troops stopped working together, began fighting among themselves, and no longer performed the tasks that were asked of them. Company K became completely demoralized. As Shibutani explained, "Ethnic segregation facilitates internal conflict by creating divergent perspectives." Since the policy of segregation was "already seen as an insult, members of minorities become hypersensitive to slights, and many common grievances become magnified and placed on an ethnic basis."[40]

Shibutani used this experience with Japanese Americans as a vehicle to explore general theories of social interaction. In describing the men of Company K, he pointed out: "Most of their reactions were characteristically human. Most of the behavior patterns described have been observed before and are likely to develop again." In other words, the fact that the men were Japanese Americans was de-emphasized. They just happened to be a "case study" that would serve as a vehicle for "broader" investigations.[41]

Shibutani's study drew a fine line. On the one side, his de-emphasis of the unique nature of Japanese American society countered the tendency of Oriental Problem theories to exoticize Asian Americans. On the other side, Shibutani, like Paul Siu, was asserting that white racial prejudice and physical segregation had been the root cause of the demoralization of Company K. The fact that Shibutani's subjects of study were Japanese American was an arbitrary accident to him, and yet the most significant factor in his analysis was the discriminatory treatment of Japanese Americans. What was behind this subtle distinction?

The initial need to distance himself and his subjects of study from their ethnic identity was driven by the need for a sociological perspective to be from a point as far as possible outside the group being studied. Therefore, the fact that Shibutani was a Japanese American being interned along with his subjects was downplayed. The fiction was that Shibutani was an outside observer to the social phenomena. Like Paul Siu, Shibutani was in practice an insider, yet his analysis needed to sound as detached as possible.

Shibutani had not always been such a general theorist. As an under-graduate at Berkeley, he had written a paper analyzing the problems of American-born Japanese, and his study could have easily been one of the projects that so typified research into the Oriental Problem.[42] By the time he wrote his dissertation, however, Shibutani was a general theorist. For example, he extrapolated from one element of Robert Park's theories of social interaction that other sociologists involved in the Oriental Prob-lem had mostly neglected—how the very rise of racial and ethnic conscious-ness was never a given and always part of a continual social process. For most of the Oriental Problem researchers since the time of the Survey of Race Relations, the distinctiveness of the Chinese or the Japanese within the United States was almost always presumed. Shibutani tried to explain how ethnic identity itself arose.[43]

In this way, his work rhetorically sounded the same as that of his ad-viser, Herbert Blumer—detached, objective, removed. Frank Miyamoto also exhibited this change in emphasis in his doctoral dissertation. Like Shibutani, he chose to organize his study around the investigation of gen-eral processes of group conflict and tension. The fact that his data were based almost solely on notes taken at the Tule Lake concentration camp where he was interned along with his family became incidental in a way that was strikingly different from his master's thesis on Seattle's Japanese community. What he and Shibutani had learned was the importance of de-emphasizing their connection to their subjects of study.

Considering the emotionally disturbing character of some of the events Tamotsu Shibutani experienced in the internment camps and in the U.S. Army, it is amazing how dispassionate his discussion of those events could be. Partly, this was the result of his use of the technique of participant observation. *The Derelicts of Company K* and Paul Siu's *Chinese Laundry-man* exhibited the same contrast between the colorful description of tran-scribed excerpts and the dry analysis of the detached observer. Shibutani was adept at capturing the rich language of his research subjects, in par-ticular the pidgin of the Hawaiian Japanese in his unit. Just as Siu's study was enlivened with Toysanese swearing, so Shibutani's soldiers cursed each other as "Buddhaheads" and "Boochies." But outside of his use of colorful quotes, his recounting of events always took place from a removed and dispassionate perspective.[44] *The Derelicts of Company K* was a perfect example of how Oriental sociologists could use the language of sociology to extricate themselves from their racialized identity as Orientals. Even though both Tamotsu Shibutani and Frank Miyamoto spent almost their entire time during World War II in the company of and studying Japanese Americans, their work had less of the character of an inside exposé than Paul Siu's study of the Chinese laundryman. Both Shibutani and Miyamoto were able to use their personal experiences in wartime relocation camps in such an abstract manner because of a quirk in the technique of participant observation.

Participant observation allowed a unique shift between inside and outside that was predicated on the secret status of the observer. Because only Shibutani, Siu, and Miyamoto knew that they were researchers, they could continually manipulate in their own minds their position vis-à-vis the people around them. They could act and feel as if they were taking part in the activities of a group but then later on erase their own participation. Or they could take part in the activities of a group with a self-conscious outlook of an outsider but actually participate, or even steer conversations toward some desired topic.

When Paul Siu became a participant observer among Chinese laundrymen during the 1930s, he deliberately kept his role as a researcher secret. The laundrymen did not know that he was conducting a study of them, nor did they know that their conversations would be used as sociological data. Most of the excerpts contained in Siu's book were transcribed after they had taken place, at a time when Siu could take notes surreptitiously. As Tamotsu Shibutani explained about his own data collection, "interviews were occasionally conducted," but he mostly relied on the technique of participant observation. "Where special information was desired, attempts were made to conduct 'hidden' interviews, i.e., unobtrusively to guide the normal flow of conversation in the desired direction." Only when such "hidden" techniques failed were direct interviews held.[45]

Participant observation did not create this sense of bifurcation between observer and observed. Indeed, it merely validated it as a valuable research method. Frank Miyamoto and Tamotsu Shibutani, in constantly taking notes on their daily lives, were no different than anyone keeping a journal or diary. They did not have to be sociologists in order to feel removed from the events around them and observe life in a detached manner; the notebooks scribbled in the cause of social science were analogous to the quiet contemplation of a diary. Participant observation as a research method abstracted and generalized this hidden observer outlook, turning it into an instrument of sociological observation. It was a professional methodology, not just a private activity.

The most powerful result of Chicago social science's affirmation of participant observation was that it allowed someone who was an inside member of a social group or community to effortlessly take on the rhetorical stance of a sociologist. Anyone, in any social setting, could take on the outlook of a sociologist by merely shifting his self-awareness from that of a participant to that of an observer. Paul Siu had worried about the possible disadvantages of being too much of an insider, but his misgivings were in some ways misplaced.

The analytical perspective of an outsider resulted from people imagining themselves as somehow removed from themselves. The very sense of being an insider was predicated on the ability to see oneself from the outside. In other words, to be a self-conscious outsider was to identify traits within oneself that could then be labeled as the characteristics of all members of a group. The very definition of what it meant to be a perfect insider was always connected to the ability to see a group from the outside.

Louis Wirth and Ernest Burgess had identified Toysanese language and origin as keys to Siu's insider status. However, Siu's own bases for identifying with the laundrymen may have been much more dynamic. He was, after all, not an isolated laundryman, and though he did identify with the men's sojourner mentality, it would have been very possible for him not to do so. Siu was married, he was a student and a social worker, and he was not growing old alone, with nothing to look forward to except going home to China. Siu's empathy with the laundrymen and his awareness of his own powerful identification with them were partly based on his ability to see a different life outside of the laundrymen's existence. He could see what it was like to be a Chinese laundry worker and also what it was like to be himself on the outside looking in. It was an indication of his great capacity for empathy that he chose to identify himself as an insider, as a fellow laundryman.

Tamotsu Shibutani's belief in seeing the world from a detached viewpoint did not mean he was a complete outsider to the world: participant observation, like Chicago sociology in general, was a constant shifting between an outside and an inside perspective. The first step was always to achieve an inside perspective, to create a sense of empathy with the subjects being studied. Shibutani explained the need to see the world from the point of view of the "derelicts" from Company K: "However bizarre their antics may appear to an outside observer, once the events are viewed through the eyes of the participants, most of them become readily comprehensible." Even when observers do not approve of the conduct described, Shibutani asserted, they could at least understand how "soldiers sharing such convictions would act as they did."[46] Only by seeing the world through the eyes of the participant, from the "inside," could the proper analysis from the "outside" view be made. However, acquiring the outsider's perspective was crucial in order to become a respected sociologist.

The imaginative estrangement of the self was not an invention of sociology. Social science merely extolled it as an ideal outlook. The technique of participant observation (or, more properly, the rhetoric of participant observation) allowed Shibutani to shift all the way to an outsider point of view, estranging himself totally from any identification with his Japanese American subjects. The outsider perspective of a sociologist was a deracinated place, where someone like Miyamoto or Shibutani could turn four years among fellow Orientals into the notebook data for a sociological study. Their studies were similar to Rose Hum Lee's in that they used the rhetorical stance of the detached sociologist to turn observations of daily life into material for analysis. Sociology allowed Lee to analyze her own hometown as if she had no personal connection to the people. It allowed Shibutani to use the same set of his experiences in differing ways, sometimes as examples of rumor circulation, at other times as examples of group demoralization.

The process of detaching oneself from life experiences could be long and drawn out, especially if those experiences had been emotionally disturbing. Shibutani waited thirty years before he could take his wartime notes and write *The Derelicts of Company K*. As he noted: "Since more than three decades have passed since these data were collected, questions will inevitably arise concerning the delay in preparing this book." Shibutani explained that when his field notes were initially organized and transcribed in 1947, he encountered "difficulties" that prevented him from writing the book. These arose because of a "deep emotional involvement in the events, the intensity of which I could not appreciate at the time." His experiences in the army had been extremely upsetting, and the anger and resentment he had felt made it virtually impossible for him to approach his notes without reliving those emotions. Shibutani "was unable to understand many things that now appear obvious," but the "passage of time has made possible a more candid appraisal of what happened." He needed time to create the distance required to analyze the events of the past, but he also needed the tools and perspective of sociology. Waiting thirty years might have been necessary in order for Shibutani to acquire the emotional distance to analyze his past in a detached manner. However, Shibutani's very effort to achieve the detachment required by sociology might also be interpreted as the process by which he overcame emotion through enlightenment and knowledge. He used the very professional need to examine those events in a detached manner to make peace with his past, explaining that "the delay has turned out to be a blessing, for it is now easier to view the materials more dispassionately."[47]

For Tamotsu Shibutani, the ability to see one emotional event from a detached perspective made it easier to see all events from the same dispassionate point of view. What happened to Company K four decades earlier was "no longer of political consequence to anyone, but many current disorders of a similar nature may prove difficult to comprehend because of our personal involvement." Thinking about other "comparable events" so that they no longer elicited "emotional reactions" would be valuable, since a "detached standpoint" was the goal of social analysis.[48] Shibutani hoped that the enlightened and unemotional perspective that he had finally gained on his wartime experiences would serve as an example for others of how to produce a similar unemotional sociological analysis.

Shibutani agreed with Park that the ability of the sociologist to shift from the outside to the inside and then back again was immensely valuable. It allowed social scientists to empathize with practically anyone, and it also allowed them to make generalizations that would be applicable to other situations. The social scientist gained different levels of understanding from the continual shifts between outside and inside. This whole process was a way to make individual experiences useful, generalizing from them to make larger scale arguments about human nature and the patterns of social interaction.

The personal gain for Shibutani, as for Paul Siu, Frank Miyamoto, and Rose Hum Lee, was to understand how human beings were sometimes subject to forces outside of their control. Their responses needed to be understood not as crazy or irrational but as very human attempts at dealing with a difficult situation. How they understood their situations was the key. In his work on rumor, Shibutani had characterized rumors as collective problem solving, pragmatic attempts by people to instill meaning into confusing situations. Rather than construing rumor as distorted communication, as so many other social scientists had, Shibutani emphasized people's need to understand what was going on around them, even when they had little information.

When Asian American sociologists tried to understand themselves and their place in the world, they acquired a removed and self-conscious perspective on themselves as objects of history and social processes. Frank Miyamoto and Tamotsu Shibutani were deeply thoughtful, contemplative men, constantly trying to understand the hows and whys of the world around them. More than any other Chinese American or Japanese American sociologist involved in the Oriental Problem, Shibutani achieved the ideal of "objective" detachment. He was able to attain the view of detached analyst, almost totally removing his individual point of view from his texts.

Like Frank Miyamoto, Shibutani had a penchant for thoughtful reflection and detachment from the world, and the role of participant observer/sociologist suited him perfectly. Perhaps he was the kind of person who had always felt a little apart from the world around him, but within social science he was amply rewarded for his ability to remove himself from the subjects he studied. Sociology suited Asian American intellectuals so well because the analytical distance of sociology also allowed them a method of therapeutic detachment from the pain and emotion of events in which they had been immersed. This was the consolation of sociology—enlightenment as a way of controlling the world and oneself through knowledge.

Such an unemotional and detached perspective on the world could engender resentment from others. In conflict situations, it was difficult to retain empathy for the enemy's point of view. As everyone began to split the world into good versus evil, right versus wrong (what Shibutani labeled "contrast conceptions"), people on one's own side tended to distrust anyone who tried to understand the other side.

The researcher's practice of metaphorically shifting between inside and outside was potentially dangerous. As valuable as it was for social science, this shifting could also prove to be volatile in certain social contexts, in particular an internment camp where there was an actual physical boundary between inside and outside marked by a barbed wire fence and armed guards. The standard practice of keeping the researchers' participant observation roles a secret became an absolute necessity during tense political crises within the internment camps.

The secrecy itself was also potentially lethal, particularly in Tule Lake camp, where tensions over the need for Japanese Americans to proclaim their loyalty to the United States led to violent factional conflict in early 1943. The researchers were in precarious positions, since the acts that their roles as participant observers entailed—taking notes, asking pointed questions, reporting to people outside the camps—made them vulnerable to suspicions of being government informers.[49]

In one of the few passages in Shibutani's sociological writings that gave a glimpse of his personal life, he tried to explain how hard it was for someone to remain neutral when everyone surrounding him was in a conflict. Read in the context of Tamotsu Shibutani at Tule Lake internment camp or in the U.S. Army at Fort Snelling, the statement becomes particularly poignant:

> One of the most difficult accomplishments for any individual is to stand back and remain dispassionate when personal interests are involved. Dispassionate analysis seems so cold and inhuman. . . . Jesus called for an appreciation of the position of one's enemy. He was much admired for it, but in the end he was lynched.[50]

Coming to America

The Oriental as an Intellectual/Object

A FINAL SETTING

The Oriental Problem as an intellectual and institutional construction dominated thinking about Asian immigrants for much of the twentieth century. Chicago sociologists set the stage for how Orientals would be understood in modern America, and they defined the roles that Chinese American and Japanese American social scientists would play in academia. Whether or not the researchers' performance was well received, there were academic rewards to be gained and accolades to be won.

The path to self-understanding for many Oriental intellectuals wound through the theories of the Oriental Problem. Time spent on stage could provide new insights and a powerful language for expressing and understanding self-identity. The Oriental Problem could also provide the big break a student needed to enter a career in academia. If a performance captured the audience, then the young scholar could parlay it into other roles and other performances. The Oriental Problem as an institutional construction was a unique opportunity for Chinese American and Japanese American intellectuals.

There was also a price to be paid. The evaluation of Chinese American and Japanese American researchers was framed by their ability to perform certain roles, and there was always a danger that they might be typecast, unable to break out of a bit role as a professional Oriental. Many of the students moved beyond their research on Orientals and went on to play other roles, to be understood and to understand themselves as theorists or sociologists. The world of the stage could be a cruel place, however, and a good performance as an Oriental researcher did not always guarantee a successful career in sociology.

The production of modern America that Chicago sociologists created in the twentieth century cast a number of meaningful roles for Orientals. They were marginal men. They were participant observers. Most of all, they joined with other sociologists as mapmakers, producing a representation of the world that defined where each person stood, where he or she had come from, and where he or she was going. This larger map would have a longer-lasting legacy than most of the individual texts produced on the Oriental Problem. Even when the curtain finally fell on the Oriental Problem as a research program, the intellectual map that was drawn to understand Orientals continued to define much of the terrain of modern America.

In retracing the paths of many of the white and Asian American sociologists who made their way through Chicago sociology's construction of the Oriental Problem, it is possible to see how complex such journeys were. Migration could involve trips backward and forward. A return could also be an advance. We can trace countless complicated paths, a complex web of crossings and recrossings, of half journeys and backtrackings. Such migrations may not have been aimless, but they certainly were not always direct or directed.

By the time Rose Hum Lee died in 1964, the place of the Oriental in American society had become very different than that surveyed by Robert Park in 1924. In 1965, new immigration laws reopened America to Asians, and an influx of new economic migrants from China, Korea, India, and the Philippines would forever change the character of Asian American populations.[1] The colonial expansion of the United States had always been a major factor in Asian immigration. Most notably, new migrants resulted from the military "opening" of China and Japan in the mid–nineteenth century, the conspiracy and coup that annexed Hawaii in 1898, the conquest and genocidal pacification of the Philippines between 1898 and 1901, and the military control of South Pacific islands such as Guam, Okinawa, and Samoa after World War II. With the continued military presence of the United States in Japan, Korea, and then Southeast Asia, refugees from American wars in Asia became one of the main sources for Asian migration.

After the end of the Vietnam War in 1975, refugees from Vietnam, Cambodia, and Laos would add even more variety to Asian immigration, further extending who would be considered Oriental. The term "Asian American" replaced the label of "Oriental," and the academic study of Asian immigrants passed out of the texts of Chicago sociologists and into the hands and mouths of Asian American activists of the civil rights era. Even with the rise of a new Asian America, however, the old map continued to guide travelers. Like an out-of-date atlas, some of the roads described still lead to the desired destinations, but others, unfortunately, do not.

8

Performers on Stage

Frank Miyamoto described the bifurcation of his identity while conducting research in a Japanese American internment camp by using the language of the theater. "One is an actor within a drama and feels the forces which shape it; but one is simultaneously an outsider, a member of the audience, who observes the drama as it is played out by others."[1] The stage analogy separated for Miyamoto the "role" of the ethnic being studied from the point of view of the nonethnic audience. The ethnic insider had a role to play, but who made up the audience that was strictly observing? It was this strange nonacting role of the audience that was the foundation of the inside/outside, observed/observer dichotomy that structured the Oriental Problem as a set of social practices. How was being the audience itself a role to be played?

The language of the theater hid social relationships of exchange. Research into the Oriental Problem was an intellectual exchange between scholars where inside knowledge was traded for sociological theories. But it was also much more. The framework of sociological theories that surrounded Orientals in America was inextricably bound with the University of Chicago's sociology department. Beyond the specific geographic setting of Chicago as the locus for the research, there were sets of relations tying mentors and students to an institutional structure. Power relations, including advising, funding, and academic advancement, controlled the professional aspects of sociology as a discipline, and it is important to see the link between the Oriental Problem as an intellectual construction and its institutional bases. The predominantly midwestern, Protestant white sociologists who originally researched the Oriental Problem dominated the ranks of academic social science in the twentieth century. Even as their definition of the problem constructed Orientals as a subject to be studied, their need for Oriental translators and insiders created an opportunity for Chinese American and Japanese American students to be trained as sociologists.

This is not to say that sociologists such as Robert Park, Emory Bogardus, and Jesse Steiner were not already interested in helping Oriental American students achieve professional careers. The sociologists and the missionaries were some of the few whites in the United States who were at all sympathetic to the difficult position of Orientals in America. Other than in sociology, the options in academia for an Oriental intellectual interested in Asian Americans in the United States were virtually nonexistent.[2] A few studied Asian history. For instance, Kazuo Kawai and another young student interviewed for the Survey of Race Relations named Yamato Ichihashi became historians of Japan. But the great majority of academic disciplines in the United States were uninterested in allowing Asian Americans into their ranks, let alone defining them as a subject matter for study.

Mentors and Students: The Oriental Problem as Institutional Opportunity

The Oriental Problem as a framework of theories and research questions created an opportunity for intelligent and well-trained Oriental students to succeed with skills they were perceived to possess as a result of their exotic cultural backgrounds.[3] Oriental students were seen by Chicago sociologists as ideal insiders, capable of providing insights into Chinese American and Japanese American communities that were inaccessible to whites. Of course, it was also necessary that the students were capable of operating within a world of academia. Therefore, it turned out that usually only those students who already had backgrounds outside of Oriental communities could take full advantage of the opportunity.

As already discussed, one of the best routes into the Oriental Problem was through sociology's historical connection to missionaries and social reformers. The Survey of Race Relations in 1924 marked the beginning of the use of universities as the recruiting ground for Oriental researchers, but Protestant church networks remained a prominent feature of the Oriental Problem. Social work, which was dominated by church ties, was an extracurricular activity for many of the Oriental students. Despite Robert Park's dislike of "do-gooders," Ernest Burgess and Louis Wirth maintained close ties with the School of Social Work at the University of Chicago, and Paul Siu and Rose Hum Lee were two of the many students to conduct research while performing social work.

Women who became involved as researchers of the Oriental Problem were especially likely to have come through church and social work connections. One student in particular illustrates how an Oriental researcher could crisscross between sociology and missionary social work all through a career. Yukiko Kimura, born in Japan in 1903, became involved with the YWCA in Japan and remained a prominent YWCA social worker in Hawaii after she emigrated there. Before and during World War II, she assisted Japanese families in and around Honolulu while at the same time completing a master's degree in sociology at the University of Hawaii. She was one of Hawaii sociologist Andrew Lind's researcher/informants, and, after the war, Lind sent her, along with a letter of recommendation, to the University of Chicago to earn a Ph.D. The primary research for Kimura's dissertation was based on her observations as a social worker in Hawaii and her participant-observation work among resettled Issei in Chicago after the war. After completing her dissertation in 1952, Kimura returned to Hawaii and worked as a researcher at the Romanzo Adams Social Research Laboratory. Although Kimura's long journey from Japan to Honolulu to Chicago and back to Honolulu is not representative of other researchers of the Oriental Problem, it does show how women in China and Japan could use missionary connections to travel away from Asia and into America.

For both Kimura and Rose Hum Lee, church networks of social work provided their initial access to sociology.[4] Within the United States, church connections could allow Chinese and Japanese women to escape from what they saw as oppressive gender roles, as the Society of Friends did for Rose Hum Lee. Through her social work in China and Chicago, Lee became a Quaker. Her network of Friends in the United States not only helped her professional career but also provided a social refuge when she came into conflict with Chinese in America.

Having a professional mentor was all-important. Without the advice and knowledge of an academic adviser, appropriate research problems were out of reach, and academic advancement nearly impossible. Although sociological theory was taught in classrooms, knowledge about where to go and what to do next to further a career was also essential. Most important of all, the evaluations of an established mentor instilled confidence and faith in a student's intellectual abilities. When Frank Miyamoto described how he had ended up in a career in sociology, he pointed to the absolute importance of having met Jesse Steiner, chairman of the sociology department at the University of Washington. Steiner was his key link to the broad network of Chicago sociologists. "Perhaps the decisive factor in giving me confidence in my choice," wrote Miyamoto, "was my contacts with Dr. Steiner at Washington, for he encouraged me, helped lay out a program for my career, and opened up possibilities which only he as a departmental head could do."[5]

Many of the Chinese American and Japanese American students who came to Chicago to pursue doctorates had finished previous degrees under advisers who themselves had graduated from the University of Chicago. Without the letters of recommendation and advice that such contacts provided, the path to graduate studies at Chicago certainly would not have been open to them. For instance, for most of its history, the sociology department of the University of Hawaii was staffed exclusively with graduates of the University of Chicago.

Like the chain migration of Chinese and Japanese immigrants who brought generations of friends and relatives from Asia to America, Chicago sociologists carried their colleagues and students back and forth between universities in Chicago, Seattle, Hawaii, Iowa, and California. For example, Romanzo Adams, who founded the department in Hawaii, brought Roderick McKenzie and Robert Park's student Andrew Lind to the university. Later, Lind managed to secure positions for in the department Chicago sociologists Clarence Glick and Bernhard Hormann. Adams, Lind, and Glick also trained a number of Chinese and Japanese students to conduct research on Orientals in Hawaii, many of whom went on to the University of Chicago for advanced degrees. Aside from Yukiko Kimura, other Asian American researchers trained at the University of Hawaii and subsequently at Chicago included Jitsuichi Masuoka, who ended up at Fisk University and was tending Robert Park when Park died; Margaret Lam, who wrote a study on the Chinese in Hawaii, as well as a paper entitled "Baseball and Race Relations"; Bung-chong Lee, the son of a Chinese store owner who conducted research on the Chinese store in Hawaii; and Douglas Yamamura and George Yamamoto, longtime members of the Hawaii sociology department who were perhaps the last of the students from Hawaii to complete the Ph.D. trek to and from Chicago.[6]

The Oriental Problem as a framework of research questions offered Chinese American and Japanese American students a topic that fit their own interests, while at the same time fulfilling the interests of the sociologists who advised and evaluated their work. It was an exchange of objects of value, a relationship that commodified information and identity and created a value for Asian American students within academia. As part of the bargain, the students acquired access to the social networks of white academia.[7]

The metaphor of commodity exchange contrasted with the students' own ideal narratives of themselves as performing the social role of a marginal man. The "role" of a translator or interpreter became the way Asian American students understood their own identity. Such a dramatic language of roles and performances was also interchangeable with the language of market exchange. The two descriptions were not mutually exclusive, nor were they in opposition to each other. The success and career rewards the sociology students achieved through performing their roles in the Oriental Problem could be understood perfectly well using both the narrative of cultural interpreters and the perspective of a market transaction. Indeed, the very value of their Oriental identity within sociology was created by the sociologists' theories about the special role of marginal racial identity.

Although the Chicago sociologists used the language of the theater to understand and describe the interactions between themselves and their students, they could just as easily have used the language of market exchanges. The Oriental students helped the established white sociologists, and the white sociologists in turn helped them. By emphasizing social roles as performance, Chicago sociologists such as Park rarely used market metaphors in their theories. But they often slipped into the language of economics because it was a perfectly commensurate way of describing the value of the knowledge that was being exchanged. The transactions of the academic market mapped perfectly onto the practices that the sociologists themselves described as the result of cultural identity and social roles. The two metaphors were functionally equivalent, but for my purposes, the actual practices of academia are better revealed through an analysis of them as market exchanges. Analyzing exchange relations helps us to understand the structure of the relationship between the Oriental students and their teachers. At the same time it reveals what was obscured by the language of the theater. Metaphors of dramatic performance hid the ways in which ethnic identity itself was an object that achieved form through the process of exchange.

The sociologists valued Oriental students because their exotic cultural background made them useful informants; conversely, most of the students understood perfectly well the value of the sociological training they were receiving. In the "Background Paper" that he wrote for Ernest Burgess in 1939, Frank Miyamoto listed four reasons he was interested in taking the course "The Study of Society" that had been designed by Park and Burgess:

a. That I consider such a course as this as fundamental in formulating a systematic point of view in sociology. Especially valuable for future teaching.
b. That Park and Burgess point of view was extremely helpful in previous research, and I should like to know more about it. Desire a systematic and critical treatment.

c. That it is probably important for taking PhD exam.

d. All of which has definite economic value.[8]

Miyamoto had given up his dream of being a novelist in order to enter a more economically secure profession. Among second-generation Orientals in America during the mid–twentieth century, there was almost a hyperawareness of the potential prospects of every professional career option. Beyond the intellectual rewards of self-enlightenment, becoming a sociologist also meant having a steady paying job.

Racial discrimination made it difficult for Orientals to obtain professional jobs, even with a college degree, and so students of color were attuned to every opportunity. Research into the Oriental Problem provided a chance for Asian American intellectuals to perform in academia at a time when there were relatively few other professional careers open to them. If being offered such an important role could be thought of as a big break onto the "stage" of academia, it was also an economic opportunity predicated on the exchange of objects. The objects traded were forms of knowledge: on the one hand, what might be called cultural identity (the very performance of exotic racial existence that the sociologists described using the language of the theater), and, on the other hand, the practical knowledge and advisers' approval that produced a successful career.

At times, Chicago sociologists used the metaphors of exchange to discuss social relationships. When Tamotsu Shibutani and his adviser, Herbert Blumer, began developing symbolic interaction theory as a way of expanding upon Park's theories of social life, they sometimes used terms such as "transaction" to describe social interactions. Similarly, Everett Hughes, in his studies of the sociology of professions and the social structures of workplaces, brought an awareness of market relations to his analysis.

But if there was one interaction that was not considered an exchange relation, it was racial and cultural identity. This was the result of the authentication of Oriental identity that the sociologists' Orientalist theories and practices demanded. In defining exotic Oriental culture, they fetishized it as an object of ultimate mystery and desire, the opposite of everything American. In so doing, they created Oriental identity as a prized commodity. Yet the sociologists' theories about culture mentioned very little about culture's ties to market society.

Cultures were authentic for the very reason that they lay outside of the capitalist market. The objects crafted by native tribes and the exotic artwork of the mysterious Orient were desired precisely because they were defined as cultural products rather than the mass-produced objects of industrial manufacture. Culture itself as a product was theoretically a matter of mind and spirit, an ethereal creation of knowledge and consciousness that was the opposite of the world of material goods. But knowledge can be an object as well, and the valuing of authentic Oriental culture paralleled its objectification as a form of exotic knowledge.

Culture and Exoticism:
The Commodification of Authentic Identity

> Rose Hum Lee, author and lecturer, brings to her audiences outstanding charm and the thought-provoking impressions of her dual perspective, a product of two civilizations—the ancient tradition-steeped culture of China and the new, virile and uninhibited culture of America. Reared by Chinese parents in the classics and traditions of China, the surroundings of her early childhood were the rugged mountains of America's Northwest.

So began a flyer advertising the lectures of Rose Hum Lee.[9] She spoke to Rotary clubs, high schools, women's clubs, anyone who was willing to listen and to pay her way. Lee was a popular speaker, and the flyer prominently displayed the rave reviews of groups ranging from the Women's Club in White Fish Bay, Wisconsin, to the Argonauts Club in San Bernardino, California. Lecture topics included "Chinese Art and Symbolism," "Chinese Customs Old and New," "America as Seen through Chinese Eyes," "America's Role in the Far East," "Generalissimo Chiang Kai-Shek," the "Chinese Nationalist Party," and, of course, the "Chinese in America." Typically, Rose Hum Lee would give her lectures in "perfectly fluent, flawless English"; afterward, dressed in the traditional Chinese *cheong sam* (a long silk dress), she would sell assorted chinoiseries and bric-a-brac as souvenirs. And so Lee put herself through college and made a lucrative living on the side while teaching.

Rose Hum Lee's career as a lecturer and import-export merchant illustrates by analogy another side of the Oriental Problem as a structure of exchange, a side that had more to do with the perceptions of Orientals as curiosities from exotic Chinatowns, replete with opium dens, gambling parlors, and silk-clad prostitutes. The perceived distance, both geographic and cultural, between whites and the Orient led to a fascination with the exoticism of things "Oriental," and the merchants of Chinatowns played that fascination for all its economic worth.

By the end of the nineteenth century, the economies of American Chinatowns had ceased to rely strictly on sales to Chinese immigrants and had begun to operate as purveyors of exotic Oriental goods and services to non-Chinese consumers. Roderick McKenzie saw this relationship clearly when he commented on how many American Chinatowns were "looked upon as a commercial asset—a sort of human zoo—which becomes a point of attraction for tourists."[10] Descriptions of Chinatowns as little pieces of the Orient in America abounded, and the physical boundaries of Chinatowns always denoted a cultural boundary as well. They were in America but not of American culture. The desire for authentic products of the Orient, whether an embroidered silk dress, a painted fan, or the services of a Chinese prostitute, heavily drove the economies of American Chinatowns (particularly the smaller ones) after the exclusionary acts of the late nineteenth century.

The commodification of exotic goods, however, was not limited to material objects. Anything can be commodified—services, acts, information, even identity. Conversely, there is never an object that is inherently valuable; what defines a commodity, and its value, is always determined together in a relationship of desire and exchange. Commodification at its simplest level describes the process within market societies by which exchange relationships create objects of value. These exchanges often, but not necessarily, involve monetary transactions. Commodification could objectify identity as a valuable form of knowledge.

In particular, the Orientalist desire for exotic identity defined the evaluation of Oriental students.[11] The power and authority of academic institutions in defining particular types of knowledge as interesting and genuine structured the categorization of the Oriental Problem. Chicago sociologists evaluated what kinds of information would be interesting scholarly knowledge. They then brought Chinese American and Japanese American intellectuals into an institutional framework that defined the value and importance of their work.

An odd parallel existed between exotic curios and the Oriental identity of the Chinese American and Japanese American students involved in sociological research. The collection of Oriental curiosities and their authentication as genuine and valuable art objects was structurally equivalent to the Survey of Race Relation's gathering and validation of knowledge about Orientals. Like the chinoiseries displayed in Chinatowns—the painted fans, the ornate sandalwood chests, even the images of the Oriental prostitute—it was the Oriental identity of students that was valued by the white sociologists. No matter how American an Oriental student seemed, it was the exotic and non-American part that made him or her interesting. Importantly, that part of the student's identity was also authenticated as being exotic and Oriental because it was valued as such. The valuation and the authentication were inseparable; each supported the other.

The Evaluation of Knowledge:
Scarcity, Exchange, and the Expert Connoisseur

The great legacy of Robert Park and the sociologists of the Oriental Problem was their categorization of knowledge about Orientals. A typology was established that gave meaning to individual objects and documents; they became indications of the second-generation Oriental Problem, examples of the marginal man, instances of and opinions about intermarriage, outbreaks of racial conflict, measurements of social distance, and epiphanies of race consciousness. Like a sorting machine, Chicago sociology transformed random information into examples of general categories.

Looking at the archival papers of the Survey of Race Relations, what is striking is the seeming arbitrary nature of some of the things the sociologists collected during their research. Anything to do with Orientals was potential knowledge, from high school annuals with pictures of Japanese students, to YMCA basketball league schedules, to random conversations with people about their dealings with Orientals, and newspaper clippings selected solely because they contained some mention of Chinese or Japanese. The almost arbitrary scope of the survey's early collecting of pertinent items and information was quickly recategorized by Park and the Chicago sociologists. Information or objects that were not considered useful or interesting within the purview of the Oriental Problem were no longer desired. Like much of the detritus contained in the Survey of Race Relations' collections, such materials were relegated to the dustbin of worthless objects.[12] Backed by the legitimacy of academia and of objective scholarship, the sociologists' expertise about the meanings and worth of knowledge became supreme. Of course, because the sociologists at first knew so little about Orientals, their judgments regarding what was useful or genuine were not very authoritative.

There was a close correlation between scarcity of knowledge and the validation of expertise. For instance, in March 1924, the organizer of the Survey of Race Relations, J. Merle Davis, asked Mary Austin, a member of the National Arts Club in New York City, what she knew of Orientals in the country. Austin remarked that thirty years before, it had been easy to buy all kinds of "good" and "interesting" Japanese pottery and chinaware. Within the last five or six years, however, there had been "a marked deterioration in the quality of the goods offered for sale." Austin suggested that perhaps the discrimination against the Japanese and Chinese had resulted in the paucity of Oriental goods available. She had recently been commissioned to buy Chinese and Japanese tableware for a friend and noticed that there were very few shops left in southern California.[13]

Why did the surveyors ask Mary Austin for her opinion? What did their very interest in her tell us about the processes of acquisition and validation of knowledge that structured the Oriental Problem in America? The surveyors had started out asking anybody and everybody, in particular important public figures, for their opinions on Orientals, and Austin was a prominent reformer and a powerful member of the eastern social elite. She was a collector. She was a connoisseur of the "strange," an authority in the matters of chinoiseries and japonaiseries, and she was an Oriental expert at a time when the Survey of Race Relations needed expertise. The surveyors' desire for Austin's opinion on Orientals in 1924 highlights the changing conceptions of what constituted expertise and valuable knowledge. As with Winifred Raushenbush, Robert Park's research assistant, explaining to an audience of academics about "Chinamen" she had met, the smallest details about the strange Orientals in America were considered valuable information.

The sociologists' very reliance on someone such as Mary Austin points to the tentative nature in the 1920s of their judgments about the value of certain kinds of information about Orientals. The sociologists appealed to universal laws to justify the types of knowledge they collected. They were connoisseurs of the strange, but it was their control over knowledge already known that gave legitimacy to their knowledge about the unknown. They certified their judgments about the importance or unimportance of new knowledge by previously possessing systematic theories about how the world operated. It did not matter what white sociologists did not know about Orientals. What granted them the authority to become experts on Orientals was that they already knew other things.

Expertise was also the product of a deliberately constructed scarcity. The Survey of Race Relations' initial structure of expertise and validation operated completely within social circles that did not contain Orientals. This had been the result of J. Merle Davis's decision to exclude Chinese or Japanese from the early stages of the survey because he was afraid the project would be seen as pro-Oriental. Thus, the scarcity of expert knowledge was the product of a particular social network that initially kept out the very people being studied. When the sociologists believed that Mary Austin possessed valuable information, it was because they thought her knowledge was rare. But the relative rarity of her knowledge depended on a situation where Orientals were deliberately not being asked about what they thought. The survey's social practices created the very scarcity of experts that validated what Austin knew as being valuable information.

The parallels between Mary Austin as an art collector and Chicago sociologists as "knowledge collectors" is striking. In each case, the expertise lay not with the artist who created the painting nor with the racial subject who experienced everyday life as an Oriental but with the collector. By the time the Chicago sociologists began recruiting Chinese American and Japanese American students as informants, the institutional practices of the Oriental Problem had already defined collecting as the activity of experts. The Orientals were just the objects being collected.

It is less important for the purposes of this discussion whether the information gathered by the Chicago sociologists was in reality good or bad information; the point is that they were the ones who could determine what was good or bad information. Knowledge that had not been evaluated by academic experts was without value as scholarly knowledge. The exotic knowledge produced by research into the Oriental Problem was always tied to a network of experts who granted themselves the professional prerogative to judge the worth and truth of knowledge. Their standards for legitimating knowledge about Orientals, which changed over time, were a key feature of the institutional practices of American Orientalism in the twentieth century.

Behind the Oriental Mask: Racial Roles and the Audience

If the Chicago sociologists considered social life an elaborate drama, then the role of sociologists was to play the audience: watching, evaluating, critiquing the performance of those on stage. The difficulty with such a theatrical metaphor was that everything should have taken place on the stage, with the actors playing their roles in front of each other, and everyone at the same time performer and audience. To have a separate audience of sociologists who were removed from the play of social life created a false division. Moreover, the audience was in practice equivalent to the white elite academics who watched everyone else in America.

The job of exotic, unknown ethnics was to play their roles on stage for the edification of the audience. Race was a performance, complete with masks and costumes and uniforms. What was most interesting to the audience was what was exotic. Elaborate costumes, funny accents, and fantastic tales of exotic origins were part of the proper role for Orientals in the playhouse of America. Who wanted to see a play about Orientals in which all the actors wore three-piece suits and acted exactly like white people?

Oddly, however, the Chicago sociologists *did* want to see exactly that performance of ordinary Americans in Oriental disguise. As an audience, they still demanded the exotic costumes, but in the end they preferred to see the mundane acts of everyday life. It was a strange performance that research into the Oriental Problem demanded of Chinese American and

Japanese American scholars. Oriental intellectuals were highly racialized, but not only because of the racial uniform Asian Americans were forced to wear. What made such a performance racial was the necessity of acting like everyone else, except with the constant constraint of not being like everyone else. An Oriental acting just like a white person was never equivalent to a white person acting like a white person.

The theatrical metaphors of identity theory resonated with the bizarre practices of race in the United States. But it was the inequity of power between performers and audience that the dramatic metaphor captured best. Playing the Oriental was a role dominated by the needs of a non-Asian audience, and, if the theater metaphor worked, it was when it described this asymmetrical relationship. In other words, the metaphor of racial performance was so compelling because it named this unequal relationship between the performer and the audience, not because racial identity was somehow really like the theater.

In using a metaphor of collecting instead, the emphasis shifts away from the stage and toward the audience. What kinds of performances did the audience want to see? Why were they so interested in certain types of roles? Most important, who was in the audience? The theatrical metaphor tended to hide the objectification and evaluation of racial performance. By using an analysis grounded in the traffic in goods, the unequal nature of these exchanges can be emphasized instead. Who judged what was a good performance, and what were the rewards for giving one? What were the objects of value? Who, in the end, was collecting the "performances"? What were they getting by watching? And what does it tell us about them?

As sociologists, Asian American intellectuals were adept performers, but they were also playwrights, creating the theories that defined the roles of ethnic identity and culture. Embodying in their own daily practices the scripted performances of race in America, they also elaborated upon its nuances. Kazuo Kawai, Paul Siu, Rose Hum Lee, Frank Miyamoto, Tamotsu Shibutani: each of them explored the possibilities of a highly limited role. Some of their performances were aesthetically astounding, complex, and difficult. They could elicit laughter and tears, spark respect and appreciation. But always, it was for an audience that would not let them forget they were Oriental.

Rose Hum Lee, by authoring a children's play, quite literally took on the role of playwright. In March 1946, the Goodman Theater of Chicago performed *Little Lee Bobo: The Chinatown Detective*. The story of a twelve-year-old Chinese American girl named Bobo, who solves the mystery of a thief in Chinatown, the play was written by Lee for a white audience. Like her own performances on the lecture circuit, Lee's play was a blend of the exotic and the mundane. There was Grandma-ma Lee, representing "old-world culture," with her Chinese costumes and accented English; Wing, a young boy "torn" by the conflict between "two cultures"; and Lee Bobo, a blend of strange Chinese and familiar American customs, just like Rose Hum Lee herself. Scenery for the play included billboards covered with exotic Chinese characters and a curio shop filled with incense sticks and firecrackers. Of the white characters, the striking contrast was between Toby, a mean-spirited thief who calls the children "chinks," and Mary, a young American friend of the children who is "curious about Chinese customs and wants to understand them."

This was Chicago school sociology reduced to its essence, a morality play about the proper way to be white. Cosmopolitan curiosity about the exotic unknown, replicated by the viewing audience of white children, would win out against ignorance and prejudice. By the play's end, Lee Bobo, allied with Mary her curious white friend, vanquishes the vile, expletive-wielding criminal who "has no appreciation of Chinese custom."[14] Lee wrote the story of the Chinese in America as one of coalition between assimilated Chinese Americans and cosmopolitan white elites. Together they would defeat racism. It was no accident, however, that all the action of the play was set in the exotic, segregated streets of a Chinatown ghetto.

The Marketplace of Ideas:
Validation, Academia, and the Intellectual

As the Chicago sociologists came to realize that some Oriental informants were providing better information than others, their criteria for evaluating the scholarly value of such knowledge changed. With Kazuo Kawai, Ching Chao Wu, and Ting-chiu Fan in the 1920s, the mere possession of an Oriental identity was enough to provide an unquestioned credibility. In their minds, the researchers of the Survey of Race Relations had constructed a situation in which reliable information about Orientals was thought to be so scarce that the musings of a connoisseur of Oriental art such as Mary Austin were considered valuable. By the time Paul Siu and Frank Miyamoto came along in the 1930s, the Chicago sociologists had begun to place the value of acquired knowledge along a spectrum ranging from insider to outsider, based on the observer's ability to participate in and penetrate a distinct social and spatial community.

Chinese American and Japanese American students who wanted to join the elite intellectual world of American universities had to travel along a particular path. It was a journey during which the ideas and information they produced were evaluated for significance at every step. In considering the history of the Oriental Problem in America and the number of

Asian Americans who became involved in it, we need to trace how the success of these people was determined. How well did they do in academia? How were they evaluated in their careers? The question of who is an intellectual in America has come to be defined by academic institutions, and so part of the Oriental Problem is the story of how a number of Chinese Americans and Japanese Americans entered the world of the university system and were validated. Scholarly acceptance was equated with success as an intellectual.

Research into the Oriental Problem validated certain kinds of knowledge as scholarship, taking information that Asian immigrants themselves might have considered mundane or even trivial and evaluating it as interesting and valuable. The scarcity of information about Orientals must be considered in light of the fact that much of this information was not scarce to the bulk of Chinese and Japanese in the United States. This evaluation of exotic information will serve to highlight how the Oriental Problem, by validating certain kinds of knowledge, structured for Orientals the very definition of what it meant to be an intellectual in America.

The difference between who knew something interesting and who did not became tied to judgments about who came from inside a cultural ghetto and therefore could claim insider knowledge. Scholarly success, however, hinged upon how well a person converted that inside knowledge into a form understandable and interesting to an outsider. The shifts that a scholar such as Paul Siu or Tamotsu Shibutani made between inside and outside were more than changes in point of view; they also reflected a change in status from an exotic native to a fellow member of academia.

In the end, moving from the role of inside informant to academic sociologist was a redefinition of self. It required traveling from everyday life in Chinatown or Little Tokyo, where knowledge about those places was uninteresting to other natives, to another place where that knowledge was unfamiliar. Within a network of white scholars interested in Orientals, that information was unknown and therefore considered valuable. But the information had to be translated from everyday knowledge into a form and language that were prized by academics. The irony is that by making this translation into the theories of sociology, an ethnic scholar often converted the knowledge into an esoteric and unknown language, unintelligible to the people who practiced it every day.

The institutional relationship between advisers and students determined what kinds of knowledge would be produced and what its value would be. Academic advisers wrote the letters of recommendation that led to research grants and academic jobs. Sociologists in Chicago, Los Angeles, Seattle, San Francisco, and Honolulu guided students through the paths of academia. Just as much as Oriental students served as the sociologists' guides to the world of Orientals, the sociologists served as the students' informants about what kinds of knowledge needed to be found, how it should be reported, and what relevance it had. The questions of what it meant to be a scholar and an intellectual in America cannot be removed from these relationships between mentor and student.

The long-term success of Oriental students depended on how well they distanced themselves from the ethnic aspect of their work. Their exotic Oriental identity, which initially had made them so valuable to the institutional sociologists, needed to be left behind. If they could not make the move to an objective, detached discourse, they were doomed as scholars. Frank Miyamoto's ability to see his own life through the theory of the marginal man, and his camp experiences through the theories of group conflict, proved his ability to acquire the distanced viewpoint of the sociological eye. Tamotsu Shibutani's long journey from his emotional experiences in Company K through the theories of demoralization showed he could do the same. Rose Hum Lee placed herself and her relatives in the general context of urban social processes. Paul Siu worked hard to see the lives of his fellow laundrymen from the distant viewpoint of the sociologist. All of the Chinese American and Japanese American students who successfully negotiated their way to careers in academia traveled a similar path away from their inside status as Orientals.

For some of the students, the quest for a scholarly outlook was easier than for others. The alienation that the students felt as Orientals in America, strangely, could help rather than hinder them in their search for intellectual detachment. African American social scientist and intellectual W.E.B. Du Bois described the "double consciousness" of racialized peoples as the result of their being forced to understand themselves as whites saw them, and at the same time knowing themselves in an utterly different manner. In many ways, the examples of Oriental researchers point to how the narratives of marginality and double consciousness made "colored" intellectuals ideal social scientists.

In the end, the definition of what was interesting knowledge could not be separated from the institutional relationships that defined its acquisition and validation. Perhaps the best example of the mentor relationship was that between Paul Siu and his adviser, Ernest Burgess. When Siu first began researching Chinese immigrants in the 1930s, he was taking classes with Burgess and Louis Wirth. Although he had been taught some English at the missionary school in China, his control of the language was still rudimentary. Burgess asked him to write a paper on swear words commonly used by Chinese immigrant men.

In a list entitled "Slangy Expressions Using Among the Chinese Immigrants," Siu described the "Bad Language" used by Chinese American laundrymen in Chicago. Most of the phrases involved insults about mothers and descriptive terms for prostitutes. For instance, Siu's list included the following:

> Chao-nei-ma-ko-hoi (fuck your mother's vagina), Chao-nei-ma (fuck your mother), Nei-ma-de (That thing of your mother), and Nei-ma-hol (your mother is impulsive sexually).

Concerning prostitution, he included:

> Chek-kai (street walker—literally "wild chicken." Used only to refer to white prostitute. For Chinese prostitute, the same Cantonese word "loo-gai" is used); Da-bo (to shot or to fuck. Commonly use among the prostitute patrons).

Most of the other insults involved an implication of homosexuality:

> See-lin (dead penis. Double meanings: 1) that a person is very foolish; 2) that a man who does not like women); Ki-doi (womanly man. It is signified homo-sexuality); Se-fat-kay (ghost of the back. Same significances as the above expression but the latter developed in America.)[15]

The Chicago sociologists found this list fascinating because they had never been privy to such inside knowledge. For Siu to merely list the curses and their meanings in English was enough to convert them into valued social scientific knowledge. That such meanings were already common knowledge to the Chinese immigrants, and to Siu, is ironic. There was a disparity between the value that Chicago sociologists gave to the English translations of the swear words and the value those definitions might have had for a Cantonese laundryman. The existence of such a disparity points to the ways in which the Oriental Problem operated as an institution for processing and evaluating information. Knowledge of the English meaning of Cantonese curses had currency only within the network of experts who were interested in the Orientals as objects of research. The transition from uninteresting information to desirable academic knowledge was a process controlled by Chicago sociologists, who were also the ones who could ultimately judge whether a person such as Paul Siu was good at producing interesting and worthwhile knowledge.

The translated list of curse words was a valuable object, but Siu wrote a paper on the subject as well. In "The Use of Bad Language among Chinese Immigrants," Siu went farther along the path to critical scholarship by trying to place the words within a social context. He differentiated between curses used by women as opposed to men and analyzed how this usage reflected gender difference among Chinese immigrants.[16] Siu attempted to use swear words as an indication of social mores, asserting that what is important to a social group or culture can be found by examining what its members defame in moments of anger and social disapprobation.

For lonely immigrant men, many of them old and weary from work and isolation, cursing was a private language of community. Siu's later depiction of "laundryman culture" in his dissertation described how this highly colorful language reinforced the men's sense of shared existence. Much of the sojourner attitude, according to Siu, was contained not in clearly articulated statements about to life goals but within the day-to-day cajoling and swearing of these men. Far from home, they sat around cursing at each other and laughing over each other's foibles.

Swear words, particularly those concerning sex and prostitution, were a language of ultimate intimacy and bonding between males. Siu's paper also revealed the fear that laundrymen had of social relations in the absence of women. In a social world dominated by physical proximity between men, the swearing reflected the possibilities of homosexual relations. In a manner analogous to other male-dominated groups (such as sports teams, military units, and boarding schools), homophobic cursing policed masculinity and proper sexual relations through a vehement and insistent proscription of perceived effeminacy.

Siu's description of laundrymen, poignant and full of insight as it is, must be understood as having exchange value because of its poignancy. The sociologists valued and validated such descriptions, and thus they recognized Siu as a good inside informant. In fact, his mere listing of the Cantonese curses may have been enough for him to have been evaluated as a good informer. However, without the "outsider's" analytical ability, Paul Siu would not be validated as a successful sociologist. Only by framing his insider status within a detached discourse could he earn the approbation given to a sociologist with an objective outlook. Siu literally had to make the laundrymen objects. At the beginning of his scholastic training, Siu looked outward from his cultural ghetto, trying to understand the inside world of academia. By the end, he was trying to look at his fellow laundrymen as if he were an outsider.

Frank Miyamoto, Rose Hum Lee, and Tamotsu Shibutani achieved success as Chinese American and Japanese American sociologists because they were intelligent and insightful but also because they most successfully acquired the detached perspective treasured by their advisers. They were not considered researchers specializing in studying their own identity, unable to get beyond their inside status. Shibutani, Lee, and Miyamoto were sociologists. But there was a price to be paid. Within the institutional practices of the Oriental Problem, it was extremely difficult to overcome the label of an Oriental. Because of the manner in which ethnic knowledge was evaluated, the roles of a participant observer and inside informant were dangerously prone to typecasting. The researchers could become so identified with the role of the inside informant that their identity could be perceived by others to be encompassed by their ethnicity. There was a very real pitfall of becoming typecast as what might be labeled a professional Oriental, the academic equivalent of Oriental bit actors in Hollywood who could only get roles playing houseboys, laundrymen, and gardeners.[17]

Students could overcome this hazard by proving their merits as researchers, theorists, and intellectuals beyond the scope of the Oriental Problem. It is a credit to those who went on to successful careers in sociology that they did. But a researcher had to go a long distance in order to leave behind the insider label. Considering how strongly Chicago sociologists identified an Oriental with actual physical ghettos such as Chinatown and Little Tokyo, escaping an ethnic identity was virtually impossible.

A SCENE FROM CHINATOWN

In 1947, Beulah Ong Kwoh wrote her master's thesis at the University of Chicago on the career prospects of Chinese American college students. In justifying her study, Kwoh wrote: "The assumption that a higher education brings a better job is probably most crucially tested when applied to minority groups." This was especially true of Chinese Americans and other Orientals who were "often not differentiated from their immigrant parents, are sometimes regarded as aliens, and to whom the expected privileges of citizenship are at times limited and denied." Kwoh studied Chinese Americans who had graduated from Berkeley between 1920 and 1942, sending out questionnaires and conducting personal interviews. Kwoh found that college degrees had helped the status mobility of the graduates, though many of those who had done well came from families with professional backgrounds. Few were from families working in laundries or chop suey restaurants.[1]

Born in Stockton, California, Beulah Ong Kwoh attended the same high school and junior college as Tamotsu Shibutani. Like him, she had transferred to Berkeley to complete her college degree and then attended the University of Chicago for graduate education, where she shared an apartment with Rose Hum Lee. After receiving her master's degree, Kwoh taught for a year at a women's college in Nanking before returning to the United States when civil war broke out in China. Kwoh settled in Los Angeles with her husband, Edwin, and began a doctorate program in sociology at UCLA. However, the demands of raising a family hindered her progress, and she never completed her degree.

Years later, Kwoh became involved in the Hollywood motion picture industry. The producer for the movie *Love Is a Many Splendored Thing* was searching for someone to help with Jennifer Jones's dialogue, since her character needed to speak with a Chinese accent. Kwoh, being Chinese American, was suggested as a possible dialect coach. It quickly became apparent, however, that she spoke English without a trace of an accent and was therefore of little use.

Despite this inauspicious start, Kwoh went on to have a long career as an actress. Under the stage name Beulah Quo, she appeared in a series of minor roles in motion pictures and television, playing Elvis Presley's adopted mother in *Girls, Girls, Girls* and nursemaid to the general's son in *MacArthur*. She retired in 1991 after a six-year stint playing a streetwise housekeeper on the daytime soap opera *General Hospital*.

Perhaps the most famous movie in which Beulah Ong Kwoh appeared was Roman Polanski's *Chinatown*. Playing Faye Dunaway's maid, Kwoh had a fairly small role, with only one spoken line. At the climax of the movie, as Jack Nicholson is frantically looking for the rich socialite played by Dunaway, he enters the house where Kwoh is working and asks for Dunaway's character. In response to Nicholson's query, Beulah Ong Kwoh, born and raised in Stockton, California, an English literature major with a master's degree in sociology from the University of Chicago, answers in accented English:

"She no here."

9

American Orientalism as a Theory of Race, Space, and Identity

The Chicago sociologists' evaluation of knowledge underwent a change between the 1920s and the 1950s as they acquired what they perceived to be better and better informants and information. They used two criteria for adjudging the worth of such information. One was an initial valuation of the exotic identity of Oriental intellectuals and their knowledge; the other was a judgment regarding the degree of inside access these Orientals were perceived to possess. By constructing a situation where information about Orientals was seen to be contained within closed Chinatowns and Little Tokyos, sociologists made Chinese American and Japanese American informants valuable.

The commodity of exotic identity was linked to its spatial expression in the metaphor of insiders and outsiders. The opposition that the sociologists imagined between an inside and an outside relationship to Oriental communities was tied to the sociologists' strong sense of the physical boundaries of Chinatowns and Little Tokyos. The informers' value as insiders was closely connected to the Chicago sociologists' emphasis on the spatial aspects of culture. The degree of inside access was tied to the degree of perceived exotic identity, and this equation led to a formula that could calculate changes in racial identity using physical measurements of space.

The Great Wall of Chinatown:
Experts from the Oriental Enclave

In the 1920s, the researchers of the Survey of Race Relations expressed their desire for Oriental informants in a very specific manner, complaining of the "Great Wall" that surrounded the Chinese community. When anyone came along who could provide an entrée into the impenetrable world of Chinatown, the surveyors seized the opportunity. Upon hearing of Ching Chao Wu, who was working on his master's degree at Chicago at that time, they immediately pressed for him to be given more research work. As Eliot Mears remarked, "I am much impressed with the thesis you sent me, prepared by C. C. Wu. . . . You realize the unusual difficulty ever present in penetrating Chinese communities, so I should be especially glad if some plan might not be worked out to utilize Mr. Wu on further studies in this general field."[1] Roderick McKenzie in Seattle agreed with Mears's characterization of the Chinese community as difficult to penetrate: "My greatest limitation is in getting information from other parts of the country, especially with reference to the Chinese . . . [who] true to their customary indifference, do nothing to help." McKenzie remarked that although the Japanese were more cooperative than the Chinese, he still saw them as a hermetic community both socially and geographically.[2]

A number of people, however, disagreed with the social scientists' portrayal of Chinese communities as closed and difficult to penetrate. For instance, E. C. Carter, former Chinese missionary and secretary of the Institute of Pacific Relations (which funded McKenzie's research into Orientals in 1927), responded indignantly to Mears's and McKenzie's conceptions of the Chinese: "I am a little disappointed that McKenzie should have already got a stereotype regarding Chinese indifference. I have always found the Chinese in this country one of the most cooperative of groups." Expressing his frustration at the social scientists' approach, Carter lamented: "If we had known that McKenzie started his study with his mind made up that the Chinese do not cooperate owing to their customary indifference, we should have been less likely to employ him for a study that involved the securing of cooperation from the Chinese."[3]

Whether, in some general way, Chinese and Japanese communities were difficult to penetrate is beside the point (and perhaps most interesting for the rather phallic imagery that it suggested as a description of social research and knowledge acquisition). The important issue is that the Chicago sociologists who constructed the Oriental Problem as a research project thought that Oriental communities were surrounded by a wall of ignorance. The ignorance, however, was the sociologists' own.

The closed nature of Chinatown had long been a theme within popular conceptions of the Chinese in America. Although Robert Park was insightful enough to realize that these attitudes toward the Chinese were born of social isolation and lack of communication, the Chicago sociologists in fact reinforced this imaginary boundary between Chinatowns and the rest of America. They saw Chinatowns as places that were difficult to know, and consequently, they evaluated information from behind Chinatown's "closed doors" as scarce and valuable. The place was exotic, and so was the knowledge associated with it.[4]

The Chicago theorists' emphasis on the spatial aspects of social interaction, expressed in their theories of human geography, carved the landscape of America into zones dominated by particular cultural groups and communities. Where people lived, and the boundaries surrounding their residences, became equated with their social life. Space and racial culture became virtually equivalent. A Chinatown was geographically distinct; sociologists could map the areas where Chinese lived and worked, and where the next neighborhood began.

The boundaries, of course, were never hermetically sealed. After all, non-Chinese often shopped and dined in Chinatown, and Chinese Americans constantly migrated in and out to work and play. But because the sociologists had such a definite awareness of the spatial dimensions of the Chinese in America, they began to see this geographic distinctiveness as equivalent to the cultural difference of the Chinese. The fact that the Chinese were so effortlessly distinguishable by physical traits made connections to their physical substantiation in the landscape all the more easy.

The spatial boundary surrounding a Chinatown was equivalent to the social barrier that isolated the Chinese within the assimilation cycle. Even if Chinese Americans moved about the city, they were still socially isolated. The social distance between cultural groups was mapped as physical separation by Chicago sociologists. In a similar manner, the clannishness, or social solidarity, as Frank Miyamoto labeled it, of Japanese American communities could also be given concrete existence in the urban landscape.

Chinatowns and Japantowns were delineated as distinctive geographic and cultural spaces within America. Because the definition of Oriental culture was tied to an opposition between American and non-American cultural traits, Oriental communities became equivalent to foreign places within America. A Chinatown was the embodiment of the exotic Orient, of all those traits and characteristics that simultaneously defined what was non-American.[5]

The Chicago sociologists' portrayal of a "Great Wall" surrounding Chinatowns, and their spatialization of the exotic nature of all Oriental communities, greatly increased their desire for inside informants. Researchers who could bring an Oriental identity to Chicago were seen as coming from a foreign place as much as a foreign culture. This explains why at first the Chicago sociologists made very little distinction between a student like Ching Chao Wu, who was from China, and someone who was born and raised in a Chinatown in the United States. They were both insiders from an exotic location, and an Oriental identity could be tied to the culturally non-American enclave of Chinatown just as easily as the foreign nation of China.

For the Chicago theorists, marginality was easily expressed in physical terms. After all, it was a spatial metaphor, denoting a location on the periphery or in the margins between two locales. As an ethnic or cultural experience, marginality as a description connected culture and urban space simultaneously. Marginality could also slip easily into being exotic or foreign, and it was this equation of marginality within the United States with the foreign location of the Orient that was the enduring spatial foundation for the theories of the Oriental Problem.

Marginality as a description also echoed with the metaphor of inside/outside that had so powerfully shaped anthropological and sociological research into the Oriental Problem. To be seen as an insider to an unknown ethnic community was valuable to Chinese American and Japanese American scholars. But they could also be considered outsiders to the social world of white academia. Was this just a curious irony of the situation, or was there something inherently misleading about the metaphor of insider/outsider?

The spatial metaphor of inside/outside became equivalent to the distinction between known and unknown. When Park and other white sociologists first came to the West Coast to study Orientals, they considered themselves outsiders to the closed inside world of Oriental culture. To be an outsider, therefore, became equal to ignorance; and to be an insider became equal to knowledge. The intellectual move for an outsider was to acquire the knowledge that insiders possessed; and the move for an insider was to translate knowledge already possessed so that ignorant outsiders could understand.

The inside/outside dichotomy also had metaphorical meaning by being value neutral. An outsider, initially knowing nothing, can view the knowledge acquired as merely an object—something that can be examined from the outside, like a shiny pebble or a glittering bauble. Because this can be done dispassionately, with no preconceptions, outsiders are often considered neutral, more objective. To be the subject of study, therefore, the insider who already possesses some knowledge is by definition unable to be neutral.

A simple formula explains these metaphorical linkages: insider = possessing knowledge = subject of study, and outsider = wanting knowledge

= studier of objects. We might think that the paths mapped by such links would be two-way streets. But they were not. Where the equivalence broke down was the last term—who was the studier and who was the studied—and it was around this issue that questions of power arose. If white sociologists were outsiders to Oriental culture, and Asian American sociologists were outsiders to American academia, these two ways of being outsiders were not the same. To be an Asian American insider meant having a commodity, specifically knowledge about Orientals, that was valuable to white outsiders. To be an Asian American outsider meant wanting a commodity—knowledge about academia—that white academic insiders possessed. Conversely, to be a white outsider meant wanting a commodity—knowledge about Orientals—that Asian American insiders possessed. So far, the equations are reversible.

But to be a white insider also meant having a commodity—knowledge about academia—that was itself built on the assumption that good scholarship was about discovering things unknown to white insiders. Scholarship was judged to be good if it was objective, in other words, understood from the point of view of white outsiders who treated all things they did not know as objects. The scholarly worth of an Oriental intellectual was judged by how well he or she acquired and practiced the perspective of white outsiders. Tamotsu Shibutani, Paul Siu, Frank Miyamoto, and Rose Hum Lee were all successful in transforming their own "subjective" knowledge into something described as if they were on the outside viewing it "objectively."

Although Asian Americans as outsiders could also be objective about what was inside knowledge to whites, such objectivity was of little value within the marketplace of academia. Park did recognize that marginal outsiders saw the inside world of American academia in interesting ways, but he considered such points of view curiosities, interesting but not as valuable as the exotic insider knowledge that Orientals were also seen to possess.

Furthermore, Orientals as the subject of study were always considered insiders to Oriental knowledge, even when they themselves knew very little about Asia or about what life was like for Orientals in America. Even if an Asian American was as ignorant about Oriental culture as a white American, he or she was always allowed to find out about him- or herself. It is because Orientals are seen as permanent outsiders to America that they are also considered permanent insiders privy to knowledge about the Orient.

Kazuo Kawai, the young UCLA student who decided to become an expert on Oriental history, initially considered himself an outsider to Asian culture and history; after all, he knew as little about it as did white outsiders. But because of his body and his permanent position as the object to be studied, he always held the privilege of being an insider to Oriental knowledge. And so Kawai was learning more about himself, and, once he learned enough to be able to supply the valuable knowledge sought by Orientalists, the question of whether he had always possessed that knowledge or acquired it only recently was uninteresting.

To take a contemporary example: imagine infants adopted from Korea by Scandinavian American parents in Minnesota. Raised in a town that was overwhelmingly white, such children might eventually go to a university and "rediscover" their ethnic culture. Even though they might know as little about Korea or Korean Americans as their adoptive parents, or even less, we might speculate that they would be presumed to be learning about themselves. Once they have learned something about themselves, their knowledge about being Korean American would go relatively unquestioned by most non-Koreans. The key is not whether their knowledge was or was not genuine; the interesting question is in what context their expertise acquires authority. Those who give them authority are those who do not know, and they do so on the grounds that the Korean Americans' physical appearances tie them to Asia.[6]

The tie between place and identity has had interesting effects on Asian American intellectuals. Because the connection between space and race was so strong within the theories of Chicago sociology, the validity of an Oriental intellectual's inside knowledge went unquestioned. As long as they were perceived to be from an Oriental location, Chinese American and Japanese American sociologists occupied an authoritative position as the expert voices for Orientals in America. They were cast in the role of inside informants and were given credibility because a close link between their bodies, their cultural identity, and their geographic origin was always assumed.

Surveying Chinatown:
The Growth and Decline of Oriental Identity

One of the most revealing examples of the tie between cultural identity and physical space was the way that Chinese American scholars at the University of Chicago portrayed Chinatowns. Starting with Ching Chao Wu and his classmate Ting-chiu Fan in 1926 and continuing through Paul Siu in the 1930s and Rose Hum Lee in the late 1940s and 1950s, each saw Chinatown through very different eyes. Their portrayals of the physical growth and decline of Chinatowns were often connected to their own hopes and desires for Chinese identity in America.

Chicago sociologists tried to trace the levels of Oriental identity by mapping the physical dimensions of Oriental communities. If the boundaries of a Chinatown were shrinking, they saw this as proof of the decline of Chinese culture and identity. Like the incipient disappearance of "savage" cultures that characterized anthropologists' portrayals of indigenous societies, the Chicago sociologists continually narrated a story about the declension of Chinese culture in America.

For example, Ting-chiu Fan, a China-born student who attended the University of Chicago at the same time as Ching Chao Wu, wrote a study on Chicago's Chinese in 1926. Like Wu, Fan was a Mandarin speaker in a city dominated by Cantonese immigrants, but, from the perspective of the Chicago sociologists, the two of them were as good insiders as could be found. Since Fan had difficulty communicating with most of the Chinese immigrants in Chicago, his study used alternative sources of information. After acquiring the addresses of all the Chinese businesses in Chicago from a telephone directory, Fan plotted their locations. Since he found the Chinese dispersed throughout the city, Fan attributed the geographic distribution of the Chinese to their desire to mingle with Americans. Eager to counter the perception that the Chinese in the United States were unable to enter into American life, he stated that "from the beginning the Chinese have learned not to live together" and therefore did not "isolate themselves from the influence of the American customs and institutions."[7]

Ten years later, Paul Siu took this same geographic pattern of the Chinese and apprehended a very different meaning. Siu's tables and maps charted the same dispersion as Fan's work, but he came to a more insightful conclusion (see figure). Only laundries and restaurants were evenly distributed throughout the city, which had more to do with the nature of the laundry and restaurant business than with any desire of the Chinese to assimilate. In fact, according to Siu, it was an even more powerful indication of their geographic and social isolation. The Chinese were not only ghettoized into Chinatowns as in most cities; they also were further isolated from one another by the necessity of living in small one- or two-man laundries. Linguistic and social barriers separated them from the non-Chinese around them, and sheer physical distance kept them from other Chinese. Only weekly trips to Chinatown for recreation and grocery shopping provided a respite from loneliness and isolation.[8]

Ting-chiu Fan, as a Chinese student with little appreciation of the social experience of the Chinese in America, could only follow the Chicago sociologists' understanding of physical dispersion as somehow weakening the physical distinctiveness of bounded Chinatowns. In contrast, Paul Siu's personal identification with the laundrymen led him to see their spatial existence not as a breaking out from the ghetto of Chinatown but

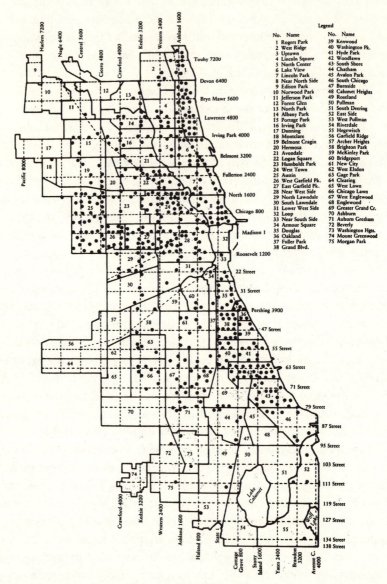

Paul Siu produced this map showing the spatial distribution of Chinese laundries throughout Chicago in 1940. His point was that the laundry men were dispersed and socially isolated by the needs of the laundry market. Ting-Chiu Fan, having seen the same dispersion of Chinese Americans through the urban space of Chicago, concluded that the Chinese were breaking down as a coherent group and becoming assimilated to American society. The key to Fan's interpretation was the conflation of geographic space and cultural identity. From Paul Siu, *The Chinese Laundryman: A Study of Social Isolation*, edited and with an introduction by John Kuo Wei Tchen (New York: New York University Press, 1987). Courtesy of New York University Press.

as a replication of its physical and social isolation. The distribution of Chinese laundries had nothing to do with a trend toward assimilation.

Rose Hum Lee, in her 1947 dissertation and in a 1950 article, provided a very different portrayal of Chinese ghettos. Although Lee was considered just as much an insider as Paul Siu (particularly when compared with Ting-chiu Fan), she agreed more with Fan's analysis than Siu's. For Lee, Chinatowns in the United States were dying, and her charting of their precipitous decline was directly related to her own desire to erase Chinese identity in America.

Like Fan, Lee saw Chinese Americans leaving the ghettos, particularly the second generation, and she took this as an indication of the eventual disappearance of Chinatowns. Rose Hum Lee observed that most American Chinatowns, which had thrived in the late nineteenth century, had long suffered as a result of immigration exclusion policies. By the time Lee wrote her article on Chicago's Chinatown in 1950, she was predicting the death of most American Chinatowns as viable communities, anticipating that they would be occupied only by the vestiges of aging sojourners and the occasional chop suey restaurant.[9] Like Roderick McKenzie's description of Chinatowns as "a sort of human zoo," catering to white tourists for their economic survival, Lee's description of Chicago's Chinese emphasized how "the community's economic structure is geared toward supplying the services demanded by the larger society, tourists, transients, and recreational seekers, who patronize the Chinatown for 'something different.'"[10]

Lee's claims for the eventual demise of American Chinatowns originated from her study of Butte, Montana, and her description of the small frontier town on the decline matched her hopes. She applied her model of Chinatown to Chicago as a place with "rapidly disappearing immigrant institutions," asking "if the geographical confines delineating the community will increase or decrease . . . and if the group's racial and cultural identity can be absorbed."[11] It was obvious to Lee that Chinatowns were in decline. "It would appear that the geographical confines of Chinatown may shrink rather than extend. . . . Moreover, as more American-born resettle, whether in Chicago or other parts of the United States, their domiciles may not be clustered within a ghetto." Lee concluded that "the reference to 'Chinatown' may be a reminder of a historical incident."[12]

With the slight increase in Chinese immigration after World War II (due to a change in the War Brides Act that allowed Chinese American veterans to bring wives into the country and to the influx of refugees after the Chinese Communist liberation of 1949), Lee's predictions for the end of Chinatown proved premature. She had recognized that a huge West Coast Chinatown like San Francisco's was large enough to sustain an internal economy and social life, but she hoped that without new immigrants even that Chinatown would eventually disappear. Lee was against the further immigration of Chinese until the present populations in the United States had completely assimilated. Therefore, she would have neither foreseen nor approved of the massive migrations of new Chinese immigrants after 1965.[13]

For Rose Hum Lee, and for Ting-chiu Fan and Paul Siu, the spatial dimensions of American Chinatowns had everything to say about the character of Chinese immigrant life in America. Lee saw the disappearance of recalcitrant ethnicity in each dying Chinatown store and every crumbling sidewalk. For Ting-chiu Fan, deaf to the bitter voices of Chinese immigrants, the fragmented spaces of Chinese existence only spoke of brave forays into white America. Paul Siu, seeing the same dispersion of Chinese through the landscape of America, heard the lonely, desperate curses of men trapped in their own private ghettos.

Movement, Space, and the Map of Culture: The Fictive Character of Exotic Origins

The decline of immigration as a factor in American life after the 1924 quota restrictions slowly transformed Chicago theories of race. American social theorists incorporated much of Park's emphasis on physical and social segregation. They created a model of American society based on structural pluralism, redefining the meanings of assimilation in such a way that the immigrant bases of Park's assimilation cycle were no longer relevant.[14] Park, Thomas, and McKenzie's emphasis on movement as the key to their social theories had lost much of its applicability in American society.

The exclusion era between 1924 and 1965, however, is an aberration in U.S. history. In every other period, large-scale migration from abroad has been the rule rather than the exception. To this day, many social theorists stubbornly cling to modes of social analysis that arose in an era when describing culture as a stagnant entity seemed to make sense. Even during the period of immigration exclusion, however, it was movement and contact in all their physical and intellectual modes that created descriptions of cultural difference.

According to the Chicago sociologists, modernity created the awareness of ethnicity. Migration and contact produced an awareness of difference. However, this contact also produced a heightened sense of similarity.[15] People who have never met strangers from somewhere else do not have a strong sense of their own place or the traits they might have in common. This local similarity is created by the awareness of being different from the foreign. The geography of similarity results from a sense of the stranger from somewhere else whose presence somehow ties everyone else to the place they live.

With a migrant, movement also creates abstract ties to a place that has been left behind, a sense of origin and having come from a location very different from the "here." Anybody else from that original location becomes identified as a fellow traveler from "there." This sense of having roots in another place, of having been transplanted, arose with an awareness of movement, and the Chicago sociologists recognized it and reinforced it in their connection of culture and space.

Robert Park, however, overstated his case in arguing that "modernity" was marked by migration and the contact of different cultures. Migration and contact between strangers did not suddenly arise in the modern age. People have been moving around and meeting strangers since time immemorial. What Park and his Chicago colleagues did do was create a new map for understanding and interpreting those contacts. In a sense, Park and the Chicago sociologists, Asian American and non-Asian, helped create a specific definition of how migration and movement were to be understood. They created the category of cultural identity as a way of understanding contacts between strangers, and they defined it as a "modern" phenomenon.

Cultural identity became a causal explanation for social interaction and behavior. That someone was Chinese or Japanese explained why they acted the way they did. However, using the culture concept as a causal explanation for social continuity and social change is analytically bankrupt. This is apparent when we consider that culture is commonly understood as a description of a group's way of doing things or understanding things.[16] To say that a group of people does something or acts in a certain way because of their culture is to say nothing. In other words, if culture is a group's way of doing things, then to say that a group does something because of its culture is equivalent to saying that it does something because that is the way it does things. The logical tautology involved in the culture concept as a causal explanation is disturbing, to say the least.

One way to think about the variability of any definition of immigrant culture might be to connect definitions of Chinese culture in the United States to notions about Chinese culture in China. The idea that there would be a timeless Chinese culture that had a causal effect on relations between the Chinese and whites in America takes on an implausible logic when we recognize that there were constant changes in society in China.

Would the Chinese culture of Chinese immigrants be their notion of Chinese culture when they left China? If they returned to China later on, how would they account for the very different society they encountered? Would their conceptions of what embodied Chinese culture have remained static in the intervening years, while China itself passed through history? What if their very notions of Chinese culture changed as they spent more time in the United States? They might become more nostalgic, or more orderly, or put greater emphasis on those qualities they saw missing from American culture. How are definitions of their own "Chineseness" and lack of Americanness predicated on the constant comparisons with Americans around them, a product of a systematic series of contrasts that gave them a sense of cultural difference from Americans?

The practices of social life achieve patterns of repetition for all kinds of reasons, the least causal of which is something called culture. People do things a certain way, and often at some point they stop doing things a certain way. Culture is as bad an explanation for why they continued to do things in the same way as it is a nonexplanation for why they started doing something else. All cultural descriptions can do in each instance is to narrate a story about the persistence of culture and, in the case of social change, the loss of culture. But that is a meaningless narrative derived from hindsight. Most Americans suffer still from the delusion that culture has causality in the social world. Cultural theory at best is a description of the way things are. By believing that it is more than that, we give it a power over us and allow it to control our actions.

The Chicago sociologists' affixing of identity to symbols such as race, culture, and place of origin created the modern map of American social thought. Our awareness of the fictive character of such categories is supposedly a postmodern consciousness. Most of this book has been devoted to exploring the constructed nature of the maps and theatrical metaphors that sociologists used.

But to stop at the act of proving that categories are constructed and therefore always fictive is a banal exercise in the obvious. The more interesting step is to see how this awareness of the arbitrary nature of categories allows us to see the very humanity of the categorizers. It is to see the ways in which categorizations and definitions connect with the desires and needs of certain people, and how the creation of theories and texts reflected those needs and desires.

Maps are human inventions. In realizing that the particular map we hold is one we may choose to accept or reject, we should be free to decide whether that map will take us to the places we want to go. If it does not, then we should make a new one. As Tamotsu Shibutani observed:

Knowledge is an instrument for living; the more accurate it is, the more effective a tool it provides . . . much like a map. If it is not reasonably accurate, it cannot serve as an effective guide for finding one's way about the territory.

Indeed, as all those who have become lost using an out-of-date road map know well, "an inaccurate map may turn out to be worse than none at all."[17] In making a new map, however, we must realize that a map is powerful not because it represents the world but because it reflects our attempts to create and organize the social relationships of our lives.

10

Legacies and Descendents

We all need maps, in a sense, and we are all mapmakers. The maps we make come to represent the world as we understand it. Therefore, to study the intellectual constructions of other people is to see the world as they wish to see it, to travel the landscape as they do. It is, as the saying goes, to walk a mile in their shoes. We need to understand, of course, how any map also contains the methods of control and domination, of constraining and defining exactly what people and places are to mean.

There are remnants of Chicago thinking in the disciplines of geography, sociology, social psychology, history, and Asian American studies, where repudiation covers a long-standing appropriation. Life histories, theories of racial prejudice and discrimination, spatial segregation, ideas of social space, and migration studies are all dramatically different from the approaches used by the Chicago sociologists. Yet they also reflect effects of the powerful map created by the Chicago surveyors.

An old road map thrown away and full of inaccuracies still looks vaguely familiar because new maps use many of the same symbols and markings to represent the landscape. The terrain may have changed radically, but, if the analytical and descriptive tools remain remarkably similar, we need to ask why and how these techniques and tools have somehow been retained in usage. The subtle eliding of the legacy of Chicago sociology is an interesting and dangerous irony.

From Oriental Problem to Model Minority:
The Rhetoric of Overcoming Works Too Well

Asian Americans, once considered the Oriental Problem because they were stuck in the gears of the assimilation cycle, are now seen as the exemplar of American success at work. The portrayal of Asian Americans as a model minority is a particularly perverse legacy of the Oriental Problem. It came, ironically, almost directly out of a number of postwar Chicago sociology studies of Japanese Americans who had been released from wartime concentration camps.

The internment and resettlement of Japanese Americans set the stage for the final act of the Oriental Problem. The question of cultural adjustments that Asian immigrants made in America, so long the basis for the Oriental Problem, was again reiterated. Just as internment camps and the Japanese Evacuation and Resettlement Study (JERS) had provided a research project for students such as Frank Miyamoto and Tamotsu Shibutani, so resettlement created another chance to look at the acculturation of Japanese Americans into American life. Rounded up and moved off the West Coast in 1942, a limited number of Japanese Americans were gradually resettled after 1943 into supposedly safe locations such as Chicago and Minneapolis. Relocation had profound effects on the lives of young Japanese American sociology students, as it did on all those who were interned. Relocation also created a new source of Japanese American students for the University of Chicago.[1]

A number of Japanese American students attended the University of Chicago in the years immediately after the war, and many of them studied how Japanese Americans were adjusting to having been flung in small groups all across the United States. In a strange way, most of the students' initial presence in Chicago itself had been a direct consequence of resettlement. Chicago had a relatively small Japanese American population before the war. With resettlement, however, the city became a popular destination for the released internees; this new Japanese American community supplied not only some of the postwar students to Chicago's sociology department but also a new topic for study.

Among the students, several wrote studies reminiscent of the Oriental Problem as delineated by Park, but the emphasis on assimilation turned from the question of whether Japanese could enter American society to the question of why they were doing so well. Setsuko Matsunaga Nishi, whose dissertation was entitled "Japanese American Achievement in Chicago: A Cultural Response to Degradation," took part in a postwar study that tried to find out why Japanese Americans were so successful in America despite the difficulties of internment and American racism. Eugene Shigemi Uyeki, who wrote "Process and Patterns of Adjustment to Chicago" in 1953, traced the difficulties that Japanese Americans had in adjusting to Chicago, but he also indicated how well they were doing despite the situation.[2]

In a curious way, resettlement, by taking small, isolated groups of Japanese from the West Coast and spreading them across the American landscape, fit perfectly into the assimilation cycle's definition of how to expose Orientals to American society. Whatever physical and social isolation the Japanese may have suffered on the West Coast before World War II, their move to Chicago was a new migration that begged for another application of the social interaction cycle. Yukiko Kimura, who left Honolulu to obtain her Ph.D. at Chicago, wrote a comparative study of Japanese in Hawaii and Chicago, focusing on the adjustments of older, first-generation Japanese Americans. Her study reiterated the powerful effects of social isolation, linguistic competence, and group cohesion in retarding the assimilation of Issei, while also showing how American-born Nisei were adjusting well to life in Chicago.

As Chicago sociologists had done ever since the inception of the Oriental Problem in the 1920s, the postwar Japanese American sociologists tried to prove that Orientals (in the form of the Japanese) were not a problem to American society. Japanese Americans were good, loyal citizens, and the studies showed them adjusting to life after the war and indeed surviving admirably despite anti-Japanese sentiment. Neither Setsuko Matsunaga Nishi nor Eugene Uyeki pushed the point that Japanese Americans were capable of cultural assimilation; they began with that assumption. The new point that they tried to make was that whatever remnants of Japanese culture remained had in fact helped strengthen the ability of Japanese Americans to overcome the difficulties of internment. The team of anthropologists and sociologists with whom Setsuko Nishi worked tried to demonstrate how cultural traits that Japanese Americans held because of a Confucian legacy paralleled the Protestant work ethic of successful, middle-class whites.

In the end, all the attempts to prove that Orientals were not a problem came to fruition. By the late 1960s and 1970s, the positive image of Orientals had won out, and characterizations of Chinese Americans and Japanese Americans as a problem were replaced by promises of their resounding success in America. This very triumph, however, left a malignant legacy. Encapsulated best in an article by social scientist William Peterson in the *New York Times*, entitled "Success Story, Japanese-American Style" (1966), Japanese Americans were now considered an example of the proper way for immigrants and racial and ethnic minorities to behave in America. Petersen went on to write a book expanding upon his thesis that Japanese Americans had overcome the most difficult of circumstances and, in the end, were a success story to be emulated. Japanese Americans could suffer racism and the stripping of their properties, their livelihoods, their dignity, and their freedom of movement. They could be deprived of all the rights to which they were entitled as American citizens. But because they overcame such obstacles, they were now a model for success.

The apotheosis of Japanese Americans as exemplars of American immigrant success was soon extended to Chinese, Korean and other Asian Americans. By the 1980s, Asian Americans were being portrayed as the model minority, disproportionately gaining entrance into elite education and its rewards of upward social and economic mobility.[3] The lesson to other minority groups that had also suffered in American society, in particular African Americans and Latinos, was implicit but clear: "Stop complaining and be like the Asians." The success of Asians was attributed to supposed Oriental, Confucian cultural traits such as hard work, obedience to family, belief in higher education, and emphasis on economic improvement rather than political action.

Although the study in which Nishi took part (often called the Caudill study because William Caudill was the first from the team to publish his results) was flawed in assuming culture as a causal factor, its ideological purposes seemed beneficial to Asian Americans.[4] By equating Confucian culture with the Protestant work ethic, the study showed Oriental culture as a potentially valuable object, rather than the depraved pathogen described by the Yellow Peril. The traditional Japanese culture that was perceived as inhibiting immigrants' acceptance in America was no longer seen as an undesirable trait to be left behind by the assimilation cycle. Instead, Oriental culture was viewed as positive, something at least as good as Protestant culture, and potentially even better.

The extolment of Confucian culture was explicitly a response to the degradation of internment and anti-Asian racism. It served to rehabilitate Japanese Americans who had been unjustly interned as potential enemies. But it also paralleled wider attempts by anthropologists and liberal intellectuals to praise the value of exotic cultures. Melville Herskovits, in his book *Acculturation* (1958), expressed an increasingly prevalent argument that contact between cultures should be analyzed from the point of view of both sides. Using the descendants of enslaved Africans brought to the United States as one example, Herskovits argued that, despite the holocaust of slavery, some African cultural traditions remained from the process of cultural contact and indeed may have even helped African Americans survive the ordeal.[5]

The argument for the survival, and survival value, of African culture thus paralleled the argument of the Oriental Problem sociologists. Confucian culture was not impeding Japanese Americans in becoming better Americans; in fact, it had helped Japanese Americans survive and overcome the deprivations of internment. As a process of rehabilitation, the rhetorical strategy of praising Confucian culture seemed to have succeeded in burying the problem of Orientals once and for all. It would take very little work to make Asian Americans into a model for all minorities.

We might suppose that the difference between Orientals as a problem and Asian Americans as a model could not be more stark. There would seem to be little connection between the opposing portrayals. The relationship between the two, however, is intimate. In both instances, Orientals and Asians prove the validity of successful assimilation, but, more important, they vindicate Americans. This is why the model minority story is a legacy of the Oriental Problem. The fascination with the success of Asian Americans has little to do with the Asian origin of supposed cultural traits such as hard work and education.

The exoticization of Orientals belies an obsession with America, not Asia. Thinking about Orientals has always been thinking about what it means to be American. There is a perverse irony in how American social theories still use Asians as a symbol of exotic difference, asserting constantly that what makes them interesting is that which is not American about them. All the while, everything said about Asian Americans revolves around a definition of America that cannot find a sensible place for them without exoticizing them.

The need to recognize a distinction between Chinese and Chinese American, between Japanese and Japanese American, between Old World and New World, has driven the production of knowledge about Asian Americans for virtually all of the twentieth century. "A large number of people," William Smith wrote in 1925, "seem to be utterly oblivious to the fact that there are in the United States several thousand native-born Chinese and Japanese who are American citizens. These American-born persons are treated, to all intents and purposes, as if they were alien Orientals."[6] This was an obvious injustice to native-born Asian Americans, a mistake that needed to be righted for the good of all Americans. Such an idealization of American-born citizens further exacerbated a division between American and foreigner that only reinforced Orientalism. Chicago sociologists made the difference between "American citizens" and "alien Orientals" the important dividing line when studying Asian Americans. The result has been an inability ever since to see Asian Americans through anything except the bifocal lens of foreigner versus "real" American. It is, in the end, a profoundly misleading distinction.

Since the 1920s, most American intellectuals have deluded themselves with a nationalist vision that racism against Orientals could be erased through the heightening of national boundaries. But no matter how loyal or assimilated an Asian American seemed, the best he or she could garner was the status of being "one of the good ones." As part of the process, other Asian Americans were demonized as too foreign or not American enough. Such a Manichean division between good citizens and bad foreigners has only exacerbated the sense that Orientals are perpetual foreigners. The definitions of Orientalism since the 1920s have continued to exoticize anyone who looks Asian. Thus white Americans are continually fascinated by the existence of Asian Americans who somehow do not act Oriental but nevertheless are clothed in an exotic racial uniform. No matter how much such Asian Americans seem just like other Americans, they are still Orientals who look different.

When every Japanese American was interned during World War II, the failure in vision was the same as in 1999, when all Chinese American businesses were suspected by the Cox Commission of spying for Communist China. The process of sorting good Asian Americans from bad Asians is fundamentally flawed. It produces a false dualism that can never work in practice. Continually placed in the default setting of exotic Oriental, Asian Americans look over their shoulders, afraid that at some point immigrants "fresh off the boat" from Asia might do something that will get every Asian into trouble. The best that a non-Asian can do for consolation is to say, "Don't worry, I know you're different from them." But the very need for such a malignant form of sympathy indicates the continuing legacy of Orientalism in this nation.

The Curtain Falls:
Dissolution of the Oriental Problem and the
Rise of Asian American Consciousness

The Oriental Problem ended its long production amid the derision and scorn of numerous critics. Asian American historians and community activists of the 1970s rediscovered the lives of early Asian pioneers while repudiating the theories of the Oriental Problem. At the same time, new waves of migrants ended over half a century of Asian exclusion, and the new immigrants knew little about the earlier history of Orientals in the United States.

To the vast majority of Asian and Pacific Islander Americans who entered the United States after 1965, Asian American history during the exclusion era often seems archaic. When they are interested in history, it is often the story of their own families' recent countries of origin. They are often surprised when they realize the parallels between their lives and the lives of American-born Orientals in the period between 1920 and 1965. They, too, find themselves feeling in between worlds, caught in the margins and not feeling at home either in the United States or in a home country they know very little.

The parallels are no accident. The intellectual and institutional construction of the Oriental Problem, first created in the 1920s, is still with us. More important, the structures of racial hierarchy that create the feelings of marginality and exclusion are still in place. In many ways, it is a better world than it was in the 1920s, but having come to a country less than thirty years ago, young Asian Americans are often unaware of the long history of obstacles and constraints they face.

One of the main legacies of the definition of American Orientalism by Chicago sociology concerns which groups were left out. By defining the Oriental Problem as the shared experience of Chinese Americans and Japanese Americans in being excluded by whites, sociologists reinforced a lumping together of Chinese and Japanese under the rubric of Orientals. Oriental status was seldom granted to other migrants from across the Pacific. Filipino Americans, even though they had begun to appear in significant numbers during the late 1920s, were minor players in the Chicago definitions of the Oriental Problem, and very few Filipino American students were recruited to study Filipino migrants to the United States. Emory Bogardus was one of the few Chicago-trained sociologists to write about Filipino Americans, and, because USC had a number of students from elite Philippine families, he managed to direct a handful of undergraduate theses on Filipino immigrants. But there was no graduate research, and none of the students went on to become professional academics.

American missionaries began the connection of the Oriental Problem to China and Japan, and Chicago sociologists reinforced it. Within this book I have been trying to outline how Chinese American and Japanese American intellectuals were drawn into the structures of American Orientalism and, therefore, how other Asian Americans were at the same time left out. But research is needed on the very different institutional practices that have defined other Asian Americans.

Interestingly, contemporary Asian Americans who understand their problems as being related to their racial and cultural identity show a mode of consciousness that arose with their Oriental parents and grandparents. The creation of Asian American studies in the 1970s was a powerful social and political movement that tried to distance itself from the theories and texts of the early Oriental Problem researchers. It is ironic, therefore, that the very rise of cultural and ethnic identity as a means of self-description and understanding was tied to the theories of the Oriental Problem that Asian American studies was trying to repudiate. It was the Oriental Problem that took assorted moments in the lives of research subjects such as Kazuo Kawai and Flora Belle Jan and turned them into general theories explaining modern life as a racial minority in America. The desire for cultural identity as a way of self-understanding was not created by Chicago sociologists, but they supplied the dominant language through which identity would be described and analyzed.

One of the innumerable ironies of the Oriental Problem in America is that it remains with us in so many ways, all the more perverse because we are not as aware of its legacy as we should be, and therefore we miss it in many guises. The historians born of the Asian American activist movement rejected most of the theories of the Oriental Problem, but they also recognized the importance of the work done by the early social scientists.[7] Because sociologists such as Paul Siu, Rose Hum Lee, Frank Miyamoto, Clarence Glick, Andrew Lind, William Carlson Smith, Emory Bogardus, and Ching Chao Wu were among a small group of scholars to have studied Asians in the United States, their work could not simply be dismissed. Often, however, their studies were mined for "authentic" voices of Asian immigrants, as sources for firsthand quotations of Asian immigrants. When Paul Siu's study of Chinese laundrymen was rescued from archival obscurity, it was hailed for the manner in which its insider perspective reflected the genuine experience of Chinese immigrant life. Siu's sociological analysis became secondary to the rich portrayal of laundrymen.

The genesis of the quotations and their path through the interpretive frameworks of Chicago sociology (particularly the process of secret observers recording transcripts of conversations from memory) often went unaddressed. For instance, for his tapestry-like *Strangers From a Different Shore*, Ronald Takaki took many excerpts from the interviews and life histories of the Survey of Race Relations and other early Chicago studies and wove them into a narrative emphasizing the "true voices" of the Asian immigrants.[8] Although laudable as an attempt to counter scholarly traditions that had neglected the viewpoints of Asian Americans, the emphasis on authentic voices is a strange echo of the Oriental Problem and its emphasis on the authentic identity of its Oriental informants.

Asian American activists in the 1970s viewed the Chicago school's theories on race relations and immigration as backward and outdated, and they deliberately maligned many of the earlier researchers. Park was labeled a conservative and a racist.[9] Many of the Chinese American and Japanese American researchers who had become sociologists, particularly Rose Hum Lee, came under attack as pro-assimilationist apologists and not genuine enough as ethnic intellectuals. The outsider position of the Oriental sociologists, so important for their acceptance and validation as intellectuals within the American university system, came under attack as a form of "selling out" and "pandering" to whites. The participant observer was castigated as a tattletale, a gossip, and, worst of all, a traitorous informant for maintaining the secrecy of his role. Numerous Asian American and African American scholars have also attacked the whiteness of the standpoint of objectivity.

The attacks on the writings of the Asian American sociologists of the Chicago school, trenchant in their critiques of the structure of white Orientalism that had created the theories of the Oriental Problem, were rather harsh on the Chinese American and Japanese American students who were recruited to conduct research. The criticism, at heart, is misdirected when it targets individuals. The practices of American Orientalism are institutional, and it is folly to pin them on individual Asian American intellectuals. In the final analysis, these scholars did not make American Orientalism; it made them.

An apt analogy, and one that echoes the spatial metaphors of Chicago racial theory, might be to think of the institutional and intellectual construction of the Oriental Problem as a house. As a structure that defined and created the relationships between white and Asian American intellectuals, the Oriental Problem put Asian Americans in different-sized rooms than white intellectuals. As if closeted by walls, Asian Americans were constrained in what they could do, living in the tiny spaces of a racialized identity. They were not restricted to the extent that they all had to do exactly the same things. There was a certain amount of agency and freedom of choice in the actions of individuals, but they could not do all the things that a white scholar was free to do. A person in a small room can dance the lindy or even a waltz, just as a person in a large room, but he or she cannot run a fifty-yard dash.

The Oriental Problem defined Asian American intellectual life by promoting lone individuals in institutional careers. In contrast, the Chicago sociologists' theoretical descriptions of the "Negro Problem" never had the same effects on African Americans.[10] Despite the prominent work by African American intellectuals trained at Chicago, such as E. Franklin Frazier, Charles S. Johnson, St. Clair Drake, and Horace Cayton, Chicago sociology's theories about Negroes were among the myriad of explanations for problems that African Americans faced in the United States. Apart from the much larger number of African American intellectuals, compared with Asian Americans, there was also a greater variety of ideas about African Americans. This panoply of competing concepts was reflected in the amount of intellectual and political debate over what exactly the Negro Problem was and what its possible solutions might be.

The institutional domination of one school over the training and professionalization of researchers interested in Orientals was missing in the case of the Negro Problem. African American thinkers came from diverse backgrounds, just like the Chinese Americans and Japanese Americans who studied the Oriental Problem. African Americans went to a number of different schools, however, and there was never a central locus like Chicago through which most were eventually drawn.

Another interesting difference resulted from the existence of black academic institutions in America. Jonathan Holloway's study of African American social activists and intellectuals who were affiliated with Howard University offers an interesting contrast and parallel to the history of the Oriental Problem as an intellectual and institutional construction.[11] The existence of all-black institutions such as Howard University created a very different institutional life for African American intellectuals. The concentration of black scholars in segregated institutions could, of course, reinforce already existent intellectual and political marginalization. But schools such as Howard and Fisk University gave African American intellectuals places where they did not have to prove themselves as lone individuals. Institutional support in the form of finance, social validation, and scholarly legitimacy provided a haven for African American thinkers to experiment with ideas and politics. There was an enormous difference between needing to convince everyone of the validity and legitimacy of a subject of study, and the feeling that the need for research is already recognized.

Asian American intellectuals both suffered and benefited from the necessity of living such singular professional lives. That most of the Asian American intellectuals came to define themselves through their profession was connected to the ways in which academia as an institution individuated them. They came to academic institutions virtually alone as representatives of their race and culture. They depended for support on the network of Chicago sociologists who were experts on race relations and who had helped them into the profession of sociology. Their narratives of personal identity and their professional success reflected how the Oriental Problem defined who they were. They stood alone, and they succeeded or failed alone.

Asian American intellectuals in white-dominated institutions never fostered a set of students to carry on their work. In contrast, having an all-black institution meant that African American scholars were able to socially reproduce a younger generation of scholars. This new generation could be nurtured and developed in a situation very different from that in which their mentors existed.

The recruitment between 1924 and 1965 of Asian American intellectuals into the overwhelmingly white structure of academia was a positive development. Constrained in their actions or not, at least they were there. With the rise of ethnic studies in the 1970s, a new means of entry was forcibly opened. For the past twenty-five years, ethnic studies has been one of the most effective institutional means for the training of intellectuals of color, in the same ways that women's studies has been for women. We need to maintain such fertile ground for the nurturing and growth of scholars of all backgrounds.

In many ways the rise of Asian American studies was predicated on the need for a separate institutional existence in which Asian Americans as a self-identified group could define the validity of their ideas. On academic campuses at San Francisco State, at the University of California, Berkeley, and at UCLA, Americans who had long been identified as Orientals came to define themselves as Asian Americans.[12] Taking inspiration from Black Power and Third World solidarity movements, Asian American activists created institutions that rejected the goal of assimilation into a white-dominated society. They also attacked the institutional structure that had produced assimilation theories and that had kept Chinese American and Japanese American intellectuals as lone individuals within academia.

Asian American studies and ethnic studies were attempts to control the site of production of knowledge about Asians in America. In the transition from sociology's Oriental Problem to Asian American studies, the biggest difference has been the creation of a separate institutional network where research can be produced and validated. Before the 1970s, the definitions of who Asians were, and what they meant within America, lay with the theories and institutions of the Oriental Problem. Since the 1970s, researchers interested in Asian Americans have received funding from places like the Asian American Studies Center at UCLA and have been able to present their papers at the annual conference of the Association for Asian American Studies. Often, these scholars are professional historians, social scientists, and literary critics whose work is also evaluated and respected by non–Asian Americans, but a nurturing institutional network has been a powerful factor in the growth of their scholarship. Separate institutions devoted to studying Asians in America have mitigated some of the need to prove the worth and validity of research on Asian Americans. There have been some unwanted consequences, such as a need to continually guard against insularity and the danger of being dismissed as irrelevant by the powerful professional disciplines. However, the significance of what has been gained should not be underestimated.

Does this mean that separate institutions are the answer to the problems of racial inequity? No, but they have countered one of the continuing legacies of American Orientalism—the centering of what is interesting knowledge around the curiosity of non-Asians. Asian Americans will continue to be trained in the disciplines that produce human knowledge, such as sociology, history, literature, or anthropology. Without at least some separate and viable institutional networks, however, the production of knowledge will continue to be dominated by the racialized structures of Orientalism.

Within the institutional and intellectual construction of research into the Oriental Problem, white academics validated certain forms of knowledge as interesting and valuable. That system was overturned by people who wanted a say in defining what was their "genuine" culture and what was "fake" (created for the consumption of whites). They emphasized a different set of criteria for identity, one based on mutual suffering at the hands of whites. However, this ethnic identity was based on a set of definitions similar to those used by Chicago sociologists. The oppositional character of ethnicity remained disturbingly similar to the way exotic and Oriental were defined by the Oriental Problem.

To date, the reformation of Asian American intellectual life has been partial at best. Left intact was the institutional structure that placed the perspectives of whiteness at the center of academic evaluation. There has been a successful alliance of cosmopolitan, progressive whites with assorted scholars of color. But objectivity as a standard is still defined by the ignorance of a particular group of people. We need to create a universal standard that evaluates forms of knowledge not through the eyes of this highly restricted number of people but through a democratically defined dialogue that takes into account the mutual nature of ignorance and knowledge. Until then, we will continue to judge all knowledge from the point of view of curious and tolerant whiteness.

The legacies of the Oriental Problem in American intellectual history are manifold. Studying for the interests of white sociologists and studying for their own interests, Asian American scholars produced knowledge that otherwise would not have existed. Judged by criteria that asked them to both act Oriental and deny being Oriental, the intellectuals met with professional success or failure according to their ability to do the latter. In the end, however, as it was in the beginning, what individual Asian Americans have achieved has been structured by a system for producing knowledge that is little changed. Intellectuals of color face dilemmas and contradictions with which white scholars may empathize. However, their bodies inhabit at every moment the constraints of a nonwhite position in the structure of American society, and this everyday existence can only be imagined by those who do not live it.

Beyond Intentions as the Core of Intellectual Life: Orientalist Practice and the Historical Legacies of Structural Inequity

Chicago sociology's vision of the world as a melting pot is both gone and here more than ever. Robert Park had a transcendent vision of humanity, with a modern consciousness arising from movement and migration and a new world created out of the contacts between cultures and races. In coming to an awareness of differences between people, Park and white sociologists were fascinated by that which was exotic. They tried to see within the difference between cultures the reasons for the problems that plagued America. At the same time, Chicago sociologists argued for a common humanity that would overcome all such differences.

The tension between similarity and difference underlay the sociologists' understanding of America and the world. For them, to live in social isolation was to live in ignorance; only by knowing the breadth of human variation could a person glimpse the profundity of human similarity. It seemed a color-blind call to arms, but it was not. As a color-conscious dream, it appealed to whites to be modern cosmopolitans who could appreciate the racially different, and it appealed to people of color to embrace their marginal status. Each would begin with a unique form of culture, and in the end all would be civilized. This vision was where the Oriental Problem derived so much of its power and appeal.

Chicago sociology would come to define race relations theory in the twentieth century. Gunnar Myrdal, the Swedish social scientist commissioned by the Ford Foundation in the 1940s to study race relations in the United States, relied heavily on Chicago sociology's race relations research. Myrdal also echoed the outlook of the missionary social reformers who had begun the Survey of Race Relations. In his widely read and cited report *The American Dilemma*, Myrdal pinned the problem of racism on whites. In a manner similar to Paul Siu in *The Chinese Laundryman*, Myrdal argued that the difficulties of racial minorities were the direct and indirect results of the actions of whites.

If "white guilt" as a rhetorical appeal followed from such an explanation for America's race problems, its empirical evidence came from Chicago sociological research.[13] Chicago theories on race, culture, and marginality provided the textbook instruction for college education. Racial prejudice among whites became the target of the enlightenment project. In its place would be a cosmopolitan appreciation of difference. It is a battle that is still being fought, but it alone cannot bring victory in the war against racial inequality.

One of the main legacies of the Chicago theorists' emphasis on attitudes and consciousness has been a utopian delusion. The false promise of cultural theories of race that followed Robert Park's is that if everyone just stopped thinking about race, then race would disappear. Cultural consciousness, including racial consciousness, becomes a matter of thought and volition. If we think we are ethnic or racial minorities, then we are. If everybody stopped thinking about race or ethnicity, then it would just go away. While the culture concept eventually succeeded as an antiracist theory by denying the importance of biological differences, it failed to erase the continuing importance in American society of structures and relationships between bodies that had long been based on physical difference. Because Chicago sociology focused on identity formation in the present, these historical products of racial inequity remained as a legacy even after enlightened thinking had denied the original justifications for such inequities.

Human bodies matter. They have been defined by historical processes, and rethinking what they mean in the present cannot wish away how they have been controlled in the past. Some bodies were put into positions of inferiority in the United States because of ideas and laws about race, and denying the relevance of race only justifies leaving them in place. In other words, when Asian Americans, African Americans, and other racialized minorities deny the relevance of race in their own lives, it is equivalent to a protest against race and skin color being used to deny them the same treatment as anyone else. When Americans with the privileges of being considered white deny the relevance of race in their own lives, it is functionally equal to preserving the historical inequities in American society that have been built on racial exclusion.

If Americans have not stopped thinking about race, it is not somehow a product of a moral failing, as if we are not trying hard enough to forget about race. Because of the manner in which Chicago sociologists and missionary reformers made racism a matter of consciousness and attitude, we are left with the legacy of a deluded notion of race. We believe racism is a matter of intention. We believe, for instance, that if we all just tried very hard to get along, then we could. Such a false hope in the power of mere goodwill was very much a product of the missionary aspects of the race relations studies in which Chicago sociologists took part. If nothing else, the designers of research into the Oriental Problem were full of good intentions.

Life, however, often has very little to do with our intentions. We say what we mean, but others hear something else. Our purpose for performing some action is misunderstood or is apprehended in a manner utterly different than intended. There is, in the end, a great shortcoming with focusing solely on the original intent of a theorist in writing a theory, or a racist in killing a nonwhite minority. Intentions and ideas are interesting in themselves, but they do not tell the whole story. There can be a great gulf between intention and actions, between the best-laid plans of men and the complex results that make up social life, between what we mean to do and what actually happens.

Chicago sociologists intended to find out more about Orientals, and they did something about their desire to know. We can describe the contexts for their ideas, and we can delineate their intentions. There is a possibility, however, that in examining the intellectual construction of the Oriental Problem, we will have said very little about the consequences of that construction. Some of the historical legacies of the Oriental Problem have had little to do with the original intent behind its creation.

We can judge intentions, and we can judge results, but to do so may be to do very different things. The Oriental Problem was ideas and theories, the intellectual products of men and women who wanted to know something about others and themselves. But it was also a pattern of institutional practices, of mentors helping students get jobs, of colleagues evaluating each other's work, of the myriad of intentional acts and unintended consequences that make up the life of any group of people. Practices can be the product of acts of consciousness, but they can also occur and recur and have consequences that have little to do with the intentions of the people who originated a particular practice. The recurring patterns of activity that often make up social life can be bewildering in their lack of rationale.

The Poverty of Language:
Cosmopolitan Knowledge as a Practice of Whiteness

It is a profound mistake to hope that if whites just stopped thinking about race, all of America's racial problems would disappear. In the insistence of many white Americans to ignore the legacies of racial hierarchy in U.S. history, they in deed perpetuate and reinforce the inequities that were built into the foundations of this nation. All across the country, recent efforts to remove affirmative action and prohibit the consideration of race have used the rhetoric of color blindness to call for a more just and equitable society. In a misguided effort to erase racial categories that have had a long and powerful effect in American society, we risk ignoring their historical legacies and freezing the racial inequities forever.

The ultimate irony of examining a group of theories such as those defining the Oriental Problem is that we mistake the source of power if we think it lies in words. The poverty of language is that words are not power. Words can be powerful. They can be persuasive. They can shape power. They can define justifications for hierarchy and sustain the social practices that create and perpetuate power relations. But in the end power is constructed in a web of relations between people.

We cannot flee from this society into a world of pure ideas, a realm where we can dispassionately examine knowledge with a detached eye. Those who can imagine such a world are benefiting from a tremendous privilege, the privilege of an institutional structure that places some people in the center of knowledge production. Not every person who has produced knowledge has been white (in the sense of skin color), but even those who were physically marked as Oriental had to define the perspective of their knowledge from the point of view of whiteness.

Whiteness as an elite, cosmopolitan privilege was embodied in the structural position that people like Robert Park created and occupied. The luxury they had was to be fascinated by the unknown, and to be able to define as interesting all those who were unknown to them. That the exotic people whom they examined could benefit from such an interest neither excuses the constraints placed on Orientals nor erases the practices of whiteness that such relations further reinforced.

Americans constantly aspiring in the twentieth century to upward social mobility have embraced elite definitions of whiteness, abandoning the working-class racism that Chicago theories defined as ignorant and unenlightened. But we should be careful not to forget the racialized origins of such antiracism. The cosmopolitan ideal may be more inclusive, but a hierarchy between the position of the knower and the object that is known still exists. Antiracism built around cosmopolitan appreciation has promised to include all those who have been excluded by social practices built around elite white males—women, people of color, even working-class whites. But to deflect the issue of racism strictly onto working-class ignorance has promised a color-blind utopia that never materialized, an ideal of cosmopolitan equality never fulfilled because the centrality of whiteness in such a vision was always so well hidden.

In the beginning of the period examined in this book, Jewish and Catholic immigrants were just as much outsiders to academic scholarship as were Asian migrants and African Americans. At the same time that Asian Americans and African Americans were being recruited into Chicago sociology, so were Jewish, Irish, and Italian American intellectuals. They were all "ethnic" in the sense of being marginal outsiders. But their trajectory through the institutions of Chicago sociology deviated from the path of Orientals and Negroes. During the 1930s and 1940s, organizations such as the National Council of Christians and Jews created cross-denominational alliances between Jews, Catholics, and Protestants. Eventually, the conception of a Judeo-Christian Western tradition supported arguments that made practices of anti-Semitism and anti-Catholicism unacceptable.

The appeal of a cosmopolitan ideal drew Jewish and Catholic intellectuals into academia, allowing them to become elite scholars and to label those who excluded them as ignorant, prejudiced bigots of a lower social order. Asian Americans and African American intellectuals found Chicago sociology appealing for the same reasons. But by the 1950s and 1960s, the paths had diverged. Jewish and Catholic scholars had become generically white, while Orientals and Negroes remained colored. This was the essential difference that a definition of "ethnicity" centered upon "marginality" could not erase. All of the outsiders had started out marginal, but the cosmopolitan outlook of the curious intellectual was a path more open to those who could claim to be white. Jewish and Catholic scholars celebrated the success of a cosmopolitan appreciation of ethnicity, losing themselves through the warm embrace of a common whiteness. The privilege of whiteness was that ethnicity seemed a choice. One day a year, Irish Americans or Italian Americans could celebrate Saint Patrick's Day or Columbus Day. The other 364 days a year, they could be selective about displaying their ethnicity.[14] In contrast, Asian Americans and African Americans continued to find that their outsider's perspective remained an interesting but marginal position. They could not escape the markings of race.

Ultimately, many Chicago sociologists and missionaries erased the consequences of their own whiteness by fleeing the physical body. In making ethnicity purely a cultural phenomenon, they tied the position of being marginal to their limited definitions of culture. They made culture a strictly nonphysical phenomenon, and de-emphasized the body. They imagined a world of abstract spiritual and cultural identities, interacting with each other as equals. But if the utopian possibilities of such theories are still a powerful ideal, they remain scuttled, like any language denying the continued existence of racial hierarchy, on the shoals of social practice. White supremacy has consistently marked physical bodies with racial difference. The history of the United States has been that of a society building its institutions on racial and gendered inequity. Those institutions endure.

There is a trite observation that ethnic identity is like a new religion. Usually, this comment issues from those who are afraid of or do not approve of displays of ethnicity. If there is a truth in the statement for Asian Americans and other racialized minorities in the United States, it is that ethnic identity is a powerful form of group identity precisely because of a recurring and almost universal experience of being excluded. Their experience of being excluded has been different than that of white ethnics, however, since they cannot disappear into whiteness. For those seen as Oriental, realizing how racial structures have determined their lives transforms the meaning of their place in the world. The epiphanies of racial consciousness that Asian American intellectuals expressed when encountering the theories of Chicago sociology were just one variety of a common occurrence in apartheid America.

Those who call for an end to such racial identity wish for a greater civic religion that can replace what they decry as particularistic affinities. I, too, wish for a world in which a common humanity is the highest spiritual calling. Unfortunately, Americans are constantly convincing themselves that the United States has already become a place where race does not matter, and they are simply wrong. Indeed, racial identity as a calling would have no resonance if the country were truly free of racial hierarchy and exclusion. We have come a long way since the days of the Oriental Problem. But the exoticism that helps and hinders Asian Americans is still all around us, and the extolment of whiteness that centered American Orientalism still structures the way Asian American intellectuals are given meaning and value.

Asians are still exotic, still bearers of an authentic otherness that they cannot shake. Like other nonwhites, Asian Americans remain both Americans and examples through their existence of non-America. The continuing fixation with race in America, with its powers of definition and its corrosive divisions, structures American society as it did during the days of the Oriental Problem. At times, Asian Americans have embraced their ethnic status, and at other times they have tried to deny it, but if they have tried either option, it has been a fettered choice, and one that most whites do not have to make. For Asian Americans, whether you dance an exotic dance or try to waltz like everyone else, you are still exotic.

A truly democratic production of knowledge must recognize that racial practices have had a long history in the United States and have produced profound legacies that cannot be wished away as mere cultural differences. The answer is not to ignore or forget race but to confront its history and address the need to build a more equitable world that takes into account that history of racial exclusion and oppression. Every individual in the United States has been shaped by the practices of racial differentiation, whether through categorizations of black or Oriental or Hispanic—or the default category of white. The key is that we live together cognizant of these histories, yet believing that what makes life interesting are the myriad of other differences and similarities that bind us all as human.

Race divides and race makes similarity. Some of the most telling differences, however, are not the blatant and obvious ones that so often lead people to generalization but those subtle variations between people who are seemingly alike. They promise us again and again that the wonder of humanity lies not in the discernment of patterns of either similarity or difference but in the infinite varieties of human experience.

AN EPITAPH

As Robert Park did for many of the people he came across in his extensive research travels, he became a mentor to Flora Belle Jan, the young Chinese American writer discovered during the Survey of Race Relations. Park arranged for her to attend the University of Chicago to study journalism. He not only housed her while she was in town but also took an active interest in her intellectual development, constantly sending books and articles for her to read. He had great hopes for Jan as a writer and as the kind of sophisticated observer that resulted from her unique status as a marginal man. She took his hopes to heart and tried to fulfill the ideal.

Unfortunately, Jan's marriage in 1926 to a China-born student, Charles Wang, and the subsequent birth of a son ended her career ambitions, and she never lived up to her own expectations or Park's. In 1932, she followed her husband to China, where she stayed for the next sixteen years. She marked the death of Robert Park in 1944 with the sad regret of a sense of failure:

> I was depressed by a letter from Mrs. Robert E. Park, who told me of Dr. Park's death. . . . The underlying reason for my depression was that I had not accomplished anything during his lifetime. He had expected so much of me and had hope that I would write something worthwhile, but here I am beginning all over again.[1]

In 1948, Flora Belle Jan finally returned to the United States, but she died two years later at the age of forty-three.

DRAMATIS PERSONAE

Romanzo Colfax Adams, b. 1868 in Wisconsin. Ph.D., Chicago, 1904. Studied economics at the University of Michigan before earning his Ph.D. in sociology at Chicago. Created sociology at the new University of Hawaii when he arrived from the University of Nevada in 1919 to teach economics and sociology. Eventually concentrated solely on sociology. Wrote extensively on race relations, particularly interracial marriage, in Hawaii, and was chair of the University of Hawaii's Department of Sociology. Created the Social Research Laboratory, which was named for him in 1955. Died in 1942.

Herbert Blumer, b. 1900. Famous theoretician of symbolic interaction. Wrote his dissertation ("Method in Social Psychology") at the University of Chicago in 1928, expanding upon Park and Mead's observations on collective behavior. Taught at Chicago from 1925 to 1952, when he went to Berkeley. Died in 1987.

Emory Stephen Bogardus, b. 1882 in Belvidere, Illinois. B.A., 1908; M.A., Northwestern, 1909; Ph.D., Chicago, 1911. Joined University of Southern California in 1911 and was the head of the Department of Sociology from 1915 to 1946. Had a great influence because of his interest in methodology and his advising of student research. One of the few Chicago researchers to study Filipino immigrants.

Ernest Watson Burgess, b. 1886 in Tilbury, Ontario. Grew up in Whitehall, Michigan. The son of an Anglican minister, Burgess was called the "first young sociologist" because he was the first Chicago sociologist to have come straight into professional sociology as a career. Received his Ph.D. from Chicago in 1913 and, after teaching at various other universities in the Midwest, joined the faculty at the University of Chicago in 1919, remaining there until his retirement in 1951. One of the most influential of the Chicago mentors, he was particularly interested in urban studies, the family, juvenile delinquency, and social disorganization. Died in 1966.

Bingham Dai, b. 1899 in China. Graduated from Saint John's University in China, 1923. Worked as a high school teacher and researcher on opium addiction in Shanghai and Nanking. Sent in 1929 on a Fukien Provincial Government scholarship to study at the University of Chicago in the Department of Education. Switched from education to sociology after taking a course on delinquency and personality taught by Park, in which Park had singled out Dai as an exceptional thinker. His master's thesis was "Glossolalia, or Speaking with Tongues" (M.A., Chicago, 1932) and his doctoral dissertation was "Opium Addiction in Chicago" (Ph.D., Chicago, 1937). Park advised his M.A. thesis, but Blumer became his Ph.D. adviser after Park retired from Chicago. Dai returned to China in 1935 to study at the Peking Union Medical College in psychiatry, but he fled to the United States because of the Japanese occupation. Upon the advice of Park, who was retired to Nashville at the time, Charles S. Johnson offered Dai a lectureship at Fisk University. Taught there during the war (1939–1943) before moving to Duke University as a clinical psychologist.

Ellsworth Faris, b. 1874 in Salem County, Tennessee. A former minister and missionary to the Belgian Congo, he came to Chicago in 1911 and completed his Ph.D. in 1914. When W. I. Thomas was forced to resign in 1918, Faris returned to Chicago to replace him.

Clarence Elmer Glick, b. 1906 in Columbus, Indiana. B.A., DePauw, 1927; M.A., Chicago, 1928. Spent summer of 1932 in Zhongshan, Guangdong Province, China. Married Doris Lorden (Ph.D. in sociology, University of Iowa) in 1935. Wrote his dissertation ("The Chinese Migrant in Hawaii: A Study in Accommodation"; Chicago, 1938) after having taught and done research in Hawaii. Taught at the University of Hawaii for the bulk of his career. A favorite student of Robert Park, he was also friends with Ching Chao Wu and Paul Siu while at Chicago.

Lucy Jen Huang, b. 1920 in Amoy, Fukien Province, China. M.A., Marshall, 1948. Her dissertation was "Dating and Courtship Innovations of Chinese Students in America" (Chicago, 1954). Taught at Boston University from 1957 to 1961, then joined Illinois State University in 1967.

Everett Cherrington Hughes, b. 1897 in Beaver, Ohio, the son of a Methodist minister. Married fellow Chicago student Helen MacGill in 1927. Received his Ph.D. from the University of Chicago in 1928. After teaching at MacGill University in Montreal, returned to Chicago to become a professor in 1938. One of Park's favorite students and one of the most influential researchers of race relations, the family, and the sociology of the workplace. Died in 1983.

Yukiko Kimura, b. 1903 in Yokohama, Japan. Graduated from the Ferris Presbyterian Mission College and came to the United States to study at Oberlin College in 1935, receiving an M.A. in religious education. Involved in the YWCA in Japan, Australia, New Zealand, and Hawaii from 1938 to 1944, assisting Japanese immigrant families. Kimura earned an M.A. at the University of Hawaii and was one of Andrew Lind's researchers. Did her primary research for her doctorate while in Hawaii during the war and while working as a kitchen helper at the Edgewater Beach Hotel during the summer of 1948 and the Mastercrafters' Clock and Radio Company in 1950 and 1951 (both places employed a large number of Issei in service jobs). After obtaining her Ph.D. from Chicago in 1952 (her dissertation was "A Comparative Study of Collective Adjustment of the Issei: The First Generation Japanese, in Hawaii and in the Mainland United States since Pearl Harbor"), Kimura returned to Hawaii and worked as a researcher at the Romanzo Adams Social Research Laboratory.

Beulah Ong Kwoh, b. 1923 in Stockton, California. B.A., Berkeley, 1944. Majored in English at Stockton Junior College before transferring to Berkeley. Worked as a YWCA secretary in San Francisco for a year before going to Chicago in 1945. Roomed with Rose Hum Lee in 1947. After receiving her M.A. in 1947 (her thesis was "American-Born Chinese College Graduates"), she taught in China for a year at Jinling Women's College in Nanking, where her husband was the school administrator, and then returned to the United States because of the civil war. Taught at community colleges while trying to earn a Ph.D. at UCLA but was unable to finish because of the needs of family. Became an actress after leaving academia.

Margaret M. Lam. A graduate student at the University of Hawaii, Lam was a researcher for Romanzo Adams's interracial marriage project. Heavily influenced by Park when he visited Hawaii, and on his and Andrew Lind's advice attended graduate school in Chicago in 1935. Returned to Hawaii and became a high school English teacher.

Forrest LaViolette, b. 1904. B.A., Reed College. Wrote "Some Problems Relating to the Concept of Culture," M.A., Chicago, 1934; and "Americans of Japanese Ancestry: A Study of Assimilation in the American Community," Ph.D., Chicago, 1946. Student of Herbert Blumer at Chicago. Taught at the University of Washington from 1936 to 1939. Lived with Frank Miyamoto in Roderick McKenzie's house while researching the Japanese immigrant community of Seattle. Both worked with Jesse Steiner. Joined MacGill University's sociology department after World War II and published a book in 1948, *The Canadian Japanese and World War II*, concerning Canada's internment of Japanese Canadians. Like many Chicago students studying internment who were not Japanese American, LaViolette worked for the War Relocation Authority during Japanese internment.

Rose Hum Lee, b. 1904 in Butte, Montana. B.S., Carnegie Tech, 1942; M.A., Chicago, 1943; Ph.D., Chicago, 1947. Entered college at the age of thirty-seven, after having spent ten years in China. Lee wrote her master's thesis ("Maternal and Child Health and Welfare Services in Canton China") in the School of Social Work and Administration at the University of Chicago. Her dissertation ("The Growth and Decline of Chinese Communities in the Rocky Mountain Region"), written under Ernest Burgess and Louis Wirth in the sociology department, was based mostly on her hometown of Butte. Lee began teaching at Roosevelt University in Chicago and was the chair of the sociology department from 1956 to 1961. Died in 1964.

Andrew William Lind, b. 1901 in Seattle, Washington. B.A., 1924; M.A., Washington, 1925, as a student of Roderick McKenzie. Student of Robert Park at Chicago. Attended Chicago from 1925 to 1927. Went to Hawaii in 1927 on Rockefeller grant for race relations research. Brought in by Romanzo Adams to apply concepts of human ecology to the various "races" in Hawaii. Earned his Chicago Ph.D. in 1931 for "Economic Succession and Racial Invasion in Hawaii." Became chair of Department of Sociology at the University of Hawaii after Romanzo Adams, as well as director of the Social Research Institute. During World War II, Lind studied the racial situation of the Japanese in Hawaii. Brought in many Chicago graduates (Clarence Glick and Bernhard Hormann, originally a junior high school teacher in Honolulu) and sent many of his students to Chicago for doctorates (Yukiko Kimura, George Yamamoto, Douglas Yamamura). Lind's wife, born Katherine E. Niles, was a graduate student at Chicago and received her M.A. in sociology in 1935. She also served as an editorial secretary for the *American Journal of Sociology*.

Doris M. Lorden (Glick), b. 1908 in northern Illinois. Received her B.A., M.A., and Ph.D. from the University of Iowa, where she worked with E. B. Reuter and Clyde Hart (both Chicago graduates). Went with Reuter to Hawaii in 1930 for a year, doing research on the Chinese in Hawaii. Received her Ph.D. from Iowa in 1932 (her dissertation was "The Chinese Hawaiian Girl"). In 1935 married Clarence Glick (who had a Ph.D. from Chicago), returning to Hawaii when he was hired to teach at the university.

Helen MacGill (Hughes), b. 1903 in Vancouver, British Columbia. M.A., Chicago, 1927; Ph.D., Chicago, 1940. Robert Park and his family become close friends with MacGill while they were in Vancouver for the Survey of Race Relations. While an undergraduate senior at the University of British Columbia, MacGill conducted research on the Chinese in Vancouver. Park brought her to Chicago with a fellowship and housed her while she was a student. MacGill later married Everett C. Hughes (who had a Ph.D. in sociology from Chicago). For seventeen years served as one of the senior editors of the *American Journal of Sociology*. Died in 1992.

Jitsuichi Masuoka, b. 1903 in Japan. Wrote "Race Attitudes of the Japanese People in Hawaii: A Study in Social Distance," M.A., Hawaii, 1931; and "The Westernization of the Japanese Family in Hawaii," Ph.D., Iowa, 1940. Moved to Hawaii in 1917 at the age of fourteen and worked on Maui sugar plantations. Went to Maui High School, where one of his teachers arranged for him to go to a Presbyterian college in Emporia, Kansas. Returned to Hawaii and worked for Andrew Lind on racial attitudes and social distance research. Worked with both Robert Park and E. B. Reuter while they were visiting the Race Relations Institute in Hawaii. Reuter brought him to Iowa. Was Bingham Dai's successor at Fisk University. Park gave him an upstairs room in his house; Masuoka was the Parks' chauffeur and was present when Park died in 1944. One of the editors of Robert Park's papers.

Roderick Duncan McKenzie, b. 1885 in Carmen, Manitoba. B.A., Manitoba, 1912; Ph.D., Chicago, 1921. Member of the Department of Sociology at the University of Washington from 1921 until 1930, when he left to become the head of the department at the University of Michigan. One of the main researchers during the survey. Along with Park, pioneered the concepts of human ecology. Wrote on the ecological succession of the Chinese and Japanese in the Seattle area. Died in 1940.

George Herbert Mead, b. 1863 in South Hadley, Massachusetts. Educated at Oberlin and Harvard, where he studied with William James and Josiah Royce, though he never obtained a doctorate. Joined the philosophy department at the University of Chicago in 1894 and remained until his death in 1931. Elaborated concepts of social psychology in his graduate seminars, which were published posthumously in an influential book based on his lecture notes, *Mind, Self, and Society* (1934). Chicago sociologists Herbert Blumer, Frank Miyamoto, and Tamotsu Shibutani all used Mead's writings in developing their theories of symbolic interaction. Died in 1931.

Shotaru Frank Miyamoto, b. 1912 in Seattle, Washington. B.A., Washington, 1936; wrote "Social Solidarity among the Japanese in Seattle," M.A., University of Washington, 1938. Head researcher for the Japanese Evacuation and Resettlement Study. Used notes taken during internment as a researcher for JERS at Tule Lake Internment Camp for his dissertation, "The Career of Intergroup Tensions: A Study of the Collective Adjustments of Evacuees to Crises at the Tule Lake Relocation Center" (Ph.D., Chicago, 1950). Taught at the University of Washington from 1945 until his retirement in 1980.

Setsuko Matsunaga Nishi, b. 1921 in Los Angeles, California. During the late 1940s researched her dissertation ("Japanese American Achievement in Chicago: A Cultural Response to Degradation") but for family reasons did not complete her Ph.D. in sociology until 1963. A student at USC when World War II began, she relocated to Saint Louis as a student at Washington University in the fall of 1942. She received her B.A. from Washington University in February 1944 and an M.A. in sociology in October 1944. Conducted a study on relocated Japanese Americans in Saint Louis and was asked to contribute to the Japanese Evacuation and Resettlement Study. Became a student at the University of Chicago in 1946. Worked with Horace Cayton, Louis Wirth, and Tamotsu Shibutani.

Robert Ezra Park, b. 1864 in Harveyville, Pennsylvania. Grew up in Red Wing, Minnesota. Attended the University of Michigan, then Harvard as a graduate student, receiving a Ph.D. in philosophy from the University of Heidelburg in 1893. Worked as director of public relations at Booker T. Washington's Tuskegee Institute (1905–1912). Joined Department of Sociology at the University of Chicago in 1913. Was a visiting professor at the University of Hawaii (1931–1933) after making numerous extended trips there since 1925 during travels to the Orient. Retired from the University of Chicago in 1933. At the invitation of his former student Charles S. Johnson, Park moved to Nashville, Tennessee, in 1936 and acted as visiting professor at Fisk University until his death in 1944.

Edward Byron Reuters, b. 1880 in rural Missouri. Received his M.A. from the University of Missouri (where he studied under Charles Ellwood [Ph.D., Chicago, 1899]). Reuters received his Ph.D. from the University of Chicago in 1919; his dissertation was "The Mulatto in the United States: A Sociological and Psychological Study." Worked with Robert Park at Chicago. Taught at the University of Iowa's Department of Sociology. Spent time in Hawaii for research and brought students Jitsuichi Masuoka and Doris Lorden to Iowa, both of whom worked on topics concerning Orientals in Hawaii.

Tamotsu Shibutani, b. 1920 in Stockton, California. B.A., Berkeley, 1942. Wrote "Rumors in a Crisis Situation," M.A., Chicago, 1944, and "The Circulation of Rumors as a Form of Collective Behavior," Ph.D., Chicago, 1948. Raised in a predominantly Irish-Italian neighborhood. Attended Stockton Junior College to study English before transferring to Berkeley and, after graduation, worked for the Japanese Evacuation and Relocation Study. Took a reading course with W. I. Thomas while at Berkeley; studied with Blumer, Wirth, and Hughes at Chicago. Drafted into the U.S. Army (1944–1946). Taught at Chicago from 1948 to 1951, with students such as Setsuko Nishi, Yukiko Kimura, and Eugene Uyeki, and then went to Berkeley (1951–1957). Finished his career from 1961 to 1991 at UC-Santa Barbara.

Paul Chan Pang Siu, b. 1906 in Toyshan district, Guangdong Province, China. The son of a Chinese laundryman, Siu worked as a social worker among Chinese laundry workers in Chicago during the 1930s, taking notes on what he saw and writing "The Chinese Laundryman: A Study of Social Isolation," for which he received his Chicago Ph.D. fifteen years later in 1953. Siu had great difficulty finding academic placement, even with the support of his adviser, Ernest Burgess. Eventually obtained a faculty position in 1959 at the Detroit Institute of Technology, retiring in 1972. Died in 1986.

William Carlson Smith, b. 1883. Graduated in 1907 from Grand Island College, Grand Island, Nebraska, and received his Ph.D. from Chicago in 1920. Performed extensive missionary work before attending the University of Chicago. Held various positions—high school principal, teacher, Red Cross worker, field-worker, and probation officer—before doing educational work in Assam, India, under the American Baptist Foreign Mission Society from 1912 to 1915. Smith used his experience in India for his doctoral dissertation, "Conflict and Fusion of Cultures as Typified by the Ao Nagas of India." Joined USC's Department of Sociology in 1919. During the Survey on Race Relations concentrated his research on second-generation Orientals and anti-Asian agitation in Los Angeles. Also conducted research on second-generation Orientals in Hawaii in 1927. Later became the head of the Department of Sociology at the University of Oregon, at Eugene.

Jesse Frederick Steiner, b. 1880. Before entering graduate school, spent seven years in Japan as a teacher in a mission college in Sendai. Robert Park supervised his dissertation, "The Japanese Invasion: A Study in the Psychology of Interracial Contacts," Ph.D., Chicago (Divinity School), 1917. Taught at the University of North Carolina before taking over Roderick McKenzie's job at the University of Washington in 1930 when McKenzie went to the University of Michigan. Remained at Washington until 1948 and was the chair of Department of Sociology when Frank Miyamoto and Forrest LaViolette conducted their research.

William Isaac Thomas, b. 1863 in Russell County, Virginia. Graduated in 1884 from the University of Tennessee, pursued graduate studies in Germany, and received Ph.D. from the University of Chicago in 1896, where he was already an instructor in sociology. Became a full professor in 1910 and brought Park to the department three years later. Pioneered the use of "social disorganization" and the "life history" as analytical categories. Forced to leave the University of Chicago in the same year because of a scandal but continued to be an important intellectual colleague and friend of Park. Died in 1947.

Eugene Shigemi Uyeki, b. 1926 in Seattle, Washington. B.A., Oberlin. Wrote "Public Opinion and Administration: A Case Study, the War Relocation Authority," M.A. Chicago, 1952; and "Process and Patterns of Nisei Adjustment to Chicago," Ph.D. Chicago, 1953. Although a sociology student, Uyeki used political science theories in writing his master's thesis. Later joined the faculty at Case Western Reserve University.

Louis Wirth, b. 1897 in Gemünden, Germany. Came to the United States in 1911 and entered the University of Chicago in 1914, completing his famous dissertation, "The Ghetto: A Study in Isolation," in 1925. Returned to Chicago as a full-time professor in 1931. One of the most important of the Chicago thinkers on urban studies and race relations until his death in 1952.

Ching-Chao Wu, b. 1901 in Anhui Province, China. Graduated from Tsinghua University in Peking before leaving to study at Chicago. Wrote "Chinese Immigration in the Pacific Area," M.A., Chicago, 1926; and "Chinatowns: A Study of Symbiosis and Assimilation," Ph.D., Chicago, 1928. Wu made extensive use of materials collected by the Survey of Race Relations in his dissertation. Returned to China after graduating from Chicago. Taught at the Department of Sociology at Jinling (later Nanking) University and then joined Tsinghua University in 1947. Prominent intellectual and adviser in both the Nationalist government during the 1930s and 1940s and the Communist Party during the 1950s. Criticized as a Rightist in 1957 and rehabilitated in 1964. Died in 1968.

NOTES

Preface

1. Many of the best works written by historians of U.S. and Asian American history have tended to focus on one of two concerns: how whites have understood, portrayed, and treated Asian Americans, or how Asian Americans have understood their own difficult lives in the United States. I have tried to unite both emphases in this book to show how the two are so inextricably linked that they cannot be understood apart. For decades, the professional discipline of U.S. historians has been pulled from both within and without by ethnic studies scholars, prodded to move away from analyses of race that only emphasize white ideas about people of color. By expanding beyond documentary sources that record only dominant white perspectives, Asian American studies, along with other ethnic studies movements, has led the struggle to open U.S. history to multiple voices, and must continue to retrieve the silenced stories of Asian Americans. At the same time, understanding the structures of white supremacy that have so thoroughly dominated Asian American history remains an integral part of any such project.

2. Edward Said, *Orientalism* (New York: Random House, 1978); idem, "Orientalism: An Afterword," *Raritan* 14, no. 3 (winter 1995): 32–60; idem, "Third World Intellectuals and Metropolitan Culture," *Raritan* 9, no. 3 (winter 1990): 27–51; idem, "Representing the Colonized: Anthropology's Interlocutors," *Critical Inquiry* 15, no. 2 (winter 1989): 205–226.

3. Historian Yuji Ichioka helped popularize the term "Asian American" in his call to rediscover the "buried past" of Asian American history. Yuji Ichioka et al., *A Buried Past: An Annotated Bibliography of the Japanese American Research Project* (Berkeley: University of California Press, 1974).

Introduction

1. Labels for people who can trace their ancestors back to Asia or the Pacific Ocean have changed through U.S. history, from "Oriental" and "Asiatic" to "Asian American." Another current term is "Asian Pacific Islanders." "Asian American" is still a useful label for many of the people who were formerly known as Orientals, yet its emphasis on Asian is seen to marginalize Pacific Islanders who are not from the continent of Asia. The most popular description of Asian American history has been Ronald Takaki, *Strangers from a Different Shore* (New York: Penguin, 1989). For race in American society, see Michael Omi and Howard Winant, *Racial Formation in the United States* (New York: Routledge, 1986). On whiteness as a social, legal, and economic category, see George Lipsitz, *The Possessive Investment in Whiteness* (Philadelphia: Temple University Press, 1998); Matthew Frye Jacobson, *Whiteness of a Different Color: European Immigrants and the Alchemy of Race* (Cambridge, Mass.: Harvard University Press, 1998); Tomás Almaguer, *Racial Fault Lines: The Historical Origins of White Supremacy in California* (Berkeley: University of California Press, 1994); David Roediger, *The Wages of Whiteness: Race and the Making of the American Working Class* (London: Verso, 1991); Alexander Saxton, *The Rise and Fall of the White Republic* (London: Verso, 1990); Virginia Dominguez, *White by Definition* (New Brunswick, N.J.: Rutgers University Press, 1986).

2. Richard Wright's foreword to St. Clair Drake and Horace Cayton, *Black Metropolis: A Study of Negro Life in a Northern City* (New York: Harcourt, Brace, 1945), i–xxxiv. Thanks to Andrew Abbot for suggesting this example. Richard Wright, *Native Son* (New York: Grosset and Dunlap, 1940).

3. On European Orientalism, see Edward Said, *Orientalism* (New York: Random House, 1978). On the defining role of Orientalism in American culture, see Robert G. Lee, *Orientals* (Philadelphia: Temple University Press, 1999); and John Kuo Wei Tchen, *New York before Chinatown: Orientalism and the Shaping of American Culture, 1776–1882* (Baltimore: Johns Hopkins University Press, 1999).

4. Roediger, *Wages of Whiteness*.

A Setting

1. Sucheng Chan, *Asian Americans: An Interpretive History* (Boston: Twayne, 1991), and Ronald Takaki, *Strangers from a Different Shore* (New York: Penguin, 1989) for anti-Asian agitation; Alexander Saxton, *The Indispensible Enemy: Labor and the Anti-Chinese Movement in California* (Berkeley: University of California Press, 1971) for the driving out of Chinese in the West.

2. Speech of Lou Guernsey, a Los Angeles attorney and prominent leader of anti-Japanese agitation in Hollywood during 1923 and 1924, quoted by William C. Smith in an unpublished paper. William Carlson Smith Papers, University of California, Santa Barbara (UCSB) Library, microfilmed from originals in the Robert Cantwell Papers, Special Collections, University of Oregon Library.

3. Alien Land Acts of California in 1913 and in 1920. Washington State also passed a law forbidding landownership by "aliens ineligible for citizenship" (mean-

ing Asians) in 1921. Roger Daniels, *Asian America* (Seattle: University of Washington Press, 1988), 138–147.

4. Sucheng Chan, "Exclusion of Chinese Women, 1870–1943," in *Entry Denied*, ed. Sucheng Chan (Philadelphia: Temple University Press, 1991), 95.

5. Chan, *Asian Americans*, 109; Yuji Ichioka, *Issei: The World of the First Generation Japanese Immigrants, 1885–1924* (New York: Free Press, 1988).

Chapter 1

1. Descriptions and quotations are from letters, J. Merle Davis to Robert E. Park, June 1 and June 5, 1924, J. Merle Davis Correspondence Files, Papers of the Survey of Race Relations, Hoover Institution, Stanford University (henceforth PSSR). Biographical information on J. Merle Davis from his correspondence and from his biography of his father, *Soldier Missionary: A Biography of Rev. Jerome D. Davis* (Boston: Pilgrim Press, 1916). On Flora Belle Jan, in particular her doubled difficulties as a woman of Chinese background, see Judy Yung's *Unbound Feet: A Social History of Chinese American Women in San Francisco* (Berkeley: University of California Press, 1995), and idem, "It is hard to be born a woman but hopeless to be born a Chinese": The Life and Times of Flora Belle Jan," *Frontiers* 18, no. 3 (1997): 66–91.

2. For the relationship between power and knowledge, see Michel Foucault, *The Order of Things: An Archaelogy of the Human Sciences* (New York: Vintage, 1973); idem, *The History of Sexuality, Volumes One and Two* (New York: Vintage, 1990).

3. At that time the institute was also funding Robert and Helen Lynd's research in Muncie, Indiana, which would result in their famous work *Middletown: A Study in American Culture* (New York: Harcourt Brace Jovanovich, 1929).

4. Elmer Clarence Sandmeyer, *The Anti-Chinese Movement in California* (Urbana: University of Illinois, 1939), 35–36. See also Wesley Woo, "Protestant Work among the Chinese in the San Francisco Bay Area, 1850–1920" (Ph.D. diss., Graduate Theological Union, Berkeley, 1983).

5. Sidney Gulick, *The American Japanese Problem* (New York: Scribner's, 1914). Gulick also wrote a book emphasizing the danger to American ideals that mistreatment of the Chinese and Japanese presented: Gulick, *American Democracy and Asiatic Citizenship* (New York: Scribner's, 1918). Sandra C. Taylor, *Advocate of Understanding: Sidney Gulick and the Search for Peace with Japan* (Kent, Ohio: Kent State University Press, 1984).

6. Boxes 11–14, PSRR. Surveys had become a popular research and social reform device at the time, particularly after the Pittsburgh Survey, carried out between 1909 and 1914, which became a model for reform-minded research. Paul Kellogg Papers and Papers of the YMCA International, Social Welfare Archives, University of Minnesota.

7. Box 11, PSRR. The institute was to pay $30,000 of the cost of the survey, and it was hoped that private fund-raising on the West Coast would cover the other $25,000. No funds were to be taken from Japanese or Chinese organizations in the United States.

8. "This survey will . . . set a precedent for dealing with the whole terrific race question. It will also, Galen, be . . . an original contribution, to the whole question of approaching any serious problem on which opinions differ." George Gleason to Galen Fisher, May 17, 1923, Gleason Correspondence Files, Box 11, PSRR.

9. Letters between Merle Davis, George Gleason, Hugo Guy, and Galen Fisher, in Davis Correspondence Files, Box 11, PSRR.

10. Gleason to Fisher, April 20, 1923, Davis Correspondence Files, Box 11, PSRR.

11. Eliot Grinnel Mears, "The Survey of Race Relations," *Stanford Illustrated Review* (April 1925); reprint in Box 5, PSRR.

12. The best study of nineteenth-century American nativism remains John Higham, *Strangers in the Land: Patterns of American Nativism, 1860–1925* (New Brunswick, N.J.: Rutgers University Press, 1955). For discussions of how whiteness was constructed, see Alexander Saxton, *The Rise and Fall of the White Republic* (London: Verso, 1990); David Roediger, *The Wages of Whiteness: Race and the Making of the American Working Class* (London: Verso, 1991); and Ronald Takaki, *Iron Cages: Race and Culture in Nineteenth-Century America* (New York: Knopf, 1979). On the images of the Orient that Americans connected to the Chinese, see Stuart Creighton Miller, *The Unwelcome Immigrant: The American Image of the Chinese, 1785–1882* (Berkeley: University of California Press, 1969). On race as both the catalyst and the failure of labor organizing, see David Montgomery, *The Fall of the House of Labor* (New York: Cambridge University Press, 1987); Nell Painter, *Standing at Armageddon: United States, 1877–1919* (New York: Norton, 1987).

13. The Gentlemen's Agreement in 1907 between Japan and the United States had specifically been named to give the appearance of a voluntary act made by the Japanese to limit their emigration to the United States. Atypical in diplomatic relations between Western and Asian powers, Japan's status had been won by victory over a European nation in the Russo-Japanese War in 1904. Anti-Japanese legislation discussed in Roger Daniels, *Asian America* (Seattle: University of Washington Press, 1988); Jacobus tenBroek, Edward N. Barnhart, and Floyd Matson, *Prejudice, War and the Constitution: Causes and Consequences of the Evacuation of the Japanese Americans in World War II* (Berkeley: University of California Press, 1954). For anti-Chinese legislation, see Charles J. McClain, *In Search of Equality: The Chinese Struggle against Discrimination in Nineteenth-Century America* (Berkeley: University of California Press, 1994); Sucheng Chan, ed., *Entry Denied* (Philadelphia: Temple University Press, 1991).

14. One labor leader responded to Davis's suggestion for an impartial research survey with the accusation: "I know who you are and where you come from. You are from Japan and a spy of the Mikado. . . . This Survey is loaded with religion and capital. Who's going to pay for it anyway? Capital. The capitalists will pay for it and the church will run it and either way labor will get flimflammed." Although sounding paranoid, the accusation had some truth to it: Davis was from Japan, and the money did come from the Rockefeller Foundation. Winifred Raushenbush, *Robert E. Park: Biography of a Sociologist* (Durham, N.C.: Duke University Press, 1979), 108 (original found in the PSRR).

15. There were fewer than ten thousand of each of these three groups—East Indians, Koreans, Filipinos—in the United States during the mid-1920s, compared with almost one hundred thousand each of Chinese Americans and Japanese Americans.

16. Davis Correspondence, Box 11, PSRR. "Asiatic" and "Oriental" could also refer to different conglomerations of people. Emory Bogardus referred in 1919 to "Asiatic immigrants" by including Armenians and Syrians from "Western Asia" together with Chinese and Japanese from "Eastern Asia." Five years later, he was referring more specifically to Chinese and Japanese as "Oriental immigrants." Emory Bogardus, *Essentials of Americanization* (Los Angeles: University of Southern California Press, 2d ed., 1920), 201.

17. In his justification for the survey, Gleason explained the duty of returned missionaries who were on the West Coast: "It is up to us in this country to find the right way to handle the Japanese problems out here. To do this requires first of all more accurate knowledge than we now possess. After this knowledge is secured, political action and Christian Americanization efforts must follow." Gleason to Davis, October 28, 1922, Box 11, PSRR.

18. Some of the missionaries were quite pessimistic about the potential success of the survey in ameliorating this ill treatment of Orientals. Harvey H. Guy of Berkeley, California, one of the returned missionaries from Japan, referred to the impending exclusion legislation against Asians using the language of a pathologist: "The case looks very bad. As a friend of mine said about the Survey, it looks like our investigations will be too late, the diagnosis has become an autopsy. But . . . we may learn something even from a corpse, so we must go on with the Survey." Guy to Davis, November 26, 1923, Box 11, PSRR.

19. Gulick, *American Japanese Problem*, 220.

20. Davis Correspondence, Davis to Park, June 1, 1924, Box 11, PSRR.

21. David Starr Jordan, president of Stanford, was an outspoken defender of Chinese and Japanese immigrants. There had been a serious controversy at the turn of the century when E. A. Ross, a prominent social scientist, had been fired by Leland Stanford's widow because of his open stand against Chinese and Japanese labor. Stanford, though himself opposed to large-scale settlement of the West Coast by Asians, had made his fortune by using Chinese workers to build his railroads during the 1860s.

22. "We are not only promoting the idea of a survey of race relations, but we are also doing what may eventually prove the bigger thing—promoting the principle of an unbiased and scientific united approach, by all factions interested, to a controversial problem." Gleason to Davis, March 11, 1924, Box 11, PSRR. In public relations releases to the press, the special roles of the universities and research experts were touted repeatedly: "Educators here believe that the race relations survey meeting has been one of the most important gatherings in many years that the Pacific Coast has seen. The Survey, it is believed, has thrown more real light on the Asiatic situation, as it affects the Coast states, than has any other gathering in years. Educated persons experience a sense of relief when they learn of any endeavors, entirely divorced from legislative programs or special formu-

las, which center about the greatness of fact." *San Francisco Bulletin*, March 26, 1925.

23. *Chicago Daily News*, March 23, 1925.

24. E. A. Ross, *Social Control* (New York: Macmillan, 1901), extolled social science as a tool of social reform. He was also one of the sociologists with the most hierarchical conceptions of race. For the rise of sociology as a discipline, see Mary Furner, *Advocacy and Objectivity: A Crisis in the Professionalization of American Social Science, 1865–1905* (Lexington: University of Kentucky Press, 1975); and Dorothy Ross, *The Origins of American Social Science* (Cambridge: Cambridge University Press, 1991).

25. The enlightenment project of American social reformers at the turn of the century owed much to the eighteenth-century European Enlightenment, which spawned the notion of social science, but its alliance with organized religion differed markedly from the Enlightenment of Voltaire and Denis Diderot. The American social scientists scoured the European traditions for antecedents to their fledgling social science and found the most conducive father figures in the Scottish Enlightenment: Adam Smith and Adam Ferguson were much less anticlerical than the French philosophes. For the rise of the "science of human society," see Peter Gay, *The Enlightenment: An Interpretation*, Vol. 2, *The Science of Freedom* (New York: Vintage, 1969). In contrast, see Carl Becker, *The Heavenly City of the Eighteenth-Century Philosophers* (New Haven, Conn.: Yale University Press, 1932).

26. Chicago sociologist Ellsworth Faris was a former missionary and remained an ordained minister, and both Ernest Burgess and W. I. Thomas were the sons of ministers. Robert Park was a member of the church of Edward Scribner Ames, a pragmatist philosopher at the University of Chicago and a prominent minister of the Social Gospel. Both Albion Small and Charles Henderson, early members of the Chicago department, saw sociology as a science in the service of solving social problems, and the Department of Sociology was an important ally of the School of Social Work and Administration, which was housed across the Midway from sociology's Harper Hall. Ernest Burgess and Louis Wirth both had close connections to the social workers at the school founded by Edith Abbot and Sophonisbia Breckenridge, a reflection of their deep interest in immigrant adjustments. Perhaps the most famous social work institution with which social scientists at Chicago became associated was Jane Addams's Hull House Settlement. See Robert E. L. Faris, *Chicago Sociology, 1920–1932* (San Francisco: Chandler, 1967), for the missionary background of Chicago sociology. Robert Faris was the son of Ellsworth Faris and a sociology student and eventually a professor at Chicago. Author's interview with Robert E. L. Faris, Seattle, January 1993. For general histories of Chicago sociology, see Andrew Abbot, *Department and Discipline* (Chicago: University of Chicago Press, 1999); Barbara Ballis Lal, *The Romance of Culture in an Urban Civilization: Robert E. Park on Race and Ethnic Relations in Cities* (London: Routledge, 1990); Martin Bulmer, *The Chicago School of Sociology: Institutionalization, Diversity, and the Rise of Sociological Research* (Chicago: University of Chicago Press, 1984); Lester R. Kurtz, *Evaluating Chicago Sociology: A Guide to the Literature, with an Annotated Bibliography* (Chicago: University of Chicago Press, 1984); J. David Lewis and Richard Smith, *American Sociology and Pragmatism: Mead, Chicago, Sociology*,

and Symbolic Interaction (Chicago: University of Chicago Press, 1980); Fred H. Matthews, *Quest for an American Sociology: Robert E. Park and the Chicago School* (Montreal: McGill University Press, 1977).

27. Emory Bogardus, *A History of Sociology at the University of Southern California* (Los Angeles: University of Southern California Press, 1972), and his autobiography, *Much Have I Learned* (Los Angeles: University of Southern California Press, 1962); quotation on page 27. Bogardus also published two volumes of Shakespearean sonnets he had written throughout his life and travels: *The Traveller* (1956) and *The Explorer* (1961).

28. Smith Papers, UCSB Library.

29. Raushenbush, *Robert E. Park*, 97. See Matthews, *Quest for an American Sociology*, 79–189, for a discussion of later attacks on Park's theories. See Paul Takagi, "The Myth of Assimilation in American Life," *Amerasia Journal* 2 (fall 1973): 149–159, for an attack on Park from the point of view of the Asian American movement of the 1970s.

30. See Matthews, *Quest for an American Sociology*, 112–115, for an introduction to the Survey of Race Relations; Stow Persons, *Ethnic Studies at Chicago, 1905–45* (Urbana: University of Illinois Press, 1987), 68–72. Fred Wacker, *Ethnicity, Pluralism, and Race: Race Relations Theory in America before Myrdal* (Westport, Conn.: Greenwood Press, 1983), which unfortunately does not mention Asians or Asian Americans. John Madge, *The Origins of Scientific Sociology* (Glencoe, Ill.: Free Press, 1962); Stanford Lyman, *Militarism, Imperialism, and Racial Accommodation: An Analysis and Interpretation of the Early Writings of Robert. E. Park* (Fayetteville: University of Arkansas Press, 1992).

31. George Gleason remarked on how he was forced to use his YMCA and church contacts to do much of the research for the survey in southern California because "Dr. Bogardus' work is largely confined to the university, and Dr. Smith's largely to the city and the immediate vicinity." Gleason to Davis, September 2, 1924, Box 11, PSRR.

32. Davis to Park, June 5, 1924, Box 11, PSRR.

33. Park was particularly derisive of Davis's and the other ministers' attempts to network. These efforts to foster communication, produce harmony, and minimize misunderstandings and conflict were an essential part of the missionaries' goals. To Park, they were a waste of time. Davis wrote about how Park took "another shot at our 'over organization.' Since his arrival here in January he has lost no opportunity to ridicule and deplore what he calls the absurd amount of machinery which we have set up on this Coast for carrying on the Survey." Park believed that only a handful of expert researchers was necessary for his purposes. Davis to Fisher, March 24, 1924, Davis Correspondence, Box 11, PSRR.

34. Harvey Guy, one of the prominent returned missionaries, was particularly put off by Park's disdain for reformers, and more than once Davis was required to convince Guy to remain committed to the survey. Harvey Hugo Guy Correspondence Folder, Box 11, PSRR.

35. Because the Philippines were forcibly annexed by the United States in 1898, Filipinos could move much more freely between the Philippines, Hawaii,

and the mainland United States as wards or nationals of the United States, and particularly after 1924 they became a major labor source to replace the supply of other Asian workers cut off by exclusionary acts. South Asian migrants, mostly of the Sikh faith from the Punjab region of India, tended to migrate to dominions of the British Empire such as Hong Kong, Australia, and Canada. The few who settled in the United States mostly came through Canada and Hong Kong. Joan Jenson, *Passage from India: Asian Indian Immigrants in North America* (New Haven, Conn.: Yale University Press, 1988); Karen Leonard, *The South Asian Americans* (Westport, Conn.: Greenwood Press, 1997); idem, *Making Ethnic Choices: California's Punjabi Mexican Americans* (Philadelphia: Temple University Press, 1992).

Chapter 2

1. Robert E. L. Faris, *Chicago Sociology, 1920–1932* (San Francisco: Chandler, 1967). In 1924, the department's teaching professors were Robert Park, Ellsworth Faris, Ernest Burgess, an aging Albion Small, George Herbert Mead from philosophy, and several anthropologists, including Ralph Linton, Edward Sapir, and Fay-Cooper Cole, who would become chairman of the anthropology department when it split off in 1929.

2. Emory Bogardus, *Much Have I Learned* (Los Angeles: University of Southern California Press, 1972), 40.

3. Clarence Glick, one of Park's dearest students in the 1920s, tells how Park used to recount tales of running away from home to see the world. Interview with Clarence and Doris Glick, August 29, 1993. See Winifred Raushenbush, *Robert E. Park: Biography of a Sociologist* (Durham, N.C.: Duke University Press, 1979), 1–14, for a description of Park's childhood in Red Wing.

4. For a critique of the sociologists' descriptions of Chicago as a flawed literary vision, see Eugene Rochberg-Halton, "Life, Literature, and Sociology in Turn-of-the-Century Chicago," in *Consuming Visions*, ed. Simon Bronner (New York: Norton, 1989), 311–338.

5. For descriptions of urbanization, see Howard Chudacoff and Judith Smith, *The Evolution of American Urban Society*, 3d ed. (Englewood Cliffs, N.J.: Prentice-Hall, 1988); Howard Chudacoff, *Mobile Americans* (New York: Oxford University Press, 1972); Eric Monkkonen, *America Becomes Urban: The Development of U.S. Cities and Towns, 1780–1980* (Berkeley: University of California Press, 1988); and Sam Bass Warner, *The Urban Wilderness: A History of the American City* (New York: Harper and Row, 1972); see also Thomas Bender, *Community and Social Change in America* (Baltimore: Johns Hopkins University Press, 1978), on how American social thinkers decried the breakdown of social ties and community which gesellschaft represented.

6. The phrase is borrowed from Robert A. Heinlein's 1961 novel, *Stranger in a Strange Land* (New York: Putnam, 1961).

7. E. E. Evans-Pritchard, *Witchcraft, Oracles, and Magic among the Azande* (Oxford: Clarendon Press, 1937), based on fieldwork done in the Sudan during the 1920s; and Bronislaw Malinowski, *Argonauts of the Western Pacific* (New York:

E. P. Dutton, 1922). For critical approaches to narrative in ethnography, see James Clifford and George Marcus, eds., *Writing Culture: The Poetics and Politics of Ethnography* (Berkeley: University of California Press, 1986); James Clifford, *The Predicament of Culture: Twentieth-Century Ethnography, Literature, and Art* (Cambridge, Mass.: Harvard University Press, 1988). See also George Stocking Jr., *Victorian Anthropology* (New York: Free Press, 1987).

8. Raushenbush, address to Tentative Findings Conference of the Survey of Race Relations, March 21–26, 1925, Findings Conference Folder, PSRR. Father and daughter spelled their family names differently. Winifred Raushenbush was also the mother and grandmother of pragmatist philosophers James Rorty and Richard Rorty.

9. For instance, the narrative device contained in Baron de Montesquieu's eighteenth-century novel *Lettres Persanes* (Persian letters), where an imaginary Persian describes European society from the point of view of a stranger unfamiliar with European customs. Montesquieu also wrote *L'Esprit des lois* (The spirit of the laws), published in 1748, considered by many sociologists as one of the first works of social science. Both were forms of travelogue, the first of an imagined outsider to one's own society, and the other a comparative survey of all societies based on travelers' accounts.

10. See M. H. Abrams, *The Mirror and the Lamp: Romantic Theory and the Critical Tradition* (New York: Oxford University Press, 1953); idem, *Natural Supernaturalism: Tradition and Revolution in Romantic Literature* (New York: Norton, 1971), for discussions of Romantic aesthetics concerning the strange.

11. Full quotation: "If wandering, considered as the liberation from every given point in space, is the conceptual opposite to fixation at such a point, then surely the sociological form of 'the stranger' presents the union of both of these specifications. It discloses, indeed, the fact that relations to space are only, on the one hand, the condition, and, on the other hand, the symbol, of relations to men. The stranger is not taken here, therefore, in the sense frequently employed, of the wanderer who comes today and goes tomorrow, but rather of the man who comes today and stays tomorrow, the potential wanderer, so to speak, who, although he has gone no further, has not quite got over the freedom of coming and going. He is fixed within a certain spatial circle, but his position within it is peculiarly determined by the fact that he does not belong in it from the first, that he brings qualities into it that are not, and cannot be, native to it." Passage translated by Park from Georg Simmel's *Soziologie* (Leipzig: Duncker und Humblot, 1908), 685–691; found in Robert E. Park and Ernest W. Burgess, *Introduction to the Science of Sociology* (Chicago: University of Chicago Press, 1921), 322. Philosophy and social science as a branch of philosophy were considered by most educated elites to be at their highest levels of development in Germany, and before World War I many Chicago sociologists went there to study. W.E.B. Du Bois had studied in Germany. For the fascination of American intellectuals with German social science, see Daniel T. Rodgers, *Atlantic Crossings: Social Politics in a Progressive Age* (Cambridge, Mass.: Harvard University Press, 1998).

12. On the use of context, see Dominick LaCapra, *Rethinking Intellectual History: Texts, Contexts, Language* (Ithaca, N.Y.: Cornell University Press, 1983), 55.

13. Raushenbush, *Robert E. Park*, 57.

14. Robert Park and Herbert Miller, *Old World Traits Transplanted* (New York: Harper, 1921). The book had been commissioned by the Carnegie Corporation as part of a series on Americanization. Park was called in when his friend Miller, the head of sociology at Oberlin, was unable to finish the project. In the end, the book was mostly researched and written by William I. Thomas, whose contributions remained anonymous because of a scandal in 1918. Raushenbush, *Robert E. Park*, 88. William I. Thomas and Florian Znaniecki, *The Polish Peasant in Europe and America*, 4 vols. (Chicago: University of Chicago Press, 1918–1920).

15. Horace Kallen, *Culture and Democracy in the United States: Studies in the Group Psychology of the American Peoples* (New York: Boni and Liveright, 1924; reprint, New York: Arno Press, 1970), containing his famous essay "Democracy and the Melting Pot," which appeared in two parts in the *Nation* in 1915. David Hollinger, "How Wide the Circle of 'We'? American Intellectuals and the Problem of the Ethnos since World War II," *American Historical Review* 98 (April 1993): 317–338.

16. All information on Asian immigrants came from the U.S. Immigration Commission and from H. A. Millis's *The Japanese Problem in the United States*, a study commissioned by Sidney Gulick and the Federal Council of Churches of Christ and published in 1915. Raushenbush states that Park had spent a month in 1918 on the West Coast "interviewing Orientals" (108), but nothing from this trip seems to have had any impact on the book. Raushenbush, *Robert E. Park*, 89. The strong influence of eastern European immigration on the production of a normative model of American immigration in general, especially conceptions of ethnicity and ethnic community, was to continue into Oscar Handlin's classic immigration history, *The Uprooted: The Epic Story of the Great Migrations That Made the American People* (New York: Macmillan, 1951).

17. Davis quoted Park as saying: "My idea of the report on this Survey is to get out a volume very similar to 'Old World Traits Transplanted.' I expect to handle the Pacific Coast as the racial frontier of the two races and show the factors that limit and condition the mingling of the two races as they are living here side by side." Davis to Fisher, April 9, 1924, Box 13, PSRR.

18. Park and Burgess, *Introduction to the Science of Sociology*, 252–254, 622. Original quotation from Park's introduction to Jesse Frederick Steiner, *The Japanese Invasion: A Study in the Psychology of Inter-racial Contacts* (Chicago: A. C. McClurg, 1917). Steiner's book was adapted from his 1914 Ph.D. dissertation.

19. Full quotation: "Analogies made between Orientals on the Pacific Coast and Negroes in the Southern States fail to provide the desired clues because of the marked points of difference, among which may be mentioned: eligibility to citizenship, social status, language difficulties, organization, industry, thrift, attitude towards women, pride, psychology, and human geography." Mears paper, "California's Attitude towards the Oriental," page 2, Box 19, PSRR.

20. Park and Burgess, *Introduction to the Science of Sociology*, 619.

21. Park's colleague in the philosophy department, George Herbert Mead, was the most important theorist of social psychology at Chicago, and Park applied many of Mead's insights in his description of race psychology.

22. Park and Burgess, *Introduction to the Science of Sociology*, 761. The quotation was from Robert Park, "Racial Assimilation in Secondary Groups," *Publications of the American Sociological Society* 8 (1914): 66–72.

23. Raushenbush, *Robert E. Park*, 113.

24. Ibid., 63. After his retirement from Chicago in 1933, at the age of sixty-nine, Park followed his friend and former student Charles S. Johnson to Fisk University, teaching sociology and race relations without remuneration. He also donated his entire collection of academic books and research to Fisk for use in its library. Robert Park Papers, Fisk University Special Collections, Nashville, Tennessee.

25. For example, in the work of Ching Chao Wu, one of the handful of Asian sociology students at the University of Chicago at the time of the survey, there is a marked difference between his master's thesis, completed in 1926, and his doctoral dissertation, completed in 1928. The master's thesis contained arguments about the relation of climate and geography to racial and cultural traits, an emphasis on physical environment as cause of cultural difference that was different from biological race theories but nothing like the outlook of Park and Thomas. The ideas of geographers such as Ellsworth Huntington and Ellen Semple, who argued for the impact of geography on human development, were strong in Wu's early work, but by the time of his dissertation, "Chinatowns: A Study of Symbiosis and Assimilation," Wu was squarely in the Park tradition of social interaction theory, with cultural differences being wholly dependent on social causes, and with environment restricted to the social world. For a recent book in the Huntington tradition of analyzing the environmental effects of geography on social development, see Jared Diamond, *Guns, Germs, and Steel: The Fates of Human Societies* (New York: Norton, 1997).

26. Henry Pratt Fairchild, *Immigration, A World Movement, and Its Significance* (New York: Macmillan, 1913); idem, *The Melting-Pot Mistake* (Boston: Little, Brown, 1926). On Francis Galton, see Carl Degler, *In Search of Human Nature* (Oxford: Oxford University Press, 1991), 41; Robert C. Bannister, *Social Darwinism: Science and Myth in Anglo-American Social Thought* (Philadelphia: Temple University Press, 1979); George W. Stocking Jr., *Race, Culture and Evolution* (New York: Free Press, 1968); and idem, "American Social Scientists and Race Theory: 1890–1915" (Ph. D. diss., University of Pennsylvania, 1960) for rhetorical power of appeals to Darwin.

27. George W. Stocking Jr., ed., *The Shaping of American Anthropology, 1883–1911: A Franz Boas Reader* (New York: Basic Books, 1974); Franz Boas, *The Mind of Primitive Man* (1911; Westport, Conn.: Greenwood Press, 1963); and for Boas on the Negro Problem around the time of the Survey of Race Relations, "The Problem of the American Negro," *Yale Review* 10 (January 1921): 392. Degler, *In Search of Human Nature*, 89. W. I. Thomas and his Chicago colleague Mead had come to similar conclusions about race, and Thomas's *Source Book for Social Origins* (Chicago: University of Chicago Press, 1909), required reading for all Chicago sociology students, was remarkably similar to Boas's *Mind of Primitive Man* in its arguments against the inferiority of certain races.

28. William Smith, "The Ao Naga of India: Conflict and Fusion of Cultures" (Ph.D. diss., University of Chicago, 1920). Course on eugenics listed in the William C. Smith Papers. Although sociologists did not believe in racial inferiority based on biological or mental grounds, they often held opinions about the hierarchy of cultural attainments. Like some anthropologists, many believed in the progress of civilization (Progressive reform entailed the idea that improvement in society and civilization was attainable) and considered some forms of cultural and civilizational achievement superior to others. Stow Persons argues that E. B. Reuters, one of Park's foremost students, underwent a long transformation from his early views on the inferiority of Negro culture. All the sociologists' opinions about race and culture were in great flux during the early years of their interest in race relations. Persons, *Ethnic Studies at Chicago*, 111.

Chapter 3

1. The recent hire at USC of Earle Fiske Young, a mapping expert who had just received his Ph.D. from Chicago for his 1924 dissertation, "Race Prejudice," solidified the hold of Chicago-trained methodology in urban studies of Los Angeles. On the Los Angeles research program, see Emory Bogardus, ed., *Graduate Studies in a World Reborn* (Los Angeles: University of California Press, 1945).

2. For histories of racial segregation in Los Angeles and Seattle, see Quintard Taylor, *In Search of the Racial Frontier* (New York: Norton, 1998); idem, *The Forging of a Black Community* (Seattle: University of Washington Press, 1994); Robert D. Bullard, J. Eugene Grigsby, and Charles Lee, eds., *Residential Apartheid: The American Legacy* (Los Angeles: Center of Afro-American Studies Publications, 1994); Keith E. Collins, *Black Los Angeles* (Los Angeles: Century Twenty One Publishing, 1978). For relations between African Americans and Asian Americans in Los Angeles, see Kariann Yokota, "From Little Tokyo to Bronzeville and Back" (master's thesis, UCLA, 1996).

3. From Roderick McKenzie, "Movement and the Ability to Live," Proceedings of the Institute of International Relations, 1926; reprinted in McKenzie, *On Human Ecology*, edited and with an introduction by Amos Hawley (Chicago: University of Chicago Press, 1968), 134.

4. Roderick McKenzie, "Spatial Distance and Community Organization Pattern," *Social Forces* 5 (June 1927): 623–638; idem, "The Concept of Dominance and World-Organization," *American Journal of Sociology* 33 (July 1927): 28–42; idem, "Spatial Distance," *Sociology and Social Research* 13 (July 1929): 536–544; all reprinted in McKenzie, *On Human Ecology*.

5. William I. Thomas, "The Significance of the Orient for the Occident," *American Journal of Sociology* 13 (May 1908): 729.

6. McKenzie, "Movement and the Ability to Live," 135.

7. For the history of stages theory of civilization in social science, see Ronald L. Meek, *Social Science and the Ignoble Savage* (Cambridge: Cambridge University Press, 1976).

8. Frederick Jackson Turner, "The Significance of the Frontier in American History" (paper presented at the meeting of the American Historical Association, Chicago, July 12, 1893); reprinted in Turner, *The Frontier in American History* (New York: Henry Holt, 1920). Progressive historian Turner had argued that the frontier had been pivotal in the history of America and, by extension, of the world. Speaking in the same year as the founding of the University of Chicago, Turner marked an intellectual fascination with the American West as a zone of contact, the boundary between untamed savagery and stagnant European civilization that produced unique American characteristics.

9. Robert Park, "The Concept of Social Distance," *Journal of Applied Sociology* 8 (1924): 340.

10. Park to Bogardus, August 18, 1924, Folder 14, Box 6, Robert E. Park Papers, Regenstein Special Collections, University of Chicago.

11. Emory Bogardus, "Social Distance: A Measuring Stick Gaging Racial Antipathies on the Coast—and Elsewhere," *Survey Graphic* 56 (May 1926): 169. For original questionnaires from the survey, see Emory Bogardus, *The New Social Research* (Los Angeles: Jesse Ray Miller, 1926), 200–218.

12. Bogardus, "Social Distance," 170.

13. It is questionable what was gained by taking the arithmetic mean to two decimal places. See Theodore Porter, *Trust in Numbers* (Princeton, N.J.: Princeton University Press, 1995), for a discussion of statistical truth. Within marketing surveys, political polling, and other developments of early attitude surveys, such calculations of subjective feeling not only have become instrumental and ubiquitous but also have come to define our social lives.

14. Bogardus, "Social Distance," 210. Bogardus was a prolific writer and an amazingly productive research director, but he never achieved the reknown of Park or McKenzie as a theorist. He once wrote an essay about "social distance in Shakespeare," an intellectual exercise that was not quite as ambitious as it might first appear. The article's interesting, though limited, insights could be connected in some way to the two autobiographical collections in Shakespearean sonnet form that Bogardus also published: in all of them, the formula of applying a structured form or theory to interpret social phenomena revealed its greatest strengths (methodological rigor, new insights, efficient production of work) and its greatest weaknesses (a loss of nuance and occasional inapt applications). Emory Bogardus, "Social Distance in Shakespeare," *Sociology and Social Research* 18 (January 1933): 58–66.

15. Robert Park, "Our Racial Frontier on the Pacific," *Survey Graphic* 56 (May 1926): 196.

16. Map is from Bogardus, *New Social Research*, 37.

17. Numbers from 1940 U.S. Census. Judy Yung, *Unbound Feet: A Social History of Chinese American Women in San Francisco* (Berkeley: University of California Press, 1995), 303; and Sucheng Chan, "Exclusion of Chinese Women, 1870–1943," in *Entry Denied*, ed. Sucheng Chan (Philadelphia: Temple University Press, 1991), 95. For a study of the transnational nature of these Chinese American fami-

lies, see Madeline Hsu's forthcoming book, *Dreaming of Gold, Dreaming of Home*, based on her dissertation, "'Living Abroad and Faring Well'": Migration and Transnationalism in Taishan County, Guangdong, 1904–1939" (Ph. D. diss., Yale University, 1996).

18. According to a newspaper story covering the wedding in the *San Francisco Chronicle* on Sunday, June 20, 1897 (p. 20), Howse was a "special student" in history at Stanford and the daughter of a Palo Alto billiard hall operator named Horace Howse. The article was based on the original dispatch from the *Denver Rocky Mountain News* (p. 7) published on the same day. Walter Fong was respected enough that when someone attacked Emma Fong by saying that she had disgraced herself, David Starr Jordan, president of Stanford University, defended her by saying that anyone should be honored to have Walter Fong as a husband. Around 7.5 percent of San Francisco Chinese men in 1900 were professionals. Yung, *Unbound Feet*, 301.

19. Yung, *Unbound Feet*, 29; Paul R. Spickard, *Mixed Blood* (Madison: University of Wisconsin Press, 1989); Dick Megumi Ogumi, "Asians and California's Anti-miscegenation Laws," in *Asian and Pacific American Experiences: Women's Perspectives*, ed. Nobuya Tsuchida (Minneapolis: Asian/Pacific American Learning Resource Center and General College, University of Minnesota, 1982), 6. California's law remained in effect until after World War II. Such punitive "anti-miscegenation" laws were the embodiments of a widespread abhorrence among both whites and Asian immigrants at the thought of interracial marriage—the immigrants, however, were not making the laws. Chan, "Exclusion of Chinese Women," 128–129, on the effects of the Cable Act.

20. For examples of stories of interracial love and marriage, see Major Documents 222, 223, and 224, Box 28, PSRR.

21. The story was published in the *San Francisco Bulletin* in installments from May 24, 1922, to June 14, 1922. Copies were collected by the survey in 1923 as Major Document 53, Box 24, PSRR. The story was reprinted in *Social Science Source Documents No. 4: Orientals and Their Cultural Adjustment. Interviews, Life Histories and Social Adjustment Experiences of Chinese and Japanese of Varying Backgrounds and Length of Residence in the United States* (Nashville, Tenn.: Social Science Institute, Fisk University, 1946). For more on the Fongs, see Henry Yu, "Mixing Bodies and Cultures: The Meaning of America's Fascination with Sex between 'Orientals' and Whites," in *Sex Love Race*, ed. Martha Hodes (New York: New York University Press, 1998).

22. Madison Grant, *The Passing of the Great Race* (New York: Scribner's, 1916); Lothrop Stoddard, *The Rising Tide of Color Against White World Supremacy* (New York: Scribner's, 1920).

23. Sax Rohmer was the pseudonym of Arthur Sarsfield Ward, who wrote a series of novels, beginning with *The Insidious Dr. Fu-Manchu* (New York: McKinlay, Stone, and McKenzie, 1913), involving the evil Oriental genius out to conquer the world.

24. On the exoticization of Orientals in America, see John Kuo Wei Tchen, "Broken Blossoms," in *Image: Independent Asian Pacific American Media Arts*, ed.

Russell Leong (Los Angeles: UCLA Asian American Studies Center and Visual Communications, 1991), 133–143; James Moy, *Marginal Sights* (Iowa City: University of Iowa Press, 1993); and Robert G. Lee, *Orientals* (Philadelphia: Temple University Press, 1999). On the portrayal of Asian women in the media, see Renee Tajima, "Lotus Blossoms Don't Bleed: Images of Asian Women," in *Making Waves*, ed. Asian Women United of California (Boston: Beacon Press, 1989), 308–317. On the exoticization of Asians in literature, see William Wu, *The Yellow Peril: Chinese Americans in American Fiction, 1850–1940* (Hamden: Archon Books, 1982); Stuart Creighton Miller, *The Unwelcome Immigrant: The American Image of the Chinese, 1785–1882* (Berkeley: University of California Press, 1969).

25. Davis to Park, November 21, 1923, Box 13, Park Correspondence, PSRR.

26. Original of the full Intermarriage Document, Box 6, PSRR. The questionnaire, which was only a portion of the larger document discussing "racial intermarriage," was reprinted in Bogardus, *New Social Research*, 157–161.

27. Park to Davis, December 1923, Box 13, Park Correspondence, PSRR.

28. Sidney Gulick to Davis, July 12, 1923, Box 11, Davis Correspondence, PSRR.

29. There was a long debate in 1924 among the survey organizers over the desirability of using the "red flag" of interracial sex to provoke interest. George Gleason, one of the original organizers in Los Angeles, produced a pledge card that quickly provoked reactions from the other organizers. As one of them warned, the "illustration which depicts a Chinese married to an American with three children and attending the Methodist Church, seems to us to unnecessarily wave a red flag in the faces of our exclusionist friends. . . . [W]e believe it is very important to print nothing on one of these cards which will unnecessarily arouse any suspicion in the minds of prejudiced people that the Survey is pre-judging the case." J. Merle Davis to George Gleason, March 17, 1924, General Correspondence Folder, Box 13, PSRR. Davis was afraid that the issue of intermarriage would provoke anti-Asian activists against the survey and suggested that Gleason discard the cards. Gleason wrote back (March 20): "It seems to me that one of the very important facts we are trying to get is what is happening as a result of intermarriage. We ought to have some report on all such cases here on the Coast." Davis then told Gleason that Robert Park had said to drop the cards, and so the cards were dropped. Davis to Gleason, March 25, 1924.

30. Park to Davis, April 29, 1924, Box 13, Park Correspondence, PSRR.

31. Franz Boas evinced a more pessimistic view than Park on the effectiveness of cultural assimilation, wondering if it would ever be possible to get rid of race prejudice as long as there were visual physical differences, and thus suggesting that intermarriage as a biological phenomenon was the long-term solution to racial awareness. Franz Boas, "The Problem of the American Negro," *Yale Review* 10 (January 1921): 392.

32. Burgess and Bogardus were also interested in the study of marriage, child rearing, and juvenile delinquency from the point of view of the sociology of the family. A smattering of articles appeared in sociological journals around that time about intermarriage between Jews, Catholics, and Protestants, or between Jews,

Italians, and Irish—an interest in cultural interaction that paralleled the interest in interracial marriage as a cultural phenomenon.

33. From "Chinese Slavery: Is it Fact, or Fiction?" address by Donaldina Cameron, Superintendant of the Presbyterian Mission Home, 920 Sacramento Street, from *Oriental Mission Work on the Pacific Coast of the United States of America, Addresses and Findings of Conferences in Los Angeles and San Francisco, CA., Oct. 13, 14, 15, 1920* (New York: Home Missions Council and Council of Women for Home Missions, 1920. Much has been written about Donaldina Cameron, including Carol Green Wilson's hagiographic *Chinatown Quest: The Life Adventures of Donaldina Cameron* (Stanford, Calif.: Stanford University Press, 1931); see also Peggy Pascoe, *Relations of Rescue* (New York: Oxford University Press, 1990); idem, "Gender Systems in Conflict: The Marriages of Mission-Educated Chinese American Women, 1874–1939," in *Unequal Sisters*, ed. Vicki Ruiz and Ellen DuBois (New York: Routledge, 1994), 139–156; for a quick overview, see Laurene Wu McClain, "Donaldina Cameron: A Reappraisal," *Pacific Historian* 27 (1983): 25–35.

34. "The Jap is not the right color. The fact that the Japanese bears in his features a distinctive racial hallmark, that he wears, so to speak, a racial uniform, classifies him." From Robert E. Park, "Racial Assimilation in Secondary Groups," *Publications of the American Sociological Society* 8 (1914): 66–72.

35. Robert E. Park, "Behind Our Masks," *Survey Graphic* 56 (May 1, 1926): 136.

36. Park, "Our Racial Frontier on the Pacific," 192.

37. Ibid., 195.

Chapter 4

1. Minutes of a meeting of the Research Council of the Survey of Race Relations on the Pacific Coast, Stanford Union building, March 25, 1925. PSRR.

2. *Tentative Findings of the Survey of Race Relations: A Canadian-American Study of the Oriental on the Pacific Coast, Prepared and Presented at the Findings Conference at Stanford University, California* (March 21–26, 1925), 18. PSRR.

3. Winifred Raushenbush, *Robert E. Park: Biography of a Sociologist* (Durham, N.C.: Duke University Press, 1979), 116; original telegram in the PSRR.

4. McKenzie, "The Oriental Invasion," *Journal of Applied Sociology* 10 (1925): 125–126.

5. Quoted from telegram in note 3.

6. Park stressed the difference between the subjective attitudes and the objective facts that many people seemed to assume were the stuff of science. Early on in the survey he startled Emory Bogardus and his group of researchers by "declaring that sociology is not interested in facts, not even in social facts as they are commonly understood in their objective aspects. Sociology wants to know how people re-act to so-called facts, to what is happening to them." Attitudes, beliefs, and what W. I. Thomas called people's "definition of a situation" were the facts that Park wanted to use to understand the behavior of individuals and social groups. Raushenbush, *Robert E. Park*, 112.

7. Memorandum from Akagi to Fisher, June 30, 1925, Fisher Correspondence, Box 11, PSRR.

8. Michael Omi and Howard Winant, *Racial Formation in the United States* (New York: Routledge, 1986); George Lipsitz, *The Possessive Investment in Whiteness* (Philadelphia: Temple University Press, 1998).

9. Research materials gathered during the survey were eventually used by Bogardus, Smith, and McKenzie in their own work, and all three would go on to write books based on the collected data. Emory Bogardus, *The New Social Research* (Los Angeles: Jesse Ray Miller, 1926); idem, *Immigration and Race Attitudes* (Boston: D. C. Heath, 1928; William C. Smith, *Americans in Process: A Study of Our Citizens of Oriental Ancestry* (Ann Arbor, Mich.: Edwards Bros., 1937); Roderick McKenzie, *Oriental Exclusion: The Effect of American Immigration Laws, Regulations, and Judicial Decisions upon the Chinese and Japanese on the American Pacific Coast* (Chicago: University of Chicago Press, 1928). The Institute of Social and Religious Research subsidized Smith's book *Americans in Progress*. Eliot Mears, secretary of the survey after Davis left in late 1924, finished a manuscript summing up the Survey of Race Relations, entitled *Resident Orientals on the American Pacific Coast: Their Legal and Economic Status* (Chicago: University of Chicago Press, 1928). Park, who had planned to write a book about the survey along the lines of *Old World Traits Transplanted*, never did.

10. Paul Kellogg, the editor of *Survey Graphic*, was a prominent social reformer who had directed the famous Pittsburgh Survey. Paul Kellogg Papers and the YMCA International Papers, Special Collections, University of Minnesota. Kellogg pointed to Hawaii as the most significant place for international and race relations in his editor's preface to the "East Meets West" edition of *Survey Graphic* 56 (May 1926): 133. Park's quotation is from his article "Our Racial Frontier on the Pacific," *Survey Graphic* 56 (May 1926): 196.

11. Islands are isolated, discrete entities that could be compared and contrasted. But the social scientists' sense that the social variables in their studies were somehow more controlled than in other places was spurious—the Hawaiian Islands were one of the busiest thoroughfares in all the Pacific, more akin to Hong Kong and San Francisco than the Galapagos Islands.

12. Kellogg, editor preface, 133. On American Orientalism and the Institute of Pacific Relations, see Henry Yu, "Orientalizing the Pacific Rim: The Production of Exotic Knowledge by American Missionaries and Sociologists in the 1920's," *Journal of American-East Asian Relations* 5 (fall 1996).

13. Park, "Our Racial Frontier on the Pacific," 192.

14. R. David Arkush, *Fei Xiaotong and Sociology in Revolutionary China*, Council on East Asian Studies (Cambridge, Mass.: Harvard University Press, 1981).

15. I am indebted to Kariann Yokota, whose work on the early history of American fascination with the Orient and how it defined American identity in the postcolonial era of the early Republic forms part of the material of her Ph.D. dissertation. See also John Kuo Wei Tchen, *New York before Chinatown: Orientalism and the Shaping of American Culture, 1776–1882* (Baltimore: Johns Hopkins University Press, 1999).

16. Mary Roberts Coolidge, *Chinese Immigration* (New York: Henry Holt, 1909). Coolidge was a suffragette, as well as a birth control and sex education activist, and taught at Mills College south of San Francisco. Biographical information can be found in the Dane Coolidge Papers, Bancroft Library Special Collections, University of California, Berkeley.

17. Park, "Our Racial Frontier on the Pacific," 196.

18. Raushenbush, Address to Tentative Findings Conference, March 21–26, 1925, Findings Conference Folder, PSRR.

19. My thanks to Matthew Dennis for helping me elaborate this point during a talk at the University of Oregon.

20. The hunger for the exotic that the Protestant elite of the Northeast exhibited at the turn of the century has been described by historian Jackson Lears. Lears tied such desires for authentic encounters with the exotic to a cultural trope of emptiness that was seen to afflict the bored elites of industrial society. Jackson Lears, *No Place of Grace: Antimodernism and the Transformation of American Culture, 1880–1920* (New York: Pantheon, 1981). Thanks to Nell Painter for the suggestion of narcissism as the metaphor for describing the structure of cosmopolitan whiteness.

21. Stow Persons, *Ethnic Studies at Chicago, 1905–45* (Urbana: University of Illinois Press, 1987). For a delineation of racial liberalism, see Walter Jackson, *Gunnar Myrdal and America's Conscience: Social Engineering and Racial Liberalism, 1938–1987* (Chapel Hill: University of North Carolina Press, 1990).

Chapter 5

1. Richard Wright's foreword to St. Clair Drake and Horace Cayton, *Black Metropolis: A Study of Negro Life in a Northern City* (New York: Harcourt, Brace, 1945), i.

2. Emory Bogardus, *Introduction to Social Research: A Text and Reference Study* (Los Angeles: Suttonhouse, 1936), 11.

3. During the survey itself, Bogardus had "at least fifteen persons more or less trained who will be giving systematic attention to the research side of the Race Relations Survey in Southern California during the next four months." Bogardus to Davis, September 9, 1924, Davis Correspondence, Box 11, PSRR. Bogardus was the head of the Social Research Society, an informal group of sociologists and students who met regularly to discuss research methodology, and he edited the USC sociology journal (first called the *Journal of Applied Sociology*, then *Sociology and Social Research*), which was aimed at a less educated audience than the *American Journal of Sociology*, the flagship journal for sociologists published by the Chicago department.

4. Fowler's study found in Eliot Mears Folder, PSRR.

5. Dr. Eliot Grinnel Mears's economics seminar at Stanford University on race relations produced a series of research papers written by "Oriental students," on such subjects as Japanese Associations in America, Japanese in the sugar beet industry, Oriental women and children in industry, remittances between California

and Asia, Japanese in the fruit and vegetable industry of California, and cooperative marketing as practiced by the Japanese. Mears Folder, PSRR.

6. For a Chicago sociologist's explication of the social functions of narrative
transformation in gossip and rumor, see Tamotsu Shibutani, *Improvised News: A
Sociological Study of Rumor* (Indianapolis: Bobbs-Merrill, 1966).

7. Life history of Kazuo Kawai, Los Angeles, March 2, 1925, Box 31, PSRR.
Other information on Kawai found in William C. Smith, "Interview with Kazuo
Kawai," August 7, 1924, in the same box. See also John Modell, *The Economics
and Politics of Racial Accommodation: The Japanese of Los Angeles, 1900–1942*
(Urbana: University of Illinois Press, 1977), 164–66.

8. Life history of Kazuo Kawai, 13.

9. The structuring of narratives of racial epiphany upon the model of religious
conversion is also apparent and provides a clue to the importance of missionaries
in the genres through which sociological knowledge was collected and produced.
One of the best illustrations of the confluence of social psychology case study and
religious conversion narrative is William James's highly influential model for the
study of social psychology, *The Varieties of Religious Experience* (New York:
Longmans, Green, 1902).

10. William C. Smith, "Born American, But—," *Survey Graphic* 56 (May 1,
1926): 167; idem, "The Second Generation Oriental-American," *Journal of Applied Sociology* 10 (1925–1926): 160; idem, "The Second Generation Oriental
in America" (preliminary paper prepared for the second general session, Institute of Pacific Relations, Honalulu, Hawaii, July 15–29, 1927). The papers were
based on Smith's research during the survey and in Hawaii after the end of the
survey.

11. For an interesting discussion of generational narrative in America, see
Werner Sollors, *Beyond Ethnicity* (New York: Oxford University Press, 1986).

12. Thomas Bender, *Community and Social Change in America* (Baltimore: Johns
Hopkins University Press, 1978).

13. It also reflected the anthropologists' conception of culture as a finite and
static quality that could not change without corruption—all adaptations to Western contact were seen as the loss of indigenous ways of life. James Clifford and
George Marcus, eds., *Writing Culture: The Poetics and Politics of Ethnography*
(Berkeley: University of California Press, 1986); Shelly Errington, *The Death of
Authentic Primitive Art* (Berkeley: University of California Press, 1998). Chicago
sociologists adopted enough of this idea of culture to reinforce their zero-sum definition of the assimilation spectrum: any movement along the spectrum could only
mean the gain and loss of equivalent quantities of American and immigrant culture. Ethnic revival movements in the 1960s and 1970s assumed that this spectrum could be reversed and that the redemption of assimilated ethnic Americans
lay in their own version of saving the lost ethnicity of their grandparents. Sollors,
Beyond Ethnicity, 228.

14. Chicago sociologists such as Park on the whole resisted the primitivism into
which a nostalgic celebration of gemeinschaft could fall. Fred H. Matthews, *Quest*

for an American Sociology: Robert E. Park and the Chicago School (Montreal: McGill University Press, 1977), 74–75, passim.

15. For the connection between national identities and literacy and print technology, see Benedict Anderson, *Imagined Communities: Reflections on the Origin and Spread of Nationalism*, 2d ed. (London: Verso, 1991). For the relationship of modernity and identity, see Scott Lach and Jonathan Friedman, eds., *Modernity and Identity* (Cambridge, Mass.: Blackwell, 1992); Anthony Giddens, *Modernity and Self-Identity: Self and Society in the Late Modern Age* (Stanford, Calif.: Stanford University Press, 1991).

16. Life history of Kazuo Kawai, 16.

17. Ibid., 16, 18.

18. Ibid., 17.

19. Ibid., 18.

20. We might ask why Kawai never became a sociologist. When Kawai recounted his life story, he fit perfectly into the sociologists' need for someone to take on the role of an Oriental informant. He did fulfill his dream of becoming an Oriental historian who could interpret the East to the West, receiving an A.B. in 1926 and a Ph.D. in history in 1938 from Stanford University. After teaching at UCLA from 1932 to 1941, he left for Japan to become an editor of the *Nippon Times*, remaining through the war and returning to the United States in 1949. Modell, *Economics and Politics of Racial Accommodation*, 166. For an interesting comparison, see Gordon Chang's biographical essay on Yamato Ichihashi, a long-time Stanford University professor and also a subject of study of the Survey of Race Relations, in Gordon Chang, ed., *Morning Glory, Evening Shadow* (Stanford, Calif.: Stanford University Press, 1997).

21. For a discussion of Park's conception of mobility, see Matthews, *Quest for an American Sociology*, 143–145. In 1938, Everett Stonequist, a student of Park's at Chicago, completed his dissertation, "The Marginal Man: A Study in the Subjective Aspects of Cultural Conflict," but the original idea had been Park's. Park even sent Stonequist to Hawaii to study how marginal and second-generation Orientals played important roles in race relations. Perhaps the original American model of the marginal man was taken by Park from his student E. B. Reuter's discussion in "The Mulatto in the United States" (Ph.D. diss., University of Chicago, 1919). Park's understanding of the marginal man differed from Reuter's description of the social role and status of the mulatto, however, particularly because of Park's placement of the marginal man in the context of global migration and modernity. Robert E. Park Papers, Box 7, Folder 4, Regenstein Special Collections, University of Chicago. In the interest of spurious formalism, we might formulate Park's conception as: Simmel's stranger + second-generation Orientals + mulattoes + modern migration = marginal man theory.

Chapter 6

1. St. Clair Drake and Horace Cayton, *Black Metropolis: A Study of Negro Life in a Northern City* (New York: Harcourt, Brace, 1945). For more on Park's effect

on African American sociologists, see John H. Bracey Jr., August Meier, and Eliot Rudwick, eds., *The Black Sociologists: The First Half Century* (Belmont, Calif.: Wadsworth, 1971).

2. From a telephone interview with Clarence Glick and Doris Glick, August 29, 1993. Lind was a student of Roderick McKenzie's. Back in Seattle, McKenzie's successor as chair of the department was another Park student, Jesse Frederick Steiner, whose Chicago dissertation was "The Japanese Invasion." Steiner himself would later advise a Chicago student conducting research on Japanese Americans in Seattle, Forrest LaViolette, who wrote "Americans of Japanese Ancestry: A Study of Assimilation in the American Community" (Ph. D. diss., University of Chicago, 1946). Stanford Lyman, a sociologist who worked extensively on the Chinese in America, felt a close bond to the Chinese and Japanese with whom he grew up in San Francisco, an identification that had much to do with his own family's background as Jewish immigrants from Lithuania.

3. Robert Park, "Behind Our Masks," *Survey Graphic* 56 (May 1926): 136–137.

4. "Mask" and "role" metaphors had a long history in Chicago sociology, starting with the social psychology theories of George Herbert Mead. The stage metaphor was one with which many Chicago sociologists were fascinated, but perhaps the most famous of the theorists to use the theatrical metaphor as a model of social interaction was Erving Goffman, who received his Ph.D. in sociology from Chicago in 1953. Goffman went on to write *The Presentation of Self in Everyday Life* (Garden City, N.Y.: Doubleday, 1956), which used the histrionic analogy extensively. Park had used the theme of masks to discuss social distance between Orientals and whites, but Goffman also was fascinated with the importance of saving "face" in Chinese social life, again playing extensively on the theatricality of personal interaction. Erving Goffman, "On Face-Work," in *Interaction Ritual: Essays on Face-to-Face Behavior* (Garden City, N.Y.: Doubleday, 1967). However, the question also arises as to what was ignored or missed when all the world was considered a stage. The theatrical model of social interaction, if taken too far, is misleading. As anthropologist Clifford Geertz noted, the drama analogy for social life has been around in a casual way for a long time, but, like all metaphors, it goes both ways. Is life like the theater, or is the theater like life—and what does this do to the theater analogy's insights as social analysis? Clifford Geertz, "Blurred Genres: The Refiguration of Social Thought," in Geertz, *Local Knowledge: Further Essays in Interpretive Anthropology* (New York: Basic Books, 1983).

5. Lionel Trilling, *Sincerity and Authenticity* (Cambridge, Mass.: Harvard University Press, 1972), discussed the ways in which eighteenth-century French Enlightenment thinkers such as D'Alembert and Rousseau connected the theater and an awareness of role-playing with moral questions of sincerity. For Mead and Goffman, mask and role metaphors became useful descriptions for the myriad of social faces that social interaction constantly entailed. They transformed Rousseau's struggle with questions of how to maintain a unified self in opposition to such variation of social appearance, arguing that the individual self was purely performative. Psychologist Erik Erikson in particular envisioned the coherence of a person's self-identity as the product of a successful integration of the many social

roles accumulated from childhood through adulthood. Erik Erikson, *Childhood and Society* (New York: Norton, 1950); idem, *Identity and the Life Cycle* (New York: International Universities Press, 1959).

6. See Jean-Christophe Agnew, *Worlds Apart: The Market and the Theater in Anglo-American Thought, 1550–1750* (New York: Cambridge University Press, 1986), for a history of the relationship between languages of the theater and the market.

7. Ching Chao Wu, "Chinatowns: A Study of Symbiosis and Assimilation" (Ph.D. diss., University of Chicago, 1928), chap. 16, "The Marginal Man," 327–328.

8. Ibid., 329–330.

9. There were many students like Wu who initially had been trained in American missionary colleges like Yenching University or Tsinghua University in Beijing prior to coming to the States for advanced degrees, but before the Communist revolution in 1949, all of them, like Wu, returned to China following their American training. See Siu-lun Wong, *Sociology and Socialism in Contemporary China* (London: Routledge and Kegan Paul, 1979), for a description of "American missionary sociology." Tsinghua University was established in the 1930s from Boxer Indemnity Funds paid to the United States, with the specific goal of preparing Chinese students for study in the United States, and Yenching University had been established by American missionaries at the turn of the century. The Institute of Social and Religious Research (and, through it, the Rockefeller Foundation) was also crucial in promoting sociological research in China. In 1926, it donated enough funds to finance a new Institute of Social Research in Peking for ten years. Ching Chao Wu was one of many Chinese students who went to Chicago under the auspices of American missionary colleges in China. Those who studied topics relating to China included Ernest Ni, Ai-ti Huang, and Yung-teh Chow (none of whom practiced Park's style of sociology—they were statistical demographers in the style of Park's methodological nemesis at Chicago, William Fielding Ogburn). Those who, like Wu, studied the Chinese in America included Ting-chiu Fan, Paul Siu, and Yuan Liang (all of whom wrote on the Chinese in Chicago for Ernest Burgess). Of the group, all returned to China except Liang, who remained because of the civil war, and Paul Siu, who spent the rest of his life in the United States. James P. McGough, ed. and trans., *Fei Hsiao-t'ung: The Dilemma of a Chinese Intellectual* (White Plains, N.Y.: M. E. Sharpe, 1979); Y. C. Wang, *Chinese Intellectuals and the West: 1872–1949* (Chapel Hill: University of North Carolina Press, 1966); Tung-li Yuan, *A Guide to Doctoral Dissertations by Chinese Students in America, 1905–1960* (Washington, D.C.: Sino-American Cultural Society, 1961).

10. "Guangdong" is the modern pinyin phonetic spelling of the Cantonese word "Kwangtung." The linguistic differences extended even farther beyond Mandarin (often called *pu-tong hua*) versus Cantonese (*guangdong hua*). The Chinese immigrants in America were predominantly from the Siyup (Four Counties) region of Guangdong Province, usually from Toisan County, but many were also from Huengsan (*Xiangshan*) County (later named Chungsan [*Zhongshan*]), and they spoke a different enough dialect to make communication difficult. The city dialect of Canton, different again from Toisanese and Chungsanese, was often used as a lingua franca and had an elite and educated cachet.

11. McKenzie's students at Washington during the survey included Clarence Arai, John Isao Nishinori, Katherine Woolston, and Elton F. Guthrie.

12. At the same time that Miyamoto was completing his master's thesis in the mid-1930s, he began working with Chicago graduate student Forrest LaViolette, also conducting research on the Japanese in Seattle. Since McKenzie had left Washington to head Michigan's sociology department, LaViolette, and for a time Miyamoto, lived in McKenzie's Seattle house while conducting their research.

13. From page 3 of Shotaru Frank Miyamoto, "Background Paper," Box 170, Folder 1, Ernest W. Burgess Papers, Regenstein Special Collections, University of Chicago. Additional biographical information on Frank Miyamoto from private interviews conducted with him in January 1993 and from his "Reminiscences of JERS," in *Views from Within: The Japanese American Evacuation and Resettlement Study*, ed. Yuji Ichioka (Los Angeles: Asian American Studies Center, UCLA, 1989), 141.

14. Miyamoto, "Background Paper," 3.

15. See Miyamoto, "Reminiscences of JERS," 142, for a description of Miyamoto's lifelong feeling of being both an insider and an outsider not only to the Japanese American community in Seattle but also to the social world around him in general. In 1944, Miyamoto remarked how he had envied the dynamic personality and gregariousness of C. K. Cheng, a colleague at Washington. Although Cheng was an Oriental, he showed none of the self-conscious reserve so typical of Orientals in the United States, and he charmed everyone he met, particularly women. Miyamoto saw that he and Cheng had very different personalities: Cheng created his own excitement and always seemed to be living and telling interesting stories; Miyamoto considered his own life relatively unexciting and was occupied with an internal world of imagination. Miyamoto, "A Nisei Autobiography," June 19, 1944, Call Number 67/14, Folder T1.95, Frank Miyamoto's correspondence with JERS staff, Papers of the Japanese Evacuation and Resettlement Study, Bancroft Library Special Collections, University of California, Berkeley.

16. July 27, 1943, entry in Frank Miyamoto Journal, 1943–44, Call Number 61/14, Folder T1.94, Papers of the JERS, Bancroft Library Special Collections, University of California, Berkeley.

17. Miyamoto, "Background Paper," 1.

18. Frank Miyamoto, *Social Solidarity among the Japanese in Seattle* (1939; reprint, Seattle: University of Washington Press, 1984), 9.

19. Miyamoto, "Nisei Autobiography."

20. There has been contentious scholarly debate about the JERS almost since its inception, and much has been written about the study's ties to the federal administrators who actually carried out internment (the War Relocation Authority [WRA]), as well as the compromised position of its researchers as inside informants. Dorothy Swaine Thomas and the whole research project came under attack in the late 1980s. See Ichioka, *Views from Within*, 65, for an explanation of the debate over Morton Grodzins's work, as well as more recent issues, including the polemical Peter T. Suzuki, "The University of California Japanese Evacuation and Resettlement Study: A Prolegomenon," *Dialectical Anthropology* 10 (1986): 189–213.

21. For the influence of Park and Thomas's style of sociological research on JERS researchers, see Frank Miyamoto, "Dorothy Swaine Thomas as Director of JERS," in Ichioka, *Views from Within*, 31–64.

22. James Sakoda, "The 'Residue': The Unresettled Minidokans, 1943–1945," in Ichioka, *Views from Within*, 251. Sakoda's analysis was based on notes and papers written before and during the war. Thanks to Art Hansen and Steven O. Murray for help in understanding JERS and for transcripts of Sakoda and Miyamoto's comments at the "Views from Within" conference at Berkeley organized in 1987 by Ichioka.

23. James Sakoda, "Reminiscences of a Participant Observer," in Ichioka, *Views from Within*, 221–222.

24. Sakoda, "The 'Residue,'" 251.

25. Ibid.

26. Sakoda, "Reminiscences of a Participant Observer," 221–222.

Chapter 7

1. Information on Rose Hum Lee is from her Biographical File at Roosevelt University Archives in Chicago; from private letters and papers in the possession of her daughter, Elaine Lee; from interviews conducted in October 1992 with her younger brother, Ralph Hum; and from an interview in January 1992 with her roommate for a year at the University of Chicago, Beulah Ong Kwoh.

2. Sucheng Chan, "Exclusion of Chinese Women, 1870–1943," in *Entry Denied*, ed. Sucheng Chan (Philadelphia: Temple University Press, 1991).

3. Lee's referral to herself in the third person is contained in her work *The Chinese in the United States of America* (Hong Kong: Hong Kong University Press, 1960), 387, in her story of the social approbation received by a Chinese immigrant woman when her daughter receives a Ph.D.

4. Rose Hum Lee, "The Marginal Man: Re-evaluation and Indices of Measurement," *Journal of Human Relations* 5 (spring 1956): 27–28.

5. Ibid., 28.

6. Lee, *Chinese in the United States*, 406.

7. Two thousand copies of *The Chinese in the United States* were published in Hong Kong in February 1960, paid for partly out of Lee's own funds. Although it was one of the few books on Chinese Americans at the time, it was not judged important enough to warrant publication by university presses in the United States.

8. Lee, *Chinese in the United States*, 427–430.

9. Lee's masters thesis of 1943 was a social work study based on her experiences in China: "Maternal and Child Health and Welfare Services in Canton China."

10. Elaine Tyler May, *Homeward Bound: American Families in the Cold War Era* (New York: Basic Books, 1988).

11. Thanks to Tomo Hattori for this insight about the need for Asian American women to become masculine in order to succeed in American society. For a social history of Chinese American women, see Judy Yung, *Unbound Feet: A So-*

cial History of Chinese American Women in San Francisco (Berkeley: University of California Press, 1995).

12. Entry of July 27, 1943, Frank Miyamoto Journal, 1943–44, Folder T1.94, Papers of the JERS.

13. For a time in the late 1950s, Lee's second husband, Glenn Ginn, was living in hiding, afraid that powerful Chinatown tongs were after them. Ginn was an American-born Chinese lawyer from Phoenix, and his legal work, as well as a messy divorce from his first wife, engaged him with the tongs. Lee became almost paranoid about a conspiracy between the tongs, Communist spies, and her personal enemies, certain that her sociological work had somehow made her dangerous to them. Information on Lee and her husband's fear of tong reprisals is from the author's interviews with Ralph Hum and from private correspondence between Rose Hum Lee and her daughter Elaine Lee.

14. I am indebted to Ling-chi Wang for encouraging me to pursue an understanding of Rose Hum Lee and also for providing an alternative interpretation of Lee that emphasizes the historical context of political and ideological repression in 1950s America. Ling-chi Wang, "Politics of Assimilation and Repression: History of the Chinese in the United States, 1940–1970" (unpublished manuscript, Asian American Library, University of California, Berkeley).

15. Lee, *Chinese in the United States*, 387, from the section "The Chinese Look at Themselves."

16. Ibid.

17. Private correspondence, dated January 8, 1958, in the possession of Elaine Lee and the author.

18. Paul Chan Pang Siu, *The Chinese Laundryman: A Study of Social Isolation*, ed. John Kuo Wei Tchen (New York: New York University Press, 1987), 4. See Tchen's introduction (pp. xiii–xxxix) for Siu's biography, as well as a short sketch of the dissertation's background. I am indebted to Tchen's edition not only for introducing me to *The Chinese Laundryman* but also for the original spur to pursue this research project (see note 17 of his introduction).

19. Ibid., 4.

20. Ibid., 138.

21. There was a scholarly debate over Siu's conception of the sojourner, particularly in regard to how he defined the term in his article "The Sojourner," *American Journal of Sociology* 53 (July 1952): 34–44. Franklin Ng, "The Sojourner, Return Migration, and Immigration History," in *Chinese America: History and Perspectives* (1987), 53–71; Yuen-fong Woon, "The Voluntary Sojourner among the Overseas Chinese: Myth or Reality?" *Pacific Affairs* 56 (winter 1983–1984): 673–690; and Anthony Chan, "Orientalism and Image-Making: The Sojourner in Canadian History," *Journal of Ethnic Studies* 9 (1981): 37–46.

22. Siu, *Chinese Laundryman*, 122.

23. The immigrant economy was also a direct result of chain migration, the process that had led to the amazing fact that most Chinese immigrants to America came from the same villages or counties in Guangdong Province in southern China. For both social and legal reasons, new immigrants almost invariably tended to be

relatives, friends, or acquaintances of those already in the United States. In the case of Siu and the Chicago laundrymen, and in fact for the majority of pre-1960s Chinese immigrants to America, the place of origin was Toisan district.

24. Clarence Elmer Glick, "The Chinese Migrant in Hawaii" (Ph.D. diss., University Chicago, 1938). Siu pointed out: "The static character of the Chinese minority in this country is certainly not because they are culturally determined not to be assimilated. In a different situation, as shown by Glick in his study of the Chinese in Hawaii, a somewhat different picture is presented." Siu, *Chinese Laundryman*, 3.

25. See the special issue of *American Journal of Sociology* on social disorganization, in particular, Herbert Blumer's article "Social Disorganization and Individual Disorganization," *American Journal of Sociology* 42 (May 1937): 871. The best-known treatment of social and personal disorganization was William I. Thomas and Florian Znaniecki, *The Polish Peasant in Europe and America*, 4 vols. (Chicago: University of Chicago Press, 1918–1920). The Chicago sociologists also often cited Charles H. Cooley's *Social Organization* (New York: Scribner's Sons, 1909).

26. Chicago sociologist Robert Faris explained the term "life-organization" in his textbook, *Social Disorganization* (New York: Ronald Press, 1948), 63.

27. Siu, *Chinese Laundryman*, 255.

28. "Obviously sex is always associated with other vices—gambling, opium addiction, and more recently, betting on the horses. Sex, therefore, becomes a social problem." Ibid., 271.

29. Ibid.

30. Ibid., 259.

31. Ibid., 6.

32. Many of the famous Chicago studies exposing the bohemian underworld of American society were insider accounts: Nels Anderson, *The Hobo: Sociology of the Homeless Man* (Chicago: University of Chicago Press, 1923); Clifford Shaw, *The Jack Roller: A Delinquent Boy's Own Story* (Chicago: University of Chicago Press, 1930); or an outsider view after acquiring an insider perspective, William Whyte, *Street Corner Society: The Social Structure of an Italian Slum* (Chicago: University of Chicago Press, 1943).

33. There has been a large and fascinating literature exploring the question of how ethnographers have created a sense of exotic difference at the same time that they produced meaningful descriptions that explained them. Clifford Geertz, *The Interpretation of Cultures* (New York: Basic Books, 1973); idem, and *Local Knowledge: Further Essays in Interpretive Anthropology* (New York: Basic Books, 1983); James Clifford and George Marcus, eds., *Writing Culture: The Poetics and Politics of Ethnography* (Berkeley: University of California Press, 1986); James Clifford, *The Predicament of Culture: Twentieth-Century Ethnography, Literature, and Art* (Cambridge, Mass.: Harvard University Press, 1988); Renato Rosaldo, *Culture and Truth: The Remaking of Social Analysis* (Boston: Beacon Press, 1989); Roger Sanjek, ed., *Fieldnotes: The Makings of Anthropology* (Ithaca, N.Y.: Cornell University Press, 1990); Michaela di Leonardo, *Exotics at Home: Anthropologies, Others, and American Modernity* (Chicago: University of Chicago Press, 1998).

34. Both quotations are from the wonderful ending of Tchen's introduction to Siu, *Chinese Laundryman*, xxxiv.

35. Beulah Ong Kwoh, who attended the same high school and junior college as Shibutani, recalled that even though she did not know him personally, the older Shibutani's reputation was common knowledge. Interview with Kwoh, January 28, 1992. To meet tight deadlines, Shibutani completed his master's thesis at Chicago in less than ten days, a feat that reflected his intellectual quickness and self-confidence. One of Shibutani's students at the University of Chicago, where he taught for three years, remarked that Shibutani taught his adviser's (Herbert Blumer's) courses better than Blumer did. Setsuko Matsunaga Nishi, interview, September 24, 1993.

36. All biographical information on Tamotsu Shibutani is from interviews conducted with him in September and October 1992 and from John D. Baldwin, "Advancing the Chicago School of Pragmatic Sociology: The Life and Work of Tamotsu Shibutani," *Sociological Inquiry* 60 (May 1990): 115–126.

37. Tamotsu Shibutani, "The Circulation of Rumors as a Form of Collective Behavior" (Ph.D. diss., University of Chicago, 1948), iii.

38. Tamotsu Shibutani, *The Derelicts of Company K: A Sociological Study of Demoralization* (Berkeley: University of California Press, 1978); idem, *Social Processes: An Introduction to Sociology* (Berkeley: University of California Press, 1986); and idem, *Improvised News: A Sociological Study of Rumor* (Indianapolis: Bobbs-Merrill, 1966).

39. Shibutani, *Derelicts of Company K*, 411.

40. Ibid., 285.

41. Ibid., vii.

42. Tamotsu Shibutani, "A Racial Minority in California," written for Mr. Kidner, Economics 188a, University of California, Berkeley, December, 1941, Call Number 61/14, Folder A.108, Papers of the JERS, Bancroft Special Collections. The essay dealt "with four different, though closely related, problems which face the American-born Japanese at the present time—economic insecurity, marriage problems, social disorganization, and personality maladjustments."

43. Especially in his textbook, written with Kian Kwan, *Ethnic Stratification* (New York: Macmillan, 1965).

44. As Shibutani described during interviews in the fall of 1992, he did not take sides during the various political battles and crises that occurred in the internment camps. He found it comforting to work hard just taking notes and recording his observations. Sociology as a daily practice, therefore, not only allowed, and encouraged, him to take the neutral standpoint that removed him from the social conflicts surrounding him but also provided him an activity tiring enough to accomplish the same end. According to him, he was literally too tired to choose sides.

45. Shibutani, "Circulation of Rumors," iii.

46. Shibutani, *Derelicts of Company K*, 411.

47. Ibid., x–xi.

48. Ibid.

49. Frank Miyamoto, "Reminiscences of JERS," in *Views from Within: The Japanese American Evacuation and Resettlement Study*, ed. Yuji Ichioka (Los Angeles: Asian American Studies Center, UCLA, 1989), 141; Peter T. Suzuki, "The University of California Japanese Evacuation and Resettlement Study: A Prolegomenon, *Dialectical Anthropology* 10 (1986): 189–213. For another critique of the JERS, see Lane Ryo Hirabayashi, *The Politics of Fieldwork: Research in an American Concentration Camp* (Tucson: University of Arizona Press, 1999).

50. Shibutani, *Social Processes*, 452.

A Final Setting

1. The U.S. Census of 1970 and 1980 showed a leap in population during those ten years from 435,000 to 806,000 Chinese; 343,000 to 774,600 Filipino; 76,000 to 361,500 Asian Indian; 68,100 to 354,500 Korean; and from almost no Vietnamese to over 261,700. Roger Daniels, *Asian America* (Seattle: University of Washington Press, 1988), 322.

Chapter 8

1. Frank Miyamoto, "Reminiscences of JERS," in *Views from Within: The Japanese American Evacuation and Resettlement Study*, ed. Yuji Ichioka (Los Angeles: Asian American Studies Center, UCLA, 1989), 142.

2. An academic career as an expert on China or Japan was possible, but for Orientals, discrimination in most academic disciplines severely limited their employment possibilities. This difficulty in pursuing professional careers in the humanities was the subject of much study by the Chicago sociologists. William C. Smith, "The Second Generation Oriental in America" (preliminary paper prepared for the second general session, Institute of Pacific Relations, Honolulu, Hawaii, July 15–29, 1927); idem, *Americans in Process: A Study of Our Citizens of Oriental Ancestry* (Ann Arbor, Mich.: Edwards Bros., 1937); and Beulah Ong Kwoh, "American-Born Chinese College Graduates" (M.A. thesis, University of Chicago, 1947).

3. As Ernest Burgess noted about the Chicago sociologists' interest in Chinese immigrants: "The Chinese population attracted sociological research attention for two reasons: as one of the cultural groups most deviant from the typical native American culture it provided sharp contrasts which clarified theoretical issues which otherwise might be vague." More important for practical purposes, however, Burgess noted that "the attendance of Chinese graduate students provided an opportunity for insightful research." Ernest Burgess and Donald Bogue, *Contributions to Urban Sociology* (Chicago: University of Chicago Press, 1964), 326, from the introduction to Paul Siu's chapter on the Chinese laundryman.

4. Jane Hunter, *The Gospel of Gentility* (New Haven, Conn.: Yale University Press, 1984), 229–255. Converted Chinese women used the social networks of Christian missions to obtain independence from Chinese gender roles, creating what Hunter calls "oases beyond the deserts of conventional familial expectation" (255).

5. Shotaru Frank Miyamoto, "Background Paper," Box 170, Folder 1, Ernest W. Burgess Papers, Regenstein Special Collections, University of Chicago, 5.

6. Robert Park and many other Chicago sociologists also spent time in Honolulu as visiting faculty on grants from the Rockefeller Foundation, and Park encouraged Hawaiian students to go to Chicago for advanced degrees.

7. For an explicit analysis of such social networks as a form of capital that can be converted to other forms of economic and cultural capital, see Pierre Bourdieu, *Homo Academicus*, trans. Peter Collier (Stanford, Calif.: Stanford University Press, 1988).

8. Miyamoto, "Background Paper," 7.

9. Lee, Biographical File, Roosevelt University Archives.

10. McKenzie, "The Oriental Invasion," *Journal of Applied Sociology* 10 (1925): 126.

11. This discussion of commodification and authenticity owes much to James Clifford, *The Predicament of Culture: Twentieth-Century Ethnography, Literature, and Art* (Cambridge, Mass.: Harvard University Press, 1988); and Arjun Appadurai and Igor Kopytoff, eds., *The Social Life of Things: Commodities in Cultural Perspective* (Cambridge: Cambridge University Press, 1986). For Marx on commodification and the commodity form, see Karl Marx, "1844 Manuscripts," and "Capital," in *Marx-Engels Reader*, ed. Robert Tucker, 2d ed. (New York: Norton, 1978). On the validation of knowledge, see Karl Mannheim, *Ideology and Utopia: An Introduction to the Sociology of Knowledge*, trans. Louis Wirth and Edward Shils (New York: Harcourt, Brace, 1936); also Jürgen Habermas, *Knowledge and Human Interests*, trans. Jeremy Shapiro (Boston: Beacon Press, 1971); idem, *Theory and Practice*, trans. John Viertel (Boston: Beacon Press, 1973); and Michel Foucault, *The Order of Things: An Archaelogy of the Human Sciences* (New York: Vintage, 1973). Another interesting issue deals with the opposition within Chinese American communities between "genuine" Chinese and "fake" Chinese (those things produced for consumption by non-Chinese, as argued by the writer Frank Chin).

12. For discussions of collecting and the authority of collectors in adjudging the authenticity and worth of their objects, see Shelly Errington, *The Death of Authentic Primitive Art* (Berkeley: University of California Press, 1998); Clifford, "On Collecting Art and Culture," in *Predicament of Culture*, 215; Sally Price, *Primitive Art in Civilized Places* (Chicago: University of Chicago Press, 1989); and Walter Benjamin, "Unpacking My Library," in *Illuminations*, ed. Hannah Arendt (New York: Schocken Books, 1969), 59. Also, for theoretical discussions concerning cultural and social capital in the fields of art and culture, see Pierre Bourdieu, *Distinction*, trans. Richard Nice (Cambridge, Mass.: Harvard University Press, 1984).

13. Mary Austin to Davis, March 31, 1924, Davis Correspondence File, PSRR. For a discussion of Mary Austin, see Joyce Antler, "'The Making of a New Mind': American Women and Intellectual Life in the 1920s," in *The Mythmaking Frame of Mind*, ed. James Gilbert, Amy Gilman, and Donald Scott (Belmont, Calif.: Wadsworth, 1993), 239–269.

14. Rose Hum Lee and Charlotte B. Charpenning, *Little Lee Bo-Bo: The Chinatown Detective* (Anchorage, Ky.: Children's Theatre Press, 1948), 4–7. An

original edition can be found in Rose Hum Lee's Biographical File, Roosevelt University Library.

15. Spelling and grammar are as in the original and stand uncorrected. Ernest W. Burgess Papers, Folder 1, Box 137, Regenstein Library Special Collections, University of Chicago.

16. Paul Siu, "The Use of Bad Language among Chinese Immigrants," Ernest W. Burgess Papers, Folder 1, Box 137, Regenstein Library Special Collections, University of Chicago.

17. Thanks to Edgar Wickberg for a note referring to "professional Chinese" in comments on a previous paper. This discussion grew out of that paper and his criticisms.

A Scene from Chinatown

1. Beulah Ong Kwoh, "Occupational Status of the American-Born Chinese College Graduates" (M.A. thesis, University of Chicago, 1947), 1.

Chapter 9

1. Eliot G. Mears to E. C. Carter, Secretary of the Institute of Pacific Relations, March 27, 1927, Mears Correspondence File, PSRR.

2. McKenzie quotation from letter, Carter to Mears, April 9, 1927, Mears Correspondence File, PSRR.

3. Carter to Mears, April 11, 1927, Mears Correspondence File, PSRR.

4. The theme of Chinatown as a closed world needing a daring outsider to expose its exotic secrets still structures many books. For example, see the eager and embarrassingly dim-witted book by Gwen Kinkead, *Chinatown: A Portrait of a Closed Society* (New York: HarperCollins, 1992).

5. *Genthe's Photographs of San Francisco's Old Chinatown*, selection and text by John Kuo Wei Tchen (New York: Dover, 1984). Tchen shows how Arnold Genthe's photographs reflect a selective eye that maintained an illusion of an exotic Chinatown, taking most photos at the few times of the year when traditional dress was worn and actively airbrushing out non-Chinese people in some shots. James Moy, *Marginal Sights* (Iowa City: University of Iowa Press, 1993), expands on Tchen's point to discuss the exoticization of the Chinese in America in film and theater.

6. Current discussion about ethnic identity formation should not revolve around whether such children ought to be allowed or encouraged to discover their ethnicity. What these children have been discovering, ever since similar discoveries by Oriental students such as Kazuo Kawai, has little to do with Asia. The discovery being made has always been about the terrain of race relations in America. Continually seen as permanent outsiders to the United States, Asian Americans will always be presented with this malignant benefit of inside privilege to Oriental "culture." As an aside to cultural politics within Asian American communities, others who see themselves as more genuine insiders to Korean American his-

tory than an adoptee—a Korean American raised in Seoul or Los Angeles or New York perhaps—might question or even deride the quality of knowledge possessed by a Korean American from Minnesota. In the end, however, any truly democratic vision of knowledge production for the study of Asian Americans must recognize the intrinsic importance of all such forms of knowledge.

7. Ting-chiu Fan, "Chinese Residents in Chicago" (M.A. thesis, University of Chicago 1926), 29. Fan had taken a class with Elleworth Faris and had produced a paper in conjunction with Ching Chao Wu about Chinese festivals, but he was not a sociology student. He attended the social welfare school, and, except for the theory of the assimilation cycle, he only once used a sociological term; even then it was in passing and not a part of any analysis ("secondary type" on page 87). Fan's lack of interest in sociological analysis is clearly indicated by his dismissal of intermarriage as an uninteresting phenomenon, even though there were at least "eighty such marriages which are not unsuccessful" (88). If he had been a Robert Park student, he never would have passed intermarriage off as a statistically irrelevant phenomenon.

8. Paul Chan Pang Siu, *The Chinese Laundryman: A Study of Social Isolation*, ed. John Kuo Wei Tchen (New York: New York Univeristy Press, 1987), 31–32.

9. Rose Hum Lee, "The Growth and Decline of Rocky Mountain Chinatowns" (Ph.D. diss., University of (Chicago, 1947), 39; idem, "Chicago Chinatown," *Chicago Schools Journal: An Education Magazine for Chicago Teachers* 31 (January–February 1950): 153–156. Lee discussed how the Chinese had long been taking advantage of white tourism with "novel atmosphere" and curio shops.

10. Lee, "Chicago Chinatown," 155.

11. Ibid., 156.

12. Ibid. One other Chinese American student conducted a study on the spatial dimensions of a Chinese community in America: Pao Yun Liao, "A Case Study of a Chinese Immigrant Community" (M.A. thesis, University of Chicago, 1951). His thesis researched Chinese immigrants in Arkansas and found that though they were spread throughout the state in small pockets, they retained a sense of community by visiting each other on holidays and maintaining social ties.

13. Chinatowns have again thrived, and new commercial centers of Chinese American life have appeared since the 1965 immigration reforms. For discussions of post-1965 and pre-1965 Chinatowns, see Peter Kwong, *The New Chinatown* (New York: Noonday Press, 1987); idem, *Chinatown, New York: Labor and Politics, 1930–1950* (New York: Praeger, 1977). See also Min Zhou, *Chinatown* (Philadelphia: Temple University Press, 1992).

14. Milton M. Gordon, *Assimilation in American Life* (New York: Oxford University Press, 1964).

15. Werner Sollors, *Beyond Ethnicity* (New York: Oxford University Press, 1986); Edward W. Soja, *Postmodern Geographies: The Reassertion of Space in Critical Social Theory* (New York: Verso, 1989); Akhil Gupta and James Ferguson, "Beyond 'Culture': Space, Identity, and the Politics of Difference," *Cultural Anthropology* 7 (February 1992): 6–23; and James Duncan and David Ley, eds., *Place/Culture/Representation* (London: Routledge, 1993).

16. Perhaps the best example of the culture concept as an explanatory device is Ruth Benedict, *The Chrysanthemum and the Sword* (Boston: Houghton Mifflin, 1946).

17. Tomatsu Shibutani, *Social Processes: An Introduction to Sociology* (Berkeley: University of California Press, 1986), 390.

Chapter 10

1. A number of dissertations in the postwar period used Japanese Americans as the research subjects, though not all of them were directly informed by the theories of Robert Park and William I. Thomas. Other than Miyamoto and Shibutani, there were Rachel Reese Sady, "The Function of Rumors in Relocation Centers" (Ph.D. diss., anthropology, 1947); William Abel Caudill, "Japanese American Acculturation and Personality" (Ph.D. diss., anthropology, 1950); Setsuko Matsunaga Nishi, "Japanese American Achievement in Chicago: A Cultural Response to Degradation" (Ph.D. diss., 1963). Both Caudill's and Nishi's dissertations came out of a joint research project conducted in the late 1940s. In addition, Yukiko Kimura, Ph.D. (1952); Eugene Shigemi Uyeki, Ph.D. (1953); and Dave M. Okada, M.A. (1947), full citations in Appendix.

2. With the GI Bill, economic prosperity, and the expansion of higher education, the University of Chicago, like most academic institutions in the country, experienced a postwar boom. When Tamotsu Shibutani attended graduate school in 1948, there were 175 Ph.D. students in sociology, compared with the handful who were in the department every year before the war.

3. William Petersen, "Success Story, Japanese-American Style," *New York Times Magazine*, January 9, 1966; idem, *Japanese-Americans: Oppression and Success* (New York: Random House, 1971). Martin Kasindorf, Darby Junkin, Kim Foltz, Daniel Shapiro, Paula Chih, Diane Weathers, "Asian Americans: A Model Minority," *Newsweek*, December 6, 1982, 39–43. The success of Jewish Americans in losing their ethnic status, for instance, is often hailed as the precedent for hope that Asian Americans will do the same. David Bell, "The Triumph of Asian Americans," *New Republic*, July 1985, 24–31. Bell drew parallels between the high education levels of Jewish and Asian Americans and noted the success of this route to social and economic mobility. The problem with this analysis, however, is that the success of ethnic whites such as Irish, Italian, and Jewish Americans in becoming indistinct has everything to do with their ability to not be colored. Anti-Semitism and anti-Catholicism were powerful in the 1920s, and the transformation of American society since then has indeed been great. But the amalgamation of ethnic whiteness has only strengthened the bonds of white supremacy, not lessened it. A civil rights alliance between Jewish Americans and African Americans, which derived from common problems of being excluded from American society, had the ironic effect of helping Jewish Americans become accepted not as an excluded racial minority but as white Americans with a conscience. The malignant hope offered by the model minority thesis is that Asian Americans might achieve an accepted status by drawing their difference from African Americans. Considering the con-

tinuing exoticization of Asian Americans, however, it is highly unlikely that Orientals will ever be seen as white.

4. My thanks to Setsuko Matsunaga Nishi for a pleasant afternoon chatting at the City University of New York in 1994. Nishi was one of the most fascinating of the Japanese American sociologists who studied at Chicago. Her career pointed to the long-standing difficulties that Asian American scholars, in particular women, faced as expert informants who ultimately received little recognition for their scholarly achievements. A daughter of a prominent member of the Japanese American community, Nishi was able to operate effectively within the liberal circle of white and African American intellectuals in Chicago. Relocation had forced her to transfer from USC to Washington University in Saint Louis, and it was there that she became involved with the JERS. After the war, her father became a leader of the Japanese Americans who resettled in Chicago, and her contributions to the study of Japanese American achievement were crucial. Unfortunately, the effects of a gendered academic system, which rewarded men for being able to ignore domestic duties, resulted in much of the acclaim for the study going to her collaborators in the study; they were able to finish their dissertations quickly while Nishi was slowed by the responsibilities of motherhood and family.

5. Melville Herskovits, *Acculturation: The Study of Culture Contact* (Gloucester, Mass.: P. Smith, 1958).

6. William Smith, "The Second Generation Oriental-American," *Journal of Applied Sociology* 10 (1925–1926): 160.

7. For instance, Shirley Hune's description of the impact of sociological theories on the understanding of Asian immigrants in "Pacific Migration to the United States: Trends and Themes in Historical and Sociological Literature," RIIES Bibliographic Studies No. 2 (Washington, D.C.: Research Institute on Immigration and Ethnic Studies, 1977); and the importance of what she calls the "assimilationist paradigm," in Shirley Hune, "Rethinking Race: Paradigms and Policy Formation," *Amerasia* 21, nos. 1–2 (1995): 29–40.

8. Ronald Takaki, *Strangers from a Different Shore* (New York: Penguin, 1989).

9. Paul Takagi, "The Myth of Assimilation in American Life," *Amerasia Journal* 2 (fall 1973): 149–159.

10. Robin Kelley, *Yo Mama's Disfunctional* (Boston: Beacon Press, 1996), for a convincing argument about the legacies of the social scientific construction of the Negro Problem.

11. Jonathan Holloway, "Confronting the Veil: New Deal African American Intellectuals and the Evolution of a Radical Voice" (Ph.D. diss., Yale University, 1995).

12. William Wei, *The Asian American Movement* (Philadelphia: Temple University Press, 1993); Karen Umemoto, "'On Strike!' San Francisco College Strike, 1968–69: The Role of Asian American Students," *Amerasia* 15, no. 1 (1989): 3–41, for the context of the rise of Asian American consciousness; and Shirley Hune, "Opening the American Mind and Body: The Role of Asian American Studies," *Change*, November/December 1989, 56–63, for a description of the academic and activist program of Asian American studies.

13. Walter Jackson, *Gunnar Myrdal and America's Conscience: Social Engineering and Racial Liberalism, 1938–1987* (Chapel Hill: University of North Carolina Press, 1990).

14. On how ethnic Americans became white, see Matthew Frye Jacobson, *Whiteness of a Different Color: European Immigrants and the Alchemy of Race* (Cambridge, Mass.: Harvard University Press, 1998); Karen Brodkin, *How Jews Became White Folks and What That Says about Race in America* (New Brunswick, N.J.: Rutgers University Press, 1998). Bruce Kuklick, *Puritans in Babylon: The Ancient Near East and American Intellectual Life, 1880–1930* (Princeton, N.J.: Princeton University Press, 1996), describes how Jewish intellectuals entered academia through biblical and Near Eastern studies. For a different view, see David Hollinger, *Science, Jews, and Secular Culture: Studies in Mid-Twentieth-Century American Intellectual History* (Princeton, N.J.: Princeton University Press, 1996).

An Epitaph

1. Thanks to Judy Yung for her permission to quote this passage from an unpublished paper on Flora Jan. Jan's unease with the effects of marriage on her career is also described in a letter from Jan to Park, January 13, 1927, Box 2, Folder 1, Robert Park Papers–Addenda, Regenstein Special Collections, University of Chicago.

BIBLIOGRAPHY OF PRIMARY SOURCES

Archival Sources

Burgess, Ernest W. Ernest W. Burgess Papers, Regenstein Special Collections, University of Chicago.

Glick, Clarence, and Doris Glick. Author interview, by telephone, on August 29, 1993.

Lee, Rose Hum. Rose Hum Lee Biographical File, Roosevelt University Library, Roosevelt University, Chicago. Private correspondence between Rose Hum Lee and her daughter Elaine Lee, in the possession of Elaine Lee.

Miyamoto, Frank. Materials in JERS Papers, Bancroft Special Collections, University of California, Berkeley, and in the Ernest W. Burgess Papers, Regenstein Special Collections, University of Chicago.

Park, Robert Ezra. Robert E. Park Papers, Regenstein Special Collections, University of Chicago. Robert E. Park Papers, Fisk University Library, Nashville, Tennessee. Papers of the Survey of Race Relations, Hoover Institution, Stanford University.

Shibutani, Tamotsu. Materials in JERS Papers, Bancroft Special Collections, University of California, Berkeley. Additional information from John D. Baldwin, "Advancing the Chicago School of Pragmatic Sociology: The Life and Work of Tamotsu Shibutani," *Sociological Inquiry* 60 (May 1990): 114–126.

Siu, Paul. Assorted letters and papers in the care of John Kuo Wei Tchen, Asian/American Studies Center, New York University, New York. Graduate research papers and notes for "The Chinese Laundryman" in Ernest W. Burgess Papers, Regenstein Special Collections, University of Chicago.

Published Sources

Publications of the Chicago sociologists are designated by asterisks.

*Adams, Romanzo C. *Interracial Marriage in Hawaii: A Study of the Mutually Conditioned Processes of Acculturation and Amalgamation*. New York: Macmillan, 1937.

*————. *The Peoples of Hawaii*. Honolulu: American Council, Institute of Pacific Relations, 1933.

Blakeslee, G. H., ed. *Japan and Japanese-American Relations: A Compilation of a Conference Held at Clark University*. New York: G. E. Stechert, 1912.

*Blumer, Herbert. "The Nature of Race Prejudice." *Social Process in Hawaii* 5 (June 1939): 14.

Boas, Franz. *The Mind of Primitive Man*. New York: Macmillan, 1911.

*Bogardus, Emory S. *Essentials of Americanization*. Los Angeles: University of Southern California Press, 1919. Revised 1920.

*————. *The New Social Research* (Los Angeles: Jesse Ray Miller, 1926).

*————. "Social Distance: A Measuring Stick Gaging Racial Antipathies on the Coast—and Elsewhere." *Survey Graphic* 56 (May 1926).

*————. *Immigration and Race Attitudes*. Boston: D. C. Heath, 1928.

*————. *The Mexican in the United States*. Social Science Series no. 8. New York: Jerome S. Ozer, 1934.

*————. *Introduction to Social Research: A Text and Reference Study*. Los Angeles: Suttonhouse, 1936.

*————. *Much Have I Learned*. Los Angeles: University of Southern California Press, 1962.

*————. *A Forty Year Racial Distance Study*. Los Angeles: University of Southern California Press, 1967.

*————. *A History of Sociology at the University of Southern California*. Los Angeles: University of Southern California Press, 1972.

*————, ed. *Trends in Scholarship: Annotations of Theses and Dissertations Accepted by the University of Southern California, 1910–1935*. Los Angeles: University of Southern California Press, 1936.

*Burgess, Ernest. *The Basic Writings of Ernest W. Burgess*. Ed. Donald J. Bogue. Chicago: Community and Family Study Center, University of Chicago, 1974.

*————, ed. *The Urban Community: Selected Papers from the Proceedings of the American Sociological Society, 1925*. Chicago: University of Chicago Press, 1926.

*Burgess, Ernest W., and Donald J. Bogue. *Contributions to Urban Sociology*. Chicago: University of Chicago Press, 1964.

Chang, Francis Y. "An Accommodation Program for Second-Generation Chinese." *Sociology and Social Research* 18 (1934): 541–553.

Coolidge, Mary Roberts. *Chinese Immigration*. New York: Henry Holt, 1909.

Corpus, Severino F. "Second Generation Filipinos in Los Angeles." *Sociology and Social Research* 22 (1938): 446–451.

Davis, J. Merle. *Soldier Missionary: A Biography of Rev. Jerome D. Davis, D.D., Lieutenant-Colonel of Volunteers and for Thirty-nine Years a Missionary of the American Board of Commissioners for Foreign Missions in Japan*. Boston: Pilgrim Press, 1916.

————. *The Institute of Pacific Relations*. New York: Carnegie Endowment for International Peace, Division of Intercourse and Education, 1926.

Department of Commerce, Bureau of the Census. *Chinese and Japanese in the United States, 1910*. Bulletin no. 127. Washington, D.C.: Government Printing Office, 1914.

*Drake, St. Clair, and Horace R. Cayton. *Black Metropolis: A Study of Negro Life in a Northern City*. With a foreword by Richard Wright. New York: Harcourt, Brace, 1945.

Evans-Pritchard, E. E. *Witchcraft, Oracles, and Magic among the Azande*. Oxford: Clarendon Press, 1937.

Fairchild, Henry Pratt. *Immigration, a World Movement, and Its Significance*. New York: Macmillan, 1913.

————. *The Melting-Pot Mistake*. Boston: Little, Brown, 1926.

Fisher, Galen M. *A Balance Sheet on Japanese Evacuation: Untruths about Japanese Americans*. Pamphlet series. Berkeley, Calif.: Committee on American Principles and Fair Play, 1943.

————. *John R. Mott: Architect of Cooperation and Unity*. New York, 1952.

————. *Citadel of Democracy: The Story of the Public Affairs Record of Stiles Hall*. Berkeley: YMCA of the University of California, 1955.

*Glick, Clarence Elmer. "Residential Dispersion of Urban Chinese." *Social Process in Hawaii* 2 (1936): 28.

*————. "Transition from Familism to Nationalism among Chinese in Hawaii." *American Journal of Sociology* 43 (1938): 734.

*————. *Sojourners and Settlers: Chinese Migrants in Hawaii*. Honolulu: University of Hawaii Press, 1980.

Gulick, Sidney L. *The American Japanese Problem: A Study of the Racial Relations of the East and the West*. New York: Scribner's, 1914.

————. *Mixing the Races in Hawaii: A Study of the Coming New-Hawaiian American Race*. Honolulu: Hawaiian Board Book Rooms, 1937.

Ichihashi, Yamato. *Japanese Immigration: Its Status in California*. San Francisco: Marshall, 1915.

————. *Japanese in the United States: A Critical Study of the Problems of the Japanese Immigrants and Their Children*. Stanford, Calif.: Stanford University Press, 1932.

Institute of Pacific Relations. *Notes from a Pacific Circuit: Report Letters of J. M. Davis, MA, General Secretary, to Ray Lyman Wilbur, Chairman of IPR*. New York: Institute of Pacific Relations, 1927.

The Institute of Social and Religious Research, 1921–1934. New York: Institute of Social and Religious Research, 1934.

Jenks, Jeremiah W., and W. Jett Lauck. *The Immigration Problem: A Study of American Immigration Conditions and Needs*. New York: Funk and Wagnalls, 1911.

Kawakami, K. K. *American-Japanese Relations*. New York: Fleming H. Revell, 1912.

*Kimura, Yukiko. *Issei: Japanese Immigrants in Hawaii*. Honolulu: University of Hawaii Press, 1988.

Lam, Margaret M. "Baseball and Racial Harmony in Hawaii." *Sociology and Social Research* 18 (1933): 58–66.

*Lee, Rose Hum. "Chinese Population Trends in the United States." *South-Western Journal* 2 (spring 1946): 97.

*———. "The Social Institutions of a Rocky Mountain Chinatown." *Social Forces* 27 (October 1948): 1.

*———. "Chinese Dilemma." *Phylon* 10 (2d quarter 1949): 137.

*———. "Research on the Chinese Family." *American Journal of Sociology* 54 (May 1949): 497.

*———. "Chinese Americans." In *One America*, edited by F. S. Brown and J. S. Roucek, 309–319. New York: Prentice-Hall, 1952.

*———. "Delinquent, Neglected, and Dependent Chinese Boys and Girls of the San Francisco Bay Region." *Journal of Social Psychology* 36 (1952): 15.

*———. *The City: Urbanism and Urbanization in Major World Regions*. Philadelphia: J. B. Lippincott, 1955.

*———. "The Chinese Abroad." *Phylon* 17 (3d quarter 1956): 257.

*———. "The Marginal Man: Re-evaluation and Indices of Measurement." *Journal of Human Relations* 5 (spring 1956): 27.

*———. "The Recent Immigrant Chinese Families of the San Francisco–Oakland Area." *Marriage and Family Living* 18 (February 1956): 14.

*———. "Chinese Immigration and Population Changes since 1940." *Sociology and Social Research* 41 (January 1957): 195.

*———. "The Established Chinese Families of the San Francisco Bay Area." *Midwest Sociologist* 20 (December 1957): 19.

*———. "The Stranded Chinese in the United States." *Phylon* 19 (2d quarter 1958): 256.

*———. *The Chinese in the United States of America*. Hong Kong: Hong Kong University Press, 1960.

*Lind, Andrew William. *A Study of Mobility of Population in Seattle*. University of Washington Publications in the Social Sciences. Vol. 3, no. 1. Seattle: University of Washington Press, 1925.

*———. *An Island Community: Ecological Succession in Hawaii*. Chicago: University of Chicago Press, 1938.

*———. "The Japanese in Hawaii under War Conditions." Study submitted by the American Council as a document of the eighth conference of the IPR to be held in December 1942. New York: American Council, Institute of Pacific Relations, 1942.

*———. *Hawaii's Japanese, An Experiment in Democracy*. Princeton, N.J.: Princeton University Press, 1946.

*———. *Hawaii's People*. With the assistance of Robert Schmitt. Honolulu: University of Hawaii Press, 1955.

*————. *Hawaii: The Last of the Magic Isles*. New York: Oxford University Press, 1969.

*————. *Nanyang Perspective: Chinese Students in Multiracial Singapore*. Honolulu: University of Hawaii Press, 1974.

*————, ed. *Papers Read at the Conference on Race Relations in World Perspective, Honolulu, 1954*. Honolulu: University of Hawaii Press, 1955.

*Lorden, Doris M. "The Chinese-Hawaiian Family." *American Journal of Sociology* 40 (1935): 635–641.

Louis, Kit King. "Problems of Second Generation Chinese." *Sociology and Social Research* 16 (1932): 250–258.

————. "Program for Second Generation Chinese." *Sociology and Social Research* 16 (1932): 455–462.

Malinowski, Bronislaw. *Argonauts of the Western Pacific*. New York: E. P. Dutton, 1922.

*Masuoka, Jitsuichi. "Race Relations and Nisei Problems." *Sociology and Social Research* 30 (1946): 452–459.

*Masuoka, Jitsuichi, and Preston Valien, eds. *Race Relations: Problems and Theory— Essays in Honor of Robert E. Park*. Chapel Hill: University of North Carolina Press, 1961.

*Matsunaga, Setsuko, *Facts about Japanese Americans*. Chicago: American Council on Race Relations, 1946.

*McKenzie, Roderick, *Oriental Exclusion: The Effect of American Immigration Laws, Regulations, and Judicial Decisions upon the Chinese and Japanese on the American Pacific Coast*. Chicago: University of Chicago Press, 1928.

*————. *On Human Ecology*. Edited and with an introduction by Amos Hawley. Chicago: University of Chicago Press, 1968.

Mears, Eliot Grinnell. *Resident Orientals on the American Pacific Coast: Their Legal and Economic Status*. Chicago: University of Chicago Press, 1928.

Millis, H. A. *The Japanese Problem in the United States: An Investigation for the Commission on Relations with Japan Appointed by the Federal Council of the Churches of Christ in America*. New York: Macmillan, 1915.

*Miyamoto, Frank. *Social Solidarity among the Japanese in Seattle*. 1939. Reprint, Seattle: University of Washington Press, 1984

Nodera, Isamu. "Second Generation Japanese and Vocations." *Sociology and Social Research* 21 (1937): 454–466.

*Park, Robert. *The Collected Papers of Robert Ezra Park*. Vol. 1: *Race and Culture*. Ed. Everett C. Hughes et al. Glencoe, Ill.: Free Press, 1950.

*————. *The Collected Papers of Robert Ezra Park*, Vol. 2: *Human Communities: The City and Human Ecology*. Ed. Everett C. Hughes et al. Glencoe, Ill.: Free Press, 1952.

*Park, Robert E., and Ernest W. Burgess. *Introduction to the Science of Sociology*. Chicago: University of Chicago Press, 1921.

*Park, Robert E., Ernest W. Burgess, and Roderick D. McKenzie. *The City*. Chicago: University of Chicago Press, 1925.

*Park, Robert, and Herbert Miller. *Old World Traits Transplanted*. New York: Harper and Brothers, 1921.

*Reuter, Edward B. *Race Mixture: Studies in Intermarriage and Miscegenation*. New York: McGraw-Hill, 1931.

Ross, Robert H., and Emory S. Bogardus. "The Second-Generation Race Relations Cycle: A Study in Issei-Nisei Relationships." *Sociology and Social Research* 24 (1940): 357–363.

*Shibutani, Tamotsu. *Society and Personality: An Interactionist Approach to Social Psychology*. Englewood Cliffs, N.J.: Prentice-Hall, 1961.

*———. *Improvised News: A Sociological Study of Rumor*. Indianapolis: Bobbs-Merrill, 1966.

*———. *The Derelicts of Company K: A Sociological Study of Demoralization*. Berkeley: University of California Press, 1978.

*———. *Social Processes: An Introduction to Sociology*. Berkeley: University of California Press, 1986.

*Shibutani, Tamotsu, and Kian M. Kwan. *Ethnic Stratification*. New York: Macmillan, 1965.

*Siu, Paul Chan Pang. "The Sojourner." *American Journal of Sociology* 53 (July 1952): 34–44.

*———. *The Chinese Laundryman: A Study of Social Isolation*. Edited and with an introduction by John Kuo Wei Tchen. New York: New York University Press, 1987.

*Smith, William Carlson. "Born American, But." *Survey Graphic* 56 (May 1926): 167–168.

*———. "The Second Generation Oriental in America." Preliminary paper prepared for the second general session, Institute of Pacific Relations, Honolulu, Hawaii, July 15–29, 1927.

*———. "Changing Personality Traits of Second Generation Orientals in America." *American Journal of Sociology* 33 (1928): 922.

Social Science Source Documents No. 4: Orientals and Their Cultural Adjustment. Interviews, Life Histories and Social Adjustment Experiences of Chinese and Japanese of Varying Backgrounds and Length of Residence in the United States. Nashville: Social Science Institute (Fisk University), 1946.

*Steiner, Jesse Frederick. *The Japanese Invasion: A Study in the Psychology of Interracial Contacts*. Chicago: A. C. McClurg, 1917.

*———. *Behind the Japanese Mask*. New York: Macmillan, 1943.

*Thomas, William I. "The Significance of the Orient for the Occident." *American Journal of Sociology* 13 (May 1908): 729.

*Thomas, William I., and Florian Znaniecki. *The Polish Peasant in Europe and America*. 4 vols. Chicago: University of Chicago Press, 1918–1920.

*Wu, Ching Chao. *Chinese Immigration in the Pacific Area*. Chicago: University of Chicago Press, 1926. Reprint, San Francisco: R and E Research Associates, 1974.

*———. "Chinese Immigration in the Pacific Area." *Chinese Social and Political Science Review* 12 (October 1928).

*Young, Kimball. *Social Psychology of Oriental-Occidental Prejudices*. New York: Institute of Pacific Relations, 1929.

Unpublished Sources

Arai, Clarence. "Cultural Conflicts in Homes of the Second-Generation Japanese." M.A. thesis, University of Washington, 1929.

Cheng, David Te-Chao. "Acculturation of the Chinese in the United States: A Case Study of Philadelphia." Ph.D. diss., University of Pennsylvania, 1948.

Fan, Ting-chiu. "Chinese Residents in Chicago." M.A. thesis, University of Chicago, 1926.

Fowler, Ruth M. "Some Aspects of Public Opinion Concerning the Japanese in Santa Clara County." M.A. thesis, Stanford University, 1934.

Fukuoko, Fumiko. "Mutual Life and Aid among the Japanese in Southern California." M.A. thesis, University of Southern California, 1937.

Greiner, Ruth. "A Comparative Study of Chinese and Japanese Traits and Attitudes." M.A. thesis, University of Washington, n.d.

Guthrie, Elton F. "Crises in Personality: A Study in Social Psychology." Ph.D. diss., University of Washington, 1932.

Kawasaki, Kanichi. "The Japanese Community of East San Pedro, Terminal Island, California." M.A. thesis, University of Southern California, 1931.

Lai, Kum-pui. "The Natural History of the Chinese Language School in Hawaii." M.A. thesis, University of Hawaii, 1935.

Lee, Bung-chong. "The Chinese Store in Hawaii." M.A. thesis, University of Hawaii, 1935.

Lee, Doris. "Juvenile Crime among the Orientals." Graduate student paper, University of British Columbia during the Survey of Race Relations, 1924–1926.

*Lee, Rose Hum. "Social Attitudes toward Chinese in the United States Expressed in Periodical Literature from 1919–1944." Private document, 1944.

Liang, Yuan. "The Chinese Family in Chicago." M.A. thesis, University of Chicago, 1951.

Liao, Pao Yun. "A Case Study of a Chinese Immigrant Community." M.A. thesis, University of Chicago, 1951.

Loh, Homer C. C. "Americans of Chinese Ancestry in Philadelphia." Ph.D. diss., University of Pennsylvania, 1945.

Louis, Kit King. "A Study of American-Born and American-Reared Chinese in Los Angeles." M.A. thesis, University of Southern California, 1931.

MacGill, Helen (later Helen MacGill Hughes). "Anti-Chinese Immigration Legislation of British Columbia" and "The Recreations of Oriental Domestic Servants." Undergraduate papers, University of British Columbia during the Survey of Race Relations, 1924–1926.

Mather, Greta. "Occupational Trends and Outlets of Chinese and Japanese in British Columbia." Graduate student paper, University of British Columbia during the Survey of Race Relations, 1924–1926.

Nishinori, John Isao. "Japanese Farms in Washington." M.A. thesis, University of Washington, 1926.

Nodera, Isamu. "Survey of the Vocational Activities of the Japanese in Los Angeles." M.A. thesis, University of Southern California, 1937.

Okada, Dave M. "A Study of Nisei Workers in Two Chicago Industrial Plants." M.A. thesis, University of Chicago, 1947.

Oshimo, Raymond Kakuchi. "The Problem of Japanese Assimilation in Hawaii." M.A. thesis, University of Chicago, 1926.

Riss, Arthur. "A Comparative Study of Chinese and Japanese Crime and Delinquency in Seattle." M.A. thesis, University of Washington, n.d.

Svensrud, Marian. "Some Factors Concerning the Assimilation of a Selected Japanese Community." M.A. thesis, University of Southern California, 1931.

Takahashi, Kyojiro. "A Social Study of Japanese Shinto and Buddhism in Los Angeles." M.A. thesis, University of Southern California, 1937.

Tanaka, Jane Tamiko. "The Japanese Language School in Relation to Assimilation." M.A. thesis, University of Southern California, 1933.

Tuthill, Gretchen L. "A Study of the Japanese in the City of Los Angeles." M.A. thesis, University of Southern California, 1924.

Uono, Koyoshi. "The Factors Affecting the Geographical Aggregation Dispersion of the Japanese Residences in the City of Los Angeles." M.A. thesis, University of Southern California, 1928.

Woolston, Katherine. "Japanese Standards of Living in Seattle." M.A. thesis, University of Washington, 1926.

Yokoyama, Hidesaburo. "Japanese Associations in America." M.A. thesis, University of Chicago, 1921.

INDEX